CORNERSTONES OF RELIGIOUS FREEDOM
IN AMERICA

BEACON PRESS STUDIES IN
FREEDOM AND POWER

1947

THOMAS JEFFERSON: *Champion of Religious
Freedom; Advocate of Christian Morals*

By HENRY WILDER FOOTE

1948

ESSAYS ON FREEDOM AND POWER

By LORD ACTON

Selected and with an introduction by Gertrude
Himmelfarb; preface by Herman Finer

1949

AMERICAN FREEDOM AND CATHOLIC
POWER

By PAUL BLANSHARD

CORNERSTONES OF RELIGIOUS FREEDOM
IN AMERICA

Selected basic documents, court decisions and
public statements.

Edited, with an introduction and interpretations,
By JOSEPH L. BLAU

Cornerstones
of *Religious Freedom*
in America

Edited, with an introduction and interpretations, by

JOSEPH L. BLAU

Boston • THE BEACON PRESS • *1949*

FOR

RACHEL AND JUDITH

AND

ALL THE CHILDREN OF THE UNITED STATES

Contents

vii

Prefatory Note

Many people have helped in many ways in the making of this collection. It is my privilege here to record my obligations: to my wife, Eleanor W. Blau, whose contribution lies not only in her constant aid and counsel, but also in her creation of the external conditions conducive to the completion of the work; to my former teachers and present colleagues in the Department of Philosophy of Columbia University, Herbert W. Schneider and Horace L. Friess, whose encouragement and criticism have helped to shape my interest in the place of religion in the social pattern of American life; to many others of my colleagues on whose special researches I have drawn for the background of these documents; to Fay Hanson, who helped to prepare the manuscript; and to the staff of the Columbia University Library, who have been generous in giving their time and their expert knowledge of the sources. In thanking all of these my friends, I do not intend to suggest that they share the responsibility for any mistakes in fact or errors in interpretation; any such slips are on my own head alone.

Much of the material incorporated into the latter part of the Introduction was brought to my attention by Edwin H. Wilson's invaluable feature, "The Sectarian Battlefront," which appears regularly in *The Humanist*. I hope Mr. Wilson will approve of the use to which I have put his data. In sections of the Introduction and of some of the interpretations, I have drawn upon articles which I have written at various times for *The Review of Religion*. My discussion of the Moulton-Myers report in the text is a condensation of a discussion which I prepared for the Columbia University Seminar on Religion and Democracy, and owes much to the friendly opposition and stimulating criticism which I received from the members of that group.

J. L. B.

February, 1949

CORNERSTONES OF RELIGIOUS FREEDOM
IN AMERICA

1

Introduction

I

"No MAN," said Samuel Taylor Coleridge, "can rightly apprehend an abuse till he has first mastered the idea of the use of an institution." Not until we have sketched an ideally perfect functioning of a system can we determine how far short present reality falls of ideal perfection. Without a clear understanding of the ideal we may possibly be able to evolve an adequate description of the history of an institution, of its present status, and of various futures suggested for it by different factions of interpreters. But we cannot evaluate its history, estimate the importance of present trends, or select among its possible future directions unless we have worked out the conceptual pattern of the institution with which we are concerned. Yet this is a hard and thankless task, for its importance is little realized, and its results likely to be shrugged aside by all factions. Factionalism and intellectual clarity are mortal enemies.

Now, if it is the case that clarification is necessary and that clarification cannot be abided with respect to any single institution, it is clear that both the necessity and the opposition are greatly heightened and intensified when we concern ourselves with areas in which two institutions overlap. If it is both necessary and thankless to attempt to think through to ideal functioning in the political realm abstractly conceived, and equally necessary and thankless to do so in the economic realm, it is easy to see how vitally necessary and how nearly impossible it is to achieve clarity on foreign policy, an area where politics and economics meet. When we add to these difficulties the network of emotional factors which surrounds our

3

every attempt to talk of religion in society, it is plain to see that we
have chosen of all subjects that one on which it is hardest to talk
without bias, and hardest to induce others to listen with open minds.

Perhaps it is as the result of such difficulties as have been sketched
that, in all the recent discussion of freedom, the most distinctive
and characteristically American of the freedoms — freedom of religion — has played a relatively minor part. Much has been said
and written in the past few years about freedom of speech, freedom
of the press, freedom of assembly, freedom of thought, freedom
from want, freedom from fear. Comparatively little interpretive
discussion of religion can be found. Unfortunately, during this very
period, there has been a great deal of obfuscation of the meaning of
freedom of religion. In addition, a great many instances have been
reported in the newspapers where clear understanding of the meaning of the term might have prevented the adoption of an undesirable
public policy. The difficulties attendant on the making of a clear
statement, and the deliberate obscuring of the major issues, have
led now to a situation in which defenders of traditional American
freedom must either speak out, or lose religious liberty in the name
of religious liberty

This book has been conceived as a basic element in this program.
It contains a number of clear statements — by American champions
of liberty in different eras — of what freedom of religion or one of
its constituent beliefs meant to them. These are the cornerstones,
the solid and substantial foundations on which we are to build. To
help the reader to understand the issues which called forth these
statements, each major group has been prefaced by an interpretation whose purpose is, as it were, to set the stage of history on
which the drama of liberty is being enacted. And this Introduction
attempts to set down the editor's sense of the possible directions and
misdirections of current thinking about religious liberty and to indicate why, in the editor's opinion, we are now faced with a critical
situation induced in part by our confusion and our timidity.

II

There is great danger of confusion in our ambiguous use of the
word "religion." The same word is commonly used in our culture

to refer to two different things — the beliefs of an individual, and the organization through which he expresses these beliefs. As a result of this ambiguity, the two things referred to are merged in our thinking, until it has become necessary to disentangle them. In its primary sense, the word "religion" is used to mean the deepest and most inward convictions of an individual about the meaning and sacredness of life. Because convictions of such depth and intensity lead to actions, to a path of life, it is possible to speak of the commitment or consecration of an individual to his religion. In this sense, the word "conscience" is often used as a synonym for "religion." We sometimes speak of freedom of conscience, as if this were what is meant by freedom of religion. But it is inaccurate to do so, because freedom of religion is a broader concept than freedom of conscience.

Freedom of conscience is actually a negative rather than a positive right. It is the right to object, on conscientious grounds, to the performance of some civil obligations. In all essentials it reflects the older view which was called the right of passive resistance. The individual is granted a limited right *not* to obey the government; the government determines, either legislatively or juridically, what forfeit or penalty is to be paid by the conscientious objector. The right of conscientious objection to military service, for example, has long been recognized. In earlier times, the objector might hire a substitute — in itself a strange device for so deep-rooted an objection — or, more recently, he might accept noncombatant service of one sort or another under conditions of imprisonment. Recent decisions of the United States Supreme Court in cases involving members of the sect known as Jehovah's Witnesses have established a conscientious right to refuse to salute the national flag. But, as Henry Thoreau discovered a little more than a century ago, there is scant consideration given to a refusal to pay taxes on conscientious grounds. This limited right to freedom of conscience may be considered as part of the broader ideal of freedom of religion, but it by no means exhausts that broader ideal.

Freedom of religion is a positive right. It is a right to *do,* not a right to refuse to do. Limited it may be, as every other right is limited, by the public interest, necessity, and convenience, or by prevailing moral standards. Freedom of religion means the right of the individual to choose and to adhere to whichever religious beliefs he may prefer, to join with others in religious associations to express these beliefs, and to incur no civil disabilities because of his choice. There is no guarantee that the individual will be permitted to carry all his religious beliefs into practice. Members of the Mormon Church of the Latter Day Saints may believe in polygamy, but may not practice it. Members of serpent-cults of one sort or another may believe in human sacrifice, but may not perform such sacrifices. Practices such as these are repulsive to the standards of contemporary American society and are, therefore, forbidden. In general, however, a very wide latitude is given the individual in respect to the forms which his worship may take. The positive side of freedom of religion is freedom of worship; with due regard to prevailing social or moral standards, it is "the right to worship God as one pleases."

Those who accept freedom of religion as a right are obligated by this acceptance to take the maintenance of freedom of religion as a duty. It should need no demonstration that taking freedom of religion as a duty means doing all that lies in our power to see to it that every other person is permitted the same right as we are. This allows of no casuistic equivocation; it is wrong and immoral to say, as certain Roman Catholic writers do, "Yes, we believe in freedom of religion but not in freedom of error, and all beliefs other than our own are error." The history of freedom of worship in the United States is in every essential the history of the development of toleration in the United States. It is not to the Calvinistic theocrats of Massachusetts Bay Colony — whose interest in freedom of worship was in the freedom to establish their own religion not *beside* other religions, but *instead* of other religions — that we must look for the parentage of freedom of worship. It is to Roger Williams and to William Penn, both of whom recognized the obligation of tolerance as well as the right of choice. To extend the right to worship God as one pleases in any existing church, and then to permit only one church to exist, is to make an empty, meaningless, and perverse gesture.

In order to guarantee that there would be no official favoritism shown to any one belief over all other beliefs, in order to assure all beliefs of equality of opportunity so far as the government was con-

cerned, the first amendment to the Constitution of the United States forbade Congress to make any laws establishing any one religious group or prohibiting the free exercise of any religion. These prohibitions were supplementary to a specific constitutional provision outlawing all religious tests for the holding of civil offices. In the wave of nationalism which followed the outbreak of the War between the States, these limitations of the Federal government in its dealings with religion were extended to the states in the fourteenth amendment to the Constitution. Thus, one side of the separation between religion and government — the prohibition of governmental interference with the religious beliefs of the citizens — was established in the United States.

The conception of freedom of religion which has been presented here has been the dominant one throughout our nation's history. It was approached gradually through the entire colonial period and was firmly entrenched in the American mind by 1787, the year of the formulation of the Constitution. The most striking statements of this position arose during the course of the struggle to disestablish the Anglican Church in Virginia. Thomas Jefferson and James Madison, both of whom were strong advocates of personal religion and equally strong opponents of church monopoly, led the fight against the established church. Jefferson's "Act for Establishing Religious Freedom" was the platform of the opponents of any other establishment; it was passed by the Virginia legislature in 1786 after a seven-year controversy. The keynote of the supporters of this act was struck in Madison's brilliant "Memorial and Remonstrance on the Religious Rights of Man." After the passage of Jefferson's measure, the long battle had been won not only for Virginia, bu for the entire country. Some last outposts remained to be cleare of the accumulated dross of centuries of intolerance; there was mu hesitation about the granting of full civil rights to Jews and Roman Catholics. But the principle had been firmly rooted firs Virginia and then in the Constitutional Convention.

Since 1787 the principle of freedom of religion has been atta but never overthrown. The right of each individual to choo own mode of worship and to suffer no civil disabilities in quence of his choice has remained one of the glorious achie of the founders of the United States. But it must be stre

the prohibition of civil discrimination by the government does not complete the task. There is still a frontier for continuing the work of the founders. For there is need to extend the ban beyond the political to the economic and social areas.

These are, of course, not the direct concern and responsibility of government. It is the place of government to say who shall vote and who may hold office; it is not the place of government to say who shall be employed outside of its own offices or who is to be permitted to live in certain areas or to attend certain educational institutions. Whatever action may be taken, either by the Federal government or by the governments of the states, to encourage fair-employment practices or non-discriminatory admission to colleges and professional schools can only be suggestive, except where the government concerned supplies all or a substantial part of the financial backing of the employer or of the educational institution. Furthermore, we have had enough experience with prohibitory legislation of a similar type to know that its result is only that the discriminators base their action on some other ground and do not give explicit statement to their true reasons. "Grandfather" clauses are easy to create and hard to destroy. Effective action against economic and social patterns of discrimination cannot be taken by direct governmental action.

Education rather than government is the organ through which an aroused public opinion can put an end to undesirable and outrageous socio-economic consequences of the free religious choice of the individual. The necessity that educational institutions be pioneers in this field creates a concomitant necessity that educational institutions be themselves completely free of the special influence of any religious group, however large may be its majority in a particular population center. Keeping education in the United States free of sectarian influence has long been one of the primary struggles of believers in freedom of religion. There can be no failure here, or the principle will fall. Public schools should in no way contribute or call attention to differences in the religious beliefs of pupils or teachers. This was in essence the view on which Horace Mann insisted during his twelve-year period as the outstanding figure in public education in Massachusetts. There was a great deal of opposition to Mann on this score, even from repre-

sentatives of minority sects, but the Board of Education remained firm in supporting him. Mann's self-vindication in the last of his annual reports is one of the finest and most searching examinations of the nature of public education in a nation which has accepted the principle of freedom of religion. It deserves to be far better known than it is, and to be carefully studied by everyone who has any connection with public education in the United States.

III

It was said above that freedom of religion is to be understood as the right of an individual to choose for himself the pattern of his deepest and most inward convictions, and, subject to considerations of public policy, to express his convictions in worship and in action. It has been suggested that unless an open field were maintained there would be an enforced choice rather than a free choice. Legislation and education have been noted as two supplementary methods of keeping the field open. Now we must consider the position under freedom of religion of those individuals who accept as their deepest beliefs and convictions — in the sense in which we have been using the word, as their *religion* — opposition to all or some features of organized religious groups. What is to be done about those whose religion is freedom from religion?

This group includes a number of sub-classes which should be carefully distinguished from one another. It includes some who desire the total abolition of all religious organization and of the belief in God; others who would retain religious organization but dispense with belief in an intervening Deity; still others whose objection is not to churches or to religious beliefs, but to the influence of churches on government; and — possibly the most numerous of these sub-classes — those who object only to the clergy. All of these are described in the churchly literature of an earlier day, along with adherents of non-Christian religions, as infidels. A better general name would be freethinkers. It might be even more profitable for our examination here to distinguish among these types of free thought, and to assign such descriptive names as "atheists," "liberal religionists," "secularists," and "anticlericals" to the four types mentioned above.

To make the distinction is important and necessary, because a very real part of the American heritage, perhaps that part which is most genuinely American, is anticlerical without being antireligious. Resentment of domination by an external, imposed power has been the core not of American political life alone, but also of its religious life. The early development of a strong congregationalism indicates a trend, though it does not prove the point, because of the strong central position of the minister within the congregation. The emergence of the frontier sects such as Methodism, with the resultant development of lay preaching, continues the trend and brings the point closer to proof. The real proof, however, is to be sought in the writings of those who, like Jefferson, believed in Jesus, possibly even in Christianity, but resented the dogmatism and the vested interests of professional clerics. The real proof is to be seen, for example, in the work of Joel Barlow, whose early *Columbiad* linked priests and kings as the twin sources of evil:

> Two settled slaveries thus the race control,
> Engross their labors and debase their soul;
> Till creeds and crimes and feuds and fears compose
> The seeds of war and all its kindred woes.

It is, perhaps, not merely fancy to feel in the anticlerical lines of Barlow a suggestion of that older Latin poet, Lucretius, who recognized so clearly that "Mankind, in Wretched Bondage held, lay groveling on the ground, galled with the Yoke of what is called *Religion;* from the Sky this Tyrant shewed her Head, and with grim Looks hung over us poor Mortals here below." For Barlow, too, talks of "the bondage of the mind" that "spreads deeper glooms and subjugates mankind."

Barlow, however, wrote hymns and published a hymnal which was fairly popular for a time among the Congregationalists. Evidently he saw no contradiction between writing *for* religion and writing *against* the clergy. Perhaps he would have gone as far as to say that, in writing against priesthood and the church, he was writing in the best interests of religion. A similar attitude appears, years later, among the New England transcendentalists, who in this, as in so many other respects, were the spokesmen for their era.

This series of quotations from Thoreau indicates the continuity of religious anticlericalism in America:

> Consider the snappish tenacity with which they preach Christianity, still. What are time and space to Christianity, eighteen hundred years, and a new world? — that the humble life of a Jewish peasant should have force to make a New York bishop so bigoted. . . . It is necessary not to be a Christian to appreciate the beauty and significance of the life of Christ. . . . The wisest man preaches no doctrine; he has no scheme; he sees no rafter, not even a cobweb, against the heavens. . . . It is remarkable that, notwithstanding the universal favor with which the New Testament is outwardly received, and even the bigotry with which it is defended, there is no hospitality shown to, there is no appreciation of, the order of truth with which it deals.

Thoreau was ready to give up his Christianity, not because of what it was inherently, but because of what the men of religion had made of it; under no circumstances, however, could he have given up his Christ. Fine, moralizing reflections, indeed, for a Sunday spent in a boat on the river!

This is radical anticlericalism, but it stems from the "freeborn mind" of America, which, in its turn, sprang from a protestant attitude that would cut through the centuries of clerical obfuscation of the Scriptures, and in its extreme expression would make every man his own interpreter. Individualism of this sort in religious teaching ties closely to the Hebrew tradition. For many centuries there was no such thing as a Jewish minister; the rabbi was a teacher only because he was a master scholar. He was not even a man of religion professionally; rather he was a man of ordinary affairs, often of very humble position, who, in his studies in both the Written and the Oral Law, had gone farther than those who sat under him. The professional religionist, the cleric, developed first almost by accident in American Jewry, and for many years had little position among his own people. The Jews were essentially democratic in worship. Partly in the light of this tradition we can explain the presence of Jews, even of rabbis, among the freethinkers. We must not, however, neglect to consider the possibility that some of these Jewish "freethinkers" supported the Free Religious Association and other such groups as an alternative to the possible loss of civil liberties, or even of the right to worship in their own way, which might have followed a successful campaign for the so-called "Christian amendment" by the National Reform Association.

Then, too, we must take into consideration the fact that members of minority groups in America have always been strongly convinced of the necessity for maintaining the separation of church and state. The Baptists, the Unitarians, the Universalists, the Christian Scientists have all made large contributions to the development of the "wall of separation" in the United States. Rabbis who took part in the activities of the American Secular Union were profoundly disturbed when they discovered members and even leaders of this organization trying to convert it into a movement for the destruction of religion rather than a movement for the prevention of a church establishment. There must have been many non-Jews who supported these Jewish leaders, whose approach to the secular movement was the same as theirs. For secularism, the absolute separation of church and state, is another concept dear to the American mind. It was organized bigotry playing upon the fear of losing this separateness that produced the ugly whispering campaign against Alfred E. Smith in 1928. It is a conscious and developed secularism which must be called into play in our age, if freedom of religion is to survive.

I say "conscious and developed" secularism because, in a day of organized pressure groups, disestablishment is not enough to guarantee the separation of the state from religious influence. When the Anglican Church in Virginia was disestablished in 1785, protagonists of this legislation felt that secularism had been achieved; when the first amendment to the Constitution forbade a national establishment, secularists felt their object had been permanently won. This was, as later events have shown, a naïvely optimistic view. By 1872, the churches were in the saddle once more; in that year, Francis Ellingwood Abbot published a formal statement of nine demands of American secularists in *The Index*. The essence of these demands is that indirect religious influence should be eliminated from the government even as direct religious influence had been. These demands have not been met: church property is still tax-exempt; chaplains are more than ever used and publicized in the armed services; public appropriations for sectarian institutions have increased; the Bible is still read in public schools; the President of the United States and the governors of the several states still proclaim religious festivals; simple affirmation has not been substituted for judicial oath; Sunday observance laws remain on the statute books; laws still look to "the enforcement of Christian morality"; in the practical administration of the government, privileges and advantages are conceded to religious bodies.

What has happened to American secularism? At the risk of restating the obvious, let me suggest that, while religion has progressed, secularism has largely remained in the same place. Secularism, except where it has been organized, has rested content in the formal elimination of church influence in government; the churches have realized that they can have as much or more influence informally, because not only an established church, but also all other churches, can exert pressure on government. Truly prophetic has come to seem Joel Barlow's warning:

> Think not, my friends, the patriot's task is done,
> Or Freedom safe, because the battle's won.
> Unnumber'd foes, far different arms that wield,
> Wait the weak moment when she quits her shield.

Of militant atheists there have been few in America; of liberal religionists there have been, and still are, many. The controversy over evolution made many new liberal religionists, for the significant difficulty in the acceptance of the developmental hypothesis was not what this belief did to man, but what it did to God. The most cursory reading of the literature of the period makes it clear that the stumbling block was the need to accompany evolutionary belief with rejection or modification of the belief in a constantly intervening, immanent Deity. God became exclusively the First Cause who set into operation the action of Natural Law; all later effects are produced mediately, through secondary causation.

This was not, however, the only way in which believers in the results of science were forced into a relaxation of some aspects of traditional religious orthodoxy. The impulse to liberal religion came as much from the dogmatism of the traditionalists as it did from the new hypotheses of science. Consider, for example, these statements by the eminent Presbyterian and Princeton professor, Charles Hodge:

> Banishing God from the world is simply intolerable, and blessed be his name, impossible. An absent God who does nothing is, to us, no God. It may be said that Christ did not teach science. True, but He taught truth; and science, so called, when it comes in conflict with truth, is what man is when he comes in conflict with God.
>
> The truth of this [the Scriptural] theory of the universe rests . . . on the infallible authority of the Word of God. . . . . The truth of this doctrine . . . rests not only on the authority of the Scriptures, but on the very constitution of our natures. The Bible has little charity for those who reject it. It pronounces them to be either derationalized or demoralized, or both.

Even granting that this is the dogmatism of hysteria, and that the more philosophical James McCosh, at the same university, in the same religious tradition, found it possible to make his peace with the developmental theory — even so, it is evident that, if this blind authoritarianism, this rigid attempt to control the human mind, is orthodoxy, there will always be many sincerely religious, but "freeborn," minds who will refuse to accept it. This type of theological one-way thinking — in America, at least — will alienate a far larger number of people than it will attract.

This is the significance of the warning that Dr. J. L. Cabell, of the University of Virginia, introduced into his *Unity of Mankind:*

> If theologians rashly stake the authority of the Bible on the adoption of a particular set of scientific opinions, each of which they hold to be the "articulus stantis aut cadentis ecclesiae," they should not be surprised if the exclusive votaries of science, accepting the issue thus inconsiderately presented, should come to regard with aversion a theology associated, as they have been led to believe, with propositions which they know to be both false and absurd. And thus it often happens, even at the present day, that the premature alarms of the timid friends of our holy religion, and their denunciations of free scientific inquiry, become the determining cause of the very infidelity they would deprecate.

There have also been those who have become liberals in religion for reasons unconnected with orthodoxy's failure to come to terms with science. Many have felt that the traditional churches have failed to provide a secure foundation for the ethical life of men. They point to the arbitrary view of the nature of God which is advocated by the traditional churches, and to the fact that this arbitrary God is described as applying a completely mechanical rule-of-thumb moral code. To subscribe to such a code, regardless of the authority claimed for it, is impossible for many people who have learned that the essential element in the ethical life is the element of choice. For such liberals, religious belief means the liberation of the highest in man; if they talk about God, they mean no omniscient, omnipotent, transcendent person, but that in man which transcends his own limitations without transcending the universe, or nature. Such liberals are not atheists, though their God-idea has little in common with that of the historic churches.

Here, then, is a large group of those who believe in freedom from religion in one sense or another. What can be said of their right to hold opinions antagonistic to religion? Under a system such as ours, which maintains the right of the individual to free choice among religious positions, freedom to reject is as allowable as freedom to accept. There is nothing in the written or unwritten traditions of the United States that limits the individual to a choice among patterns of acceptance. In fact, a limitation of this sort is undesirable. Once the precedent is established that the choice must be among prescribed alternatives, it would become easier to narrow the list of alternatives until the language of choice is used in the real absence of choice, as in totalitarian elections. The same freedom to believe, to associate, to speak, to preach, to missionize, and to prophesy must be granted to atheist and theist, agnostic and gnostic, anticlerical and clergyman, heterodox and orthodox. The rights of those who believe in unbelief must be defended in order to place a secure foundation under the rights of those who believe in belief.

IV

Thus far, in sketching what freedom of religion has meant historically in the United States, the center of attention has properly been placed in the individual. In the American tradition, rights have always been of individuals. A right is an immunity against authority; it is an area in which the individual is supreme; it is a sovereign power. Certain rights, however, and notably among them freedom of religion, entail the right to organize. Religion can be — but very rarely is — a purely personal, private matter between the individual and what he holds most sacred. For the most part, religion is expressed in group activity. For this reason we have come to the secondary use of the word "religion" to mean the church, the fellowship of believers in the same themes, the community of the like-minded. Those individuals who have a right to believe have a right to organize in furtherance of their beliefs. Freedom of religion implies the freedom to organize churches. (I use the word "churches," with apologies, to refer to associations of unbelievers as well as to associations of believers.)

Just as the state and all its agencies are committed to an indifference to the religious beliefs of individuals, save where the belief issues in a practice that is socially undesirable, the state is committed to the strictest neutrality as far as the religious associations are concerned, again with the same reservation. This must not, however, be considered as a right of the churches as such. It is, rather, the fulfillment of the rights of the individuals composing the churches. No organization as such can have rights save by a legal fiction. It may be considered to have the rights of an individual under the law, but it cannot be considered to have rights above the law. In any other sense than this it is absurd to talk about the rights of an association. The individual conscience may in certain respects be granted a position of privilege above the law, an immunity against authority. An association, even though it be a church, may not be granted such special privilege.

Actually, of course, there are certain privileges that are granted to religious, educational, and charitable organizations because of their character as non-profit-making groups. These are chiefly privileges with respect to tax exemptions and are, therefore, privileges under the law, subject to being rescinded as they were granted. Churches are not immune to taxation; they must be specifically exempted. Even this much favoritism has been subject to criticism; many Americans feel that churches and schools are engaged in profit-seeking ventures which happen to be not particularly profitable. This controversy is outside our province here. It is important here to stress the point that, even in this exemption, religious associations are not placed above the law.

In recent years there has been an increasingly vociferous movement among churchmen to proclaim that freedom of religion means freedom for religious organizations, a privileged position above the law. This we may call, to complete the pattern, "freedom for religion." As I have tried to suggest, freedom for religion has a legitimate place and an illegitimate extension. Legitimately the right to freedom of religion implies the right to associate freely for religious purposes and the duty to permit others freedom to organize. To this great end, the secular arm was forbidden to legislate concerning the establishment of any sect or the prohibition of any form of socially acceptable worship. The meaning and intention of the first amendment to the Constitution of the United States are crystal-clear.

This clarity, however, has been muddied, over a period of years, by the illegitimate extension of individual freedom to organizational freedom. This amounts to a distortion of tolerance, an ingenious and deliberate misinterpretation of the concept of religious freedom. Let any action of government, or any projected action, be objectionable to any sect for any reason; loud cries are raised to heaven criticizing the action of government as interference with religious freedom. Thus, for example, gambling in comparatively innocuous forms has long been the main support of many churches in — among other communities — New York City. Some years ago the city administration conducted a crusade against gambling. Betting parlors, gambling dens, and private homes were raided by the police to the accompaniment of clerical cheers. But when the same police, in the same crusade, attempted to stop the gambling in churches, the clerical cheers changed to protests; the all-out effort to complete the extermination of gambling was decried as persecution of religious bodies, and hence interference with religious liberty. The example may, perhaps, seem trivial, but the principle involved in it is a significant one. The protests of the clergy in this instance amounted to a declaration that religious organizations stand in a privileged position above the law.

The extent to which the exponents of such positions as this

depend upon deliberate distortion and falsification comes out forcibly in the comment of Monsignor J. S. Middleton, secretary for education of the Roman Catholic Archdiocese of New York, on the decision of the Supreme Court in the Vashti McCollum case. Middleton asserted that the articulate unbelief of one parent was placing "the rights of all parents to freedom of religious education for their children . . . in danger of being invaded in this country." This statement sounds fine; we find ourselves readily moved to sympathy with those whose rights are being invaded. Monsignor Middleton and his confreres know, however, that whatever right to freedom of religious education there may be has not been jeopardized by the McCollum decision. The churches and the home still stand, as they have throughout Western history, as the primary agencies of that education. What the McCollum case has done is to restore the wall of separation by prohibiting religious teaching in public-school buildings and hence at public expense. It is not freedom of religious education but cost-free religious education that Middleton is concerned about, and cost-free religious education has not been sanctioned in the United States for a century. When the dominance of the Protestant groups placed Roman Catholics in a small minority, how they protested against the intrusion of religious ideas in public education! John Hughes, first Archbishop of New York, was one of the loudest in protest. Now, however, the numerical proportion of Roman Catholics in the population has grown; though still representing a minority in the country as a whole, their ecclesiastical politicians find themselves in a majority in some areas, and growing in others, and are beginning to look forward to the reversal of their position which takes place as soon as they achieve numerical preponderance.

"In a state where the majority of people are Catholic, the church will require that legal existence be denied to error, and that if religious minorities exist, they shall have only a *de facto* existence without opportunity to spread their unbeliefs." This is a recent statement of an old Catholic policy, from an article by the Reverend F. Cavalli, S.J., in the April, 1948, issue of *Civiltà Cattolica,* a Jesuit publication. How this theoretical position, concealed by the smooth lip service of Catholic leaders to ideals of freedom in America, works out in practice may be seen in the sad story of the religious invasion of the public schools in New Mexico. In this as yet insufficiently publicized instance, the public-school system took over the parochial schools with the presumed intention of operating them as public, non-sectarian schools. The effect of the action of the public education authorities has been to grant state support to parochial schools. In some cases non-Catholic pupils who cannot afford private schools are forced to attend these schools.

In these schools, twenty-nine of them, in seven counties of the state, one hundred and forty-five members of Catholic religious orders have been on the public payroll as teachers. They have worn clerical garb. The program of instruction has included specifically sectarian material such as the catechism, which pupils have been forced to learn. Catholic shrines have been placed in the schoolrooms, and religious pictures and symbols on the walls: Libraries have been stocked with marked copies of Catholic periodicals. Among the textbooks in use have been some marked "Faith and Freedom Readers for Catholic Schools Only." Graduation exercises in some instances have been conducted in Catholic churches as religious ceremonies.

There have been overt acts of discrimination against teachers and pupils who protested these conditions, while special favors and prerogatives have been granted to those who go along with the authorities. Suit was brought in March, 1948, to compel the abandonment of this state-supported religious education. An affidavit submitted by one parent whose children refused to make confession and to go to Mass asserted that "they were locked up in a room and punished for about a week." In one of the counties, Rio Arriba, retaliation for the suit included the decision not to hire any more Protestant teachers. Protestant children who objected to the genuflections and religious posings prescribed for the processional at the commencement exercises of Costilla Sisters of Mercy Public High School (May 20, 1948) were told to get their "smart lawyers" to give them their diplomas. The grades of children who requested transfers to Presbyterian mission schools were lowered so that the children would not be admitted.

In the New Mexico District Court, the decision of Judge E. T. Hensley, Jr., was favorable to the complaining parents. The judge ruled that the practices of which illustrations have been given violate the separation of church and state, and that the influence of the religious orders "clearly invades the schoolroom at all times." A false tolerance, arising out of unfamiliarity with situations like this, can very easily lead to the destruction of the freedom of religion which it claims to exemplify.

It is interesting, in the face of so clear a demonstration of what can be done by a determined religious organization when it is supported by public taxation, to note in how many cases the entering wedge has already been inserted in the form of free textbooks, free bus transportation, and federal school-lunch money for parochial-school pupils, forms of public subsidy for religious education. Information provided by the United States Office of Education in 1947 indicates that free textbooks are provided in five states, free bus transportation in twelve, federal subsidy lunches in eighteen. These subsidies, however, do not satisfy the ecclesiastical hierarchy. The demand that is put forward, both by them and in their name, is for full federal aid, "without strings," for parochial schools. It was asserted, for example, by J. M. O'Neill, of Brooklyn College, in *Commentary* for June, 1947, that no bill that fails to provide for full federal aid to parochial schools is likely to pass. The political strength of the Catholic minority is being held over the heads of the public: "Aid to parochial schools or no aid to any schools." Thus the dismal story reveals an all-out effort to use political machinery to achieve a religious end.

This is particularly notable when the smear technique of name-calling is resorted to. In earlier nineteenth-century usage, the names used to discredit religious opponents were names indicative of unpopular, or presumably unpopular, religious views: infidel, Socinian, heretic. This was true even when the context was pseudo-political, as in Ezra Stiles Ely's sermon on "The Duty of Christian Freemen to Elect Christian Rulers," where direct political action was advocated to prevent the election of the non-orthodox. Today, in the changed climate of opinion, the name-callers use politically discreditable smear words. Thus Archbishop J. F. A. McIntyre, on May 18, 1947, called opponents of the program for released time for religious education "distinctly pro-Nazi." A year later, the same prelate said that those who oppose free bus transportation for parochial-school pupils are Communists and fellow travelers. The shift is an interesting sidelight on the progress of the "cold war." The more germane point is, however, that in following up his accusation that opponents of subsidy to parochial schools are Communists, the Archbishop of Los Angeles saw fit to assert by implication the political nature of his church in these words: "And to think that the strongest bulwark against the rising tide of Communism is the Catholic Church." Again using the political smear in religion, Monsignor J. J. Sheerin recently tried to prevent an address by Methodist Bishop G. Bromley Oxnam, an official of Protestants and Other Americans United for the Separation of Church and State. Oxnam was described by Sheerin as unqualified to speak to the Washington Association because "he could not be classed as a patriot."

Together with the methods that have been illustrated above, methods used to gain a foothold for sectarian teachings in public education — so extensively treated here because it is the major battleground at the present time — consider two other aspects of freedom for religion. The first is the attempt to establish "thought control" — to abolish freedom of thought — by means of censorship, carried out indirectly wherever possible, directly where no other means are available. The second is the recrudescence of the attempt to legislate the citizens of the United States into following the practices of the orthodox denominations.

The attempt to exercise "thought control" is, of course, nothing new in the history of the United States. In the last half-century, however, there have been developed media of communication to large groups in the population — radio, motion pictures, television — and there has been a vast increase in the number of books and magazines appealing to an audience of the barely literate. The increased possibility that those of a low level of literacy might get hold of material in one way or another unfavorable or distasteful to religious organizations has spurred on the advocates of censorship. In the first instance, the censorship is upheld on "moral" grounds. The depicting of certain types of scene or the broadcast of certain words and phrases was the target of attack. This, of course, is readily defended, and readily accepted as necessary even by many who do not concede its desirability. The movie industry and radio stations have recognized the force and possible legitimacy of the demand, and, to avoid pressure for official censorship, have set up their own self-censorship agencies. This, however, does not exhaust the tale; local agencies, in many sections of the country, insist upon additional censorship by local "boards of review." The standards applied by these local groups are frequently of a religious nature; the portrayal of divorce as a solution to a marital problem, for example, is frowned upon. The effect is to provide an additional area in which the standards of particular denominations are enforced on an entire community.

The situation with respect to radio is similar. Recently an attempt was made in California to prevent broadcasts by an avowed atheist. Despite the activities of religious bodies, whose leaders were unwilling to grant to others the liberty on which they and their organizations have flourished, the state authorities of California ruled in favor of the right of the atheist to continue his broadcasts. This is a first major test. Censorship on a smaller scale is applied by the radio stations under pressure from religious groups at all times. So great is the fear of retaliation that the stations have become overcautious, shying away from shadows. Thus on the radio, as in the movies, there is a lack of vigorous adult education and entertainment, in part as a result of religious pressures.

The book and magazine publishing field is passing through a censorship crisis at present. In Philadelphia, for example, a committee of Protestant ministers has led a drive described by *Publishers' Weekly* (May 8, 1948) as an attempt to "ban books for religious and political heresy as well as on moral grounds." The campaign is reminiscent of the old Comstock-law days; it is directed not only against "filthy and anti-American literature" but also against "blasphemous" books. The ultimate intention of the clerical committee is to gain the passage of a city ordinance establishing a local committee to pass on books sold. In the spring of 1948, several thousand books, including those of outstanding modern writers, were seized; while the judge presiding over the seizure trial was studying the briefs and the books, spectators prayed that he would receive divine guidance. At one of the court hearings, a priest declared from the witness stand that he appeared as the representative of Cardinal Dougherty, and called, in the name of the Cardinal, for the suppression of one of the books. If no other proof were at hand, this appearance would clearly testify to the invasion of the field of secular decision by ecclesiastical pressure.

The outstanding issue in magazine censorship concerns the banning of *The Nation* from the public high schools of New York City. *The Nation* ran a series of articles by Paul Blanshard criticizing political activities of the Catholic Church. Superintendent of Schools Jansen banned the magazine. Jansen's readiness to please the hierarchy was again shown when the June 14, 1948, issue of *Life* featured a treatment of the Reformation which certain Catholic leaders found objectionable. Jansen's comment was, "If it is offensive to any group, then it will be banned." In Rochester, New York, a request for the banning of *The Nation* — a request stemming from the Catholic War Veterans — was rejected by the Board of Education. In Massachusetts, however, Catholic pressure was more successful; the magazine was banned in a group of state teachers' colleges, but later reinstated.

Minor issues involving efforts on the part of religious organizations to impose their standards on everyone and to prevent the wide circulation of criticism of their efforts are constantly cropping up in the newspapers. For example, on December 16, 1947, *The New York Times* carried two such stories on page 35. One was an account of an attack made by the New York State Knights of Columbus on six Christmas cards distributed by the Progressive Citizens of America. The spokesman for the Knights of Columbus condemned the cards as an "atheistic attack against our Christian belief and the things we hold sacred," and described them further as "obscene," "blasphemous," and "sacrilegious." The second news story concerned a teachers' course in intercultural education which had been scheduled to be given by a well-known sociologist. The course was canceled by order of the superintendent of schools. The reason given was that the lecturer's effectiveness "had been impaired since it had become known that he wrote, under a pen-name, a pamphlet criticizing organized religions." Another area in which "thought control" is now being attempted affects large sections of the population indirectly, but seems on the face of it to apply only to a special group. It involves the dismissal of physicians from the staffs of Catholic hospitals for the presumption of disagreeing on scientific grounds with their ecclesiastical overlords by supporting a bill that would have permitted physicians to advise married persons on birth-control methods.

The examples which have been given speak for themselves. They reveal a pattern of aggression by various organizations against the free choice among beliefs which is the right of the individual in America. The aggression is marked by an attack on free communication and circulation of ideas. Not all the spokesmen for sectarian orthodoxies have the courage of their inner convictions — as had Francis Cardinal Spellman when he called the principle of separation of church and state "an outworn shibboleth." Rather the pattern is one of concealing an attack on the principle behind an assertion of the principle. In Easton, Pennsylvania, for example, high-school teachers have been censured by the school board for "talking politically and religiously to other teachers during school hours." The reason given for the censure was that the combination of politics and religion in the teachers' discussions violated the separation of church and state!

Fortunately, there has not as yet been any great pressure for reviving the old method of direct legislation of the patterns of behavior deemed acceptable by religious groups. As in the past, one major type of pressure which is still being exerted is for the enactment and enforcement of Sunday legislation. On December 7, 1948, *The New York Times* carried an account of such activity by the Lord's Day Alliance of the United States. It is particularly noteworthy that in some sections of the country pressure for Sunday observance is used mainly as a lever of oppression against the Seventh Day Adventist and other Christian sects which favor Saturday as a day of rest.

An attempt has been made by certain Lutheran groups, whose case was put to the House of Representatives by Congressman Reese of Kansas, to induce the government of the United States to insist on opening the sessions of the United Nations with prayer. An occasional overzealous official exaggerates the conventional use of the name of God in public statements. In one extreme case, the mayor and council of Fort Lee, New Jersey, directly violated the separation of church and state by proclaiming, on April 6, 1944, "This is the holy season of Lent, and it is in keeping with the American way of life that tribute be paid to the divine saviour," and requesting all businesses to close for three hours on Good Friday of that year "as a mark of respect to the passion of the divine saviour." These are isolated cases, however; this sort of pressure is not the characteristic approach of our age.

In some ways it can be said that the masking of political and economic activity behind a false front of religion is more usual. For example, in 1947, six hundred and thirty-seven Protestant clergymen signed a statement issued by the American Council of Christian Churches, asserting that the closed shop violated the basic teachings of the Bible as well as freedom of conscience. "Religious" organizations have been in the forefront of opposition to the proposed child-labor amendment to the Federal Constitution. Of recent times there has been a rash of organizations engaging in political activity under pseudo-religious names and auspices; the Christian Front and the Christian Mobilizers are two such groups whose activities have been widely heralded. The general pattern here is the attempt to abuse the widespread feeling that, because religion is sacred, religious organizations are sacrosanct and above the law, by using it as a shield for political activities and political designs.

V

The last few pages have given evidence that there is in fact in the United States a trend toward the practice of freedom *for* religion, and away from the individualistic interpretation of freedom *of* religion which was presented earlier. This movement is not, however, to be considered as a narrowly practical one. It has a theoretical foundation and an institutional orientation. Unfortunately the ideological basis of freedom for religion has not had clear statement in the United States, but has, rather, been implicit in the writings of many American clericals. There have been good presentations in the work of European thinkers, and, in recent times, the best in the writings of Jacques Maritain. To examine the theory, however, let us look to the writings of an earlier Catholic liberal, Lord Acton, because the British situation in the context of which he was writing was closely akin to the American scene.

Acton provides immediate proof that the heart of freedom of religion as it has been understood in the United States is the right of individuals to free choice among beliefs. He was no friend of this sort of freedom. He called it "the equal claim of every man to be unhindered by man in the fulfillment of duty to God — a doctrine laden with storm and havoc, which is the secret essence of the Rights of Man, and indestructible soul of Revolution." Yet he recognized that this was the Protestant ideal of religious liberty, the ideal of sectarians who were "concerned with the individual more than with the congregation." Acton interpreted the Puritans as seeing that "governments and institutions are made to pass away, like things of earth, whilst souls are immortal." However, the result of this vision, committing "that which had been done by authority . . . to the intellect and the conscience of free men," Acton disapproved, because "it has led to the superiority of politics over divinity in the life of nations."

In this passage, Acton voiced a criticism which he had made more in detail some thirty years earlier. In the earlier discussion, he made it evident that what he considered a desirable form of religious freedom was not freedom for the individual, but superlegal status for the church. The point, he asserted, at which civil and religious liberty unite, "the common root from which they derive their sustenance, is the right of self-government." He continued:

The modern theory, which has swept away every authority except that of the State . . . is the enemy of that common freedom in which religious freedom is included. It condemns, as a State within the State, every inner group and community, class or corporation, administering its own affairs; and, by proclaiming the abolition of privileges, it emancipates the subjects of every such authority in order to transfer them exclusively to its own. It recognizes liberty only in the individual, because it is only in the individual that liberty can be separated from authority, and the right of conditional obedience deprived of the security of a limited command. Under its sway, therefore, every man may profess his own religion more or less freely; but his religion is not free to administer its own laws. In other words, religious profession is free, but Church government is controlled. And where ecclesiastical authority is restricted, religious liberty is virtually denied.

Acton makes out an excellent case for organizational freedom. But there are two points in this statement which seem to be weak. First, he starts by making self-government the root of religious liberty, and ends by asserting ecclesiastical authority as the religious form of self-government. That is to say, since authority and government are virtual synonyms, he is asserting that, in the religious context, the *ecclesia,* the church, is the equivalent of the self. It is not the individual self but the corporate self, the organization, in which Acton finds the right of self-government resident. Thus he is enabled to assert that any subordination of the religious organization to the political organization, any restriction of the church by the laws of the country, is a denial of religious liberty. Freedom of religion, in Acton's use of the term, becomes, then, "the right of religious communities to the practice of their own duties, the enjoyment of their own constitution, and the protection of the law, which equally secures to all the possession of their own independence." The churches are to be above the law; political government is to be the servant of ecclesiastical government. This is the consequence of Acton's substitution of the group for the individual as the unit of freedom.

The second difficulty in the argument presented by Acton is one which I have discussed earlier in this Introduction: it is the ambiguous use of the word "religion" to mean both a set of beliefs and an organizational structure. What a man believes is not an organization, but a doctrine. It may be a doctrine calling for an organization to fulfill it. Preventing the formation of the organization may frustrate the practice of the belief, but it does not limit the belief itself. When Acton says, "Every man may profess his own religion more or less freely," the expression "his own religion" refers to the beliefs of the individual. In the phrase which follows, "his religion is not free to administer its own laws," the expression "his religion" refers to the church organization of which the individual is a member. This ambiguity leads Acton to the view that the state is obligated to defend the church — when what the state is actually obligated to under any meaningful use of the term "freedom of religion" is to defend the right of the individual to private beliefs which run counter to the tenets and dogmas of the various churches.

VI

Three interpretations of freedom of religion have been rapidly reviewed and exemplified in historic or contemporary situations.

I have called these three "freedom of worship," "freedom from religion," and "freedom for religion." "Freedom of worship" is the acknowledgment of the right of every individual to select the pattern of beliefs which is to be central to his life and to conform in practice to his beliefs, as far as is consonant with public order, with no sacrifice of civil rights. "Freedom from religion" is the right of the individual to disbelieve in the conventional patterns, in whole or in part. "Freedom for religion" is the right of the individual to found organizations to give expression to his pattern of beliefs, in so far as it is a pattern shared by others; unfortunately, this right shows a tendency to pass over into the claim that organizations so founded have a status superior to the law. This latter, unacceptable misconception of freedom of religion is one of the most serious threats to American freedom today.

It is a very persuasive misconception, because its advocates have learned to express this doctrine, which can lead only to the suppression of individual rights, in the language of individual rights. Much as business corporations in the United States have battened on their fictitious legal status as corporate persons entitled to individual rights under the "due process" clause, churches — religious corporations — are able to grow overweening and oppressive if their claim to legal status as corporate persons under the First Amendment is granted. "Due process" for corporate persons has produced the legal anomaly of violation of the rights of the very individuals whom the due process clause was intended to protect. Religious freedom for religious corporations, if it is allowed, will end in the trampling of the religious freedom of the individual under the marching feet of a remorseless and self-aggrandizing hierarchy.

The selections which follow are meant to serve as a reminder that the interpretation which has been given to freedom of religion in the United States has been the separation of church and state. The state is to show no preference for any church or anti-church group; these groups are to have no authority in the state. To the extent that education is a state function, supported by taxes, no religious organization has any shadow of a claim to determine what is to be taught in the schools. Similarly, religious organizations have no claim to determine any part of the procedures at public functions or in legislative sessions. They have no claim to a right to impose their standards of belief or behavior upon those who are not members of their organizations. The state has no right to interfere with their religious exercise, except in the interest of public safety or decency.

Both the state and the religious organizations exist to satisfy needs of individuals. The primary unit of society is the individual. The state serves the needs of the individual for political organization and for protection. The state protects the individual, among other things, against oppression by religious groups. The churches serve the needs of individuals for the institutionalization of their beliefs. The churches provide an appropriate atmosphere for worship and a social outlet. The individual conscience is in some respects superior to the state because the state is made by individuals. This claim cannot be denied by a constitutional state. Churches also claim superiority to the state, by virtue of divine authority. This claim a constitutional state cannot allow, because it is not the proper agency to decide among the conflicting divine authorities claimed by conflicting creeds.

An editorial in *The Christian Science Monitor* for October 20, 1948, in commenting upon the recent World Council of Churches at Amsterdam, said, in part, that "the Christian conscience in society, not the Christian church in politics, holds the hope for the future." This is an excellent suggestion of the direction in which American society must move to preserve itself from clerical domination, because it restores emphasis to the individual, in whose conscience, says the *Monitor*, "salvation begins but does not end." What a man believes in his heart is of great concern to society. It is of so much concern that society, through its protective institution of the state, must see to it that fanatical zeal does not have the opportunity to dictate what a man shall believe. All forms of "thought control" end in the stultification of thought. If our society is to continue to be adaptable to changing conditions in the world, it dares not allow "thought control" in any form or through any censoring agency, whether it be that of the leviathan state or that of the leviathan church. But to place our reliance on the individual conscience is to recognize that the social order is a moral order. It is to leave room for free choice in the interplay of diverse ideals, and to believe in men, not institutions.

Justice Felix Frankfurter's concurring opinion in the Vashti Mc-Collum case includes the suggestion that "the mere formulation of a relevant Constitutional principle is the beginning of the solution of a problem, not its answer." This has been particularly true of the problem of freedom of religion. The miraculous view has predominated in the writing of its history — the view according to which the First Amendment was adopted, and lo! there was religious freedom. This is a naïve account. The true history of the struggle for religious freedom is to be found after the principle of the wall of separation had been formulated. The struggle of the past century and three quarters to give substance to the formula of religious freedom is the true history of religious freedom. It is an unending struggle; it has not been finally determined by the McCollum decision, nor will any future decision determine the meaning of the principle once and for all time. Each generation must fight the battles of freedom anew in terms of the problems and powers of its time. To use unchanged the arms of tradition is to invite defeat; to see in the past a guide and instrument in the development of unfolding values and meanings is to be on the road to victory. The words of earlier fighters for freedom of religion are given here, not that they may be repeated by us or by our descendants, but that they may suggest to us new ways and new words for defending freedom of religion in our day. There are many brave words here of continuing vitality, rich in suggestive power — but the most stirring words are those yet to be spoken.

2

Colonial Stirrings

THE PENDULUM OF historical interpretation swings back and forth in a wide arc. Instead of merely correcting the extravagances of a past generation of historians, we relentlessly swing to the opposite extreme. Everything that used to be considered true we declare to be false; everything our fathers thought good we find evil. And then, since no view can remain unchanged in this world of change, before much time has passed, we find ourselves compelled to challenge our own earlier extreme statements, to recognize the kernel of truth in what our predecessors have said and we have confuted.

Thus has it gone with the tale of our colonial ancestors and their regard for freedom of religion. There was a version of the story so widespread that it could be called the authorized version, the definitive account. It went like this: A group, small and without influence, of English Puritans, dedicated to the restoration of Protestant Christianity, were persecuted cruelly by the Church of England. Unable, because of this persecution, to carry on their work and their faith in their native land, they migrated to Holland. There they found an atmosphere of tolerance which permitted the practice of their religion, but became disturbed because their children were becoming Hollanders, alienated from their parents. Again they made ready to migrate, this time to an unsettled country which their own hands would bring under cultivation for the glory of God and the mother country. Their successful venture at Plymouth led other English groups to follow them to the New World, where they created an asylum for those persecuted for the cause of religion. Thus was born the great American tradition of freedom of religion.

31

Clearly this account stands in need of correction. It is true that the settlers of both the Plymouth and the Massachusetts Bay colonies migrated, at least in part, for the sake of freedom of conscience. But it was their *own* conscience about which they were tender. They showed far less concern for the freedom of other people's consciences. Many a Quaker, many a Baptist, many a Roman Catholic bore testimony in his abbreviated ears or his foreshortened life that the Puritans persecuted others for conscience's sake, even as they had been persecuted, alongside of these others, in England. The Puritans were not interested in what we would call freedom of religion, but in their freedom to establish an exclusive monopoly of religion in the territories they occupied.

Those colonies whose settlement was dominated by the Church of England were somewhat less violent in their treatment of dissenters, but they were no less intolerant of those who differed from the prevailing view. Their religious leaders, as became leaders of a national church, were far more ready than those of New England to accept a superficial conformity in lieu of a deep spiritual attachment. But this much conformity, at least, was regarded as essential, especially in the tidewater seats of both secular and religious authority. Dissenters and nonconformists, mainly Presbyterians, found refuge in the mountainous back country, the Piedmont. Here, far away from the ecclesiastical centers, they were able to set up their own autocratic and intolerant communities.

Because the New England colonies were dominated by Puritan theocrats and the Southern colonies by Church of England formalists, recent accounts have gone to an extreme in denying to the colonial period any true examples of religious liberty. There can be no doubt that a large part of the colonial population was opposed to religious pluralism. It is possible, however, to carry this view too far, losing sight of five cases in which stirrings of a new spirit were felt even in early colonial times. In two of these garden spots of tolerance blooming in a desert of bigotry, the career of religious freedom was all too brief; in another, religious liberty was granted for the unworthy reason that it was good for business. The other two, however, remain the seedbeds of freedom of religion for the whole country.

For a short time after the death of Thomas Gorgas in 1649, the

colonists in Maine, of whose recalcitrance Cotton Mather gives
evidence, formed themselves into a tiny independent democracy.
Three months later they proclaimed religious freedom for all Christians in their "Declaration of Religious Tolerance":

> That all gode people within the jurisdiction of this province who are
> out of a Church way and be orthodox in judgment and not scandalous
> in life, shall have full liberty to gather themselves into a Church estate,
> provided they do it in a Christian way: with the due observance of
> the rules of Christ revealed in his worde: and every Church hath free
> liberty of election and ordination of all her officers from tyme to tyme
> provided they be able, pious and orthodox.

This tolerant little democracy in Maine lasted for three years; then
the territory was seized by the colony of Massachusetts and its brief
career was ended.

A similar situation existed in Maryland. While this was a proprietary colony under the Roman Catholic Calverts, the largest
measure of freedom was allowed to the various Church denominations, and — as Matthew Page Andrews, the historian of Maryland, points out — there is no record of "any persecutions or
prosecutions of any group, sect, or individual because of any religious belief, or lack of belief." This freedom was not a matter of
legislative enactment; it was the result of the liberal personal attitude of Cecil Calvert, Lord Baltimore, toward religion.

When, in 1649, the Maryland "Act Concerning Religion" was
passed by the General Assembly and approved by the Proprietor,
it retained some features of Maryland practice, but introduced
other sections which mark a decided retrogression towards intolerance, perhaps the result of the arrival of Puritans in the colony.
Thus, for example, the act included penalties for violation of "the
Sabbath," a typically Puritan term. It also specifically limited the
scope of tolerance to persons "professing to believe in Jesus Christ,"
thus effectively excluding not only the Jews, but also such early
unitarians as Socinians from its protection. Its liberal section is,
however, well worth preserving in this record:

> Whereas the inforcing of the conscience in matters of religion hath
> frequently fallen out to bee of dangerous consequence in those com-
> monwealths where it hath beene practised, and for the more quiet and

peaceable government of this province, and the better to preserve mutuall love and unity amongst the inhabitants here, Bee it therefore also by the lord proprietary with the advice and assent of this assembly ordained and enacted . . . that no person or persons whatsoever within this province . . . professing to believe in Jesus Christ, shall from henceforth be any waies troubled, molested, or discountenanced, for or in his or her religion, nor in the free exercise thereof . . . nor any way compelled to beleefe or exercise of any other religion against his or her consent.

During the Puritan regime which followed, a new limitation was introduced, in 1654, denying to Roman Catholics the very tolerance which they had permitted. From 1656 to 1675, Lord Baltimore returned to power, and attempted to lead his colony back to its earlier spirit. He was, however, not successful in the restoration of the situation as it had existed prior to the Janus-like act of 1649. After Cecil Calvert had died, his son Charles, third Lord Baltimore, proved less adept than his father in keeping on good terms with the English authorities. One of the results was the establishment of the Church of England in Maryland in 1692, and the end of this early experiment in religious liberty.

In the Dutch colony of New Amsterdam, after an early flurry of religious persecution, tolerance of all religious views was permitted, specifically sanctioned by the home authorities on the ground that such tolerance would help business. When New Amsterdam was acquired by the British and rechristened New York, it became nominally a Church of England colony. The original religious variety permitted by the Dutch, however, was never completely rooted out. Whatever may have been true in theory, New York was in practice exceptionally tolerant among the colonies.

In the largely Baptist colony of Rhode Island, under the gallant though undemocratic leadership of Roger Williams, a considerable latitude in religion was long permitted. Roman Catholics were not tolerated, however, and there was no enthusiastic reception given to Quakers. In the Quaker colony of Pennsylvania, on the other hand, William Penn insisted from the very beginning that all religious views must be permitted freely to be preached and practiced.

To represent the best in colonial thought and expression on free-

dom of religion, excerpts are here presented from the writings of
Roger Williams and of William Penn. It must be remembered in
reading these statements that neither their authors, nor any others
mentioned here, accepted any reason for extending religious freedom which later centuries would have considered valid. The best
that can be said of the colonial period is that, although the corner-
stone of religious freedom was not yet laid, the foundations were
being excavated. Williams and Penn are included here to illustrate
the method of excavation.

Roger Williams

1644

THE BLOUDY TENENT OF PERSECUTION
FOR CAUSE OF CONSCIENCE DISCUSSED IN A CONFERENCE BETWEENE TRUTH AND PEACE

The Argument

First, that the blood of so many hundred thousand souls of Protestants and Papists, spilt in the Wars of present and former Ages, for their respective Consciences, is not required nor accepted by Jesus Christ the Prince of Peace.

Secondly, Pregnant Scriptures and Arguments are throughout the Work proposed against the Doctrine of persecution for cause of Conscience.

Thirdly, Satisfactory Answers are given to Scriptures, and objections produced by Mr. Calvin, Beza, Mr. Cotton, and the Ministers of the New English Churches and others former and later, tending to prove the Doctrine of persecution for cause of Conscience.

Fourthly, The Doctrine of persecution for cause of Conscience, is proved guilty of all the blood of the Souls crying for vengeance under the Altar.

Fifthly, All Civil States with their Officers of justice in their respective constitutions and administrations are proved essentially Civil, and therefore not Judges, Governors or Defenders of the Spiritual or Christian State and Worship.

Sixthly, It is the will and command of God, that (since the coming of his Son the Lord Jesus) a permission of the most Paganish, Jewish, Turkish, or Antichristian consciences and worships, be granted to all men in all Nations and Countries: and they are only to be fought against with that Sword which is only (in Soul matters) able to conquer, to wit, the Sword of God's Spirit, the Word of God.

Seventhly, The state of the Land of Israel, the Kings and people thereof in Peace and War, is proved figurative and ceremonial, and no pattern nor precedent for any Kingdom or civil state in the world to follow.

Eighthly, God requireth not an uniformity of Religion to be inacted and inforced in any civil state; which inforced uniformity (sooner or later) is the greatest occasion of civil War, ravishing of conscience, persecution of Christ Jesus in his servants, and of the hypocrisy and destruction of millions of souls.

Ninthly, In holding an inforced uniformity of Religion in a civil state, we must necessarily disclaim our desires and hopes of the Jews' conversion to Christ.

Tenthly, An inforced uniformity of Religion throughout a Nation or civil state, confounds the Civil and Religious, denies the principles of Christianity and civility, and that Jesus Christ is come in the Flesh.

Eleventhly, The permission of other consciences and worships than a state professeth, only can (according to God) procure a firm and lasting peace, (good assurance being taken according to the wisdom of the civil state for uniformity of civil obedience from all sorts).

Twelfthly, lastly, true civility and Christianity may both flourish in a state or Kingdom, notwithstanding the permission of divers and contrary consciences, either of Jew or Gentile. . . .

Truth. I acknowledge that to molest any person, Jew or Gentile, for either professing doctrine, or practising worship merely religious or spiritual, it is to persecute him, and such a person (what ever his doctrine or practice be true or false) suffereth persecution for conscience.

But withal I desire it may be well observed, that this distinction is not full and complete: for beside this that a man may be persecuted because he holdeth or practiseth what he believes in conscience to be a Truth, (as Daniel did, for which he was cast into the Lions' den, Dan. 6) and many thousands of Christians, because they durst not cease to preach and practise what they believed was by God commanded, as the Apostles answered (Acts 4. & 5) I say besides this a man may also be persecuted, because he dares to be constrained to yield obedience to such doctrines and worships as are by men invented and appointed. So the three famous Jews were cast into the fiery furnace for refusing to fall down (in a nonconformity to the whole conforming world) before the golden Image, Dan. 3. 21. So thousands of Christ's witnesses (and of late in those bloody Marian days) have rather chose to yield their bodies to all sorts of torments, than to subscribe to doctrines, or practise worships, unto which the States and Times (as Nabuchadnezzar to his golden Image) have compelled and urged them. . . .

The Church or company of worshippers (whether true or false) is like unto a Body or College of Physicians in a City; like unto a Corporation, Society, or Company of East-Indie or Turkie-Merchants, or any other Society or Company in London: which Companies may hold their Courts, keep their Records, hold disputations; and in matters concerning their Society, may dissent, divide, break into Schisms and Factions, sue and implead each other at the Law, yea, wholly break up and dissolve into pieces and nothing, and yet the peace of the City not be in the least measure impaired or disturbed; because the essence or being of the City, and so the well-being and peace thereof is essentially distinct from those particular Societies; the City Courts, City Laws, City punishments distinct from theirs. The City was before them, and stands absolute and entire, when such a Corporation or Society is taken down. For instance further, the City or Civil state of Ephesus was essentially distinct from the worship of Diana in the City, or of the whole city. Again, the Church of Christ in Ephesus (which were God's people, converted and called out from the worship of that City unto Christianity or worship of God in Christ) was distinct from both.

Now suppose that God remove the Candlestick from Ephesus, yea though the whole Worship of the City of Ephesus should be altered: yet (if men be true and honestly ingenuous to City-covenants, Combinations and Principles) all this might be without the least impeachment or infringement of the Peace of the City of Ephesus.

Thus in the City of Smirna was the City itself or Civil estate one thing, the Spiritual or Religious state of Smirna, another; the Church of Christ in Smirna, distinct from them both; and the

Synagogue of the Jews, whether literally Jews (as some think) or mystically, false Christians (as others) called the Synagogue of Sathan, Revel. 2. distinct from all these. And notwithstanding these spiritual oppositions in point of Worship and Religion, yet hear we not the least noise (nor need we, if Men keep but the Bond of Civility) of any Civil breach, or breach of Civil peace amongst them: and to persecute God's people there for Religion, that only was a breach of Civility itself. . . .

As the Lily is amongst the Thorns, so is Christ's Love among the Daughters; and as the Apple tree among the Trees of the Forest, so is her Beloved among the Sons: so great a difference is there between the Church in a City or Country, and the Civil state, City or Country in which it is.

No less then (as David in another case, Psal. 103. as far as the Heavens are from the Earth) are they that are truly Christ's (that is, anointed truly with the Spirit of Christ) [different] from many thousands who love not the Lord Jesus Christ, and yet are and must be permitted in the World or Civil State, although they have no right to enter into the gates of Jerusalem the Church of God.

And this is the more carefully to be minded, because whenever a toleration of others' Religion and Conscience is pleaded for, such as are (I hope in truth) zealous for God, readily produce plenty of Scriptures written to the Church, both before and since Christ's coming, all commanding and pressing the putting forth of the unclean, the cutting off the obstinate, the purging out the Leaven, rejecting of Heretics. As if because briars, thorns, and thistles may not be in the Garden of the Church, therefore they must all be plucked up out of the Wilderness: whereas he that is a Briar, that is, a Jew, a Turk, a Pagan, an Antichristian today, may be (when the Word of the Lord runs freely) a member of Jesus Christ tomorrow cut out of the wild Olive, and planted into the true. . . .

Peace. The second Scripture brought against such persecution for cause of Conscience, is Matth. 15. 14. where the Disciples being troubled at the Pharisees carriage toward the Lord Jesus and his doctrines, and relating how they were offended at him, the Lord Jesus commandeth his Disciples to let them alone, and gives this reason, that the blind lead the blind, and both should fall into the ditch.

Unto which, answer is made, "That it makes nothing to the Cause, because it was spoken to his private Disciples, and not to public Officers in Church or State: and also, because it was spoken in regard of not troubling themselves, or regarding the offence which the Pharisees took."

Truth. I answer, (to pass by his assertion of the privacy of the Apostles) in that the Lord Jesus commanding to let them alone, that is, not only not be offended themselves, but not to meddle with them; it appears it was no ordinance of God nor Christ for the Disciples to have gone further, and have complained to, and excited the Civil Magistrate to his duty: which if it had been an Ordinance of God and Christ, either for the vindicating of Christ's doctrine, or the recovering of the Pharisees, or the preserving of others from infection, the Lord Jesus would never have commanded them to omit that which should have tended to these holy ends. . . .

I observe that he implies that beside the censure of the Lord Jesus, in the hands of his spiritual governors, for any spiritual evil in life or doctrine, the Civil Magistrate is also to inflict corporal punishment upon the contrary minded: whereas

First, if the Civil Magistrate be a Christian, a Disciple or follower of the meek Lamb of God, he is bound to be far from destroying the bodies of men, for refusing to receive the Lord Jesus Christ, for otherwise he should not know (according to this speech of the Lord Jesus) what spirit he was of, yea and to be ignorant of the sweet end of the coming of the Son of Man, which was not to destroy the bodies of Men, but to save both bodies and souls, vers. 55.56.

Secondly, if the Civil Magistrate, being a Christian, gifted, prophesy in the Church, 1 Corinth. 1. 14. although the Lord Jesus Christ, whom they in their own persons hold forth, shall be refused, yet they are here forbidden to call for fire from heaven, that is, to procure or inflict any corporal judgement upon such offenders, remembering the end of the Lord Jesus his coming, not to destroy men's lives, but to save them.

Lastly, this also concerns the conscience of the Civil Magistrate, as he is bound to preserve the civil peace and quiet of the place and people under him, he is bound to suffer no man to break the Civil Peace, by laying hands of violence upon any, though as

vile as the Samaritans for not receiving of the Lord Jesus Christ.
. . .

I hence observe, that there being in this Scripture held forth a
two-fold state, a Civil state and a Spiritual, Civil officers and spiritual, civil weapons and spiritual weapons, civil vengeance and
punishment, and a spiritual vengeance and punishment: although
the Spirit speaks not here expressly of Civil Magistrates and their
civil weapons, yet these States being of different Natures and Considerations, as far differing as Spirit from Flesh, I first observe, that
Civil weapons are most improper and unfitting in matters of the
Spiritual state and kingdom, though in the Civil state most proper
and suitable. . . .

It is no Argument to prove that Tertullian meant a civil sword,
by alleging 1 Cor. 5. or Gal. 5. which properly and only approve a
cutting off by the sword of the Spirit in the Church, and the purging out of the leaven in the Church in the Cities of Corinth and
Galatia.

And if Tertullian should so mean as himself doth, yet

First, that grant of his, that Heresy must be cut off with the
sword of the Spirit, implies an absolute sufficiency in the sword of
the Spirit to cut it down, according to that mighty operation of
Spiritual weapons, (2. Cor. 10. 4.) powerfully sufficient either to
convert the Heretic to God, and subdue his very thoughts into
subjection to Christ, or else spiritually to slay and execute him.

Secondly, it is clear to be the meaning of the Apostle, and of
the Spirit of God, not there to speak to the Church in Corinth or
Galatia, or any other Church, concerning any other dough, or
house, or body, or flock, but the dough, the body, the house, the
flock of Christ his Church: Out of which such sparks, such leaven,
such rotten flesh and scabbed sheep are to be avoided.

Nor could the eye of this worthy Answerer ever be so obscured,
as to run to a Smith's shop for a Sword of iron and steel to help
the Sword of the Spirit, if the Sun of Righteousness had once been
pleased to show him, that a National Church (which elsewhere he
professeth against) a state Church (whether explicit, as in Old
England, or implicit, as in New) is not the Institution of the Lord
Jesus Christ. . . .

Peace. Brentius (whom you next quote, saith he) speaketh not to your cause. We willingly grant you, that man hath no power to make Laws to bind conscience, but this hinders not, but men may see the Laws of God observed which do bind conscience.

Truth. I answer, In granting with Brentius that man hath not power to make Laws to bind conscience, he overthrows such his tenent and practice as restrain men from their Worship, according to their Conscience and belief, and constrain them to such worships (though it be out of a pretence that they are convinced) which their own souls tell them they have no satisfaction nor faith in.

Secondly, whereas he affirmeth that men may make Laws to see the Laws of God observed.

I answer, as God needeth not the help of a material sword of steel to assist the sword of the Spirit in the affairs of conscience, so those men, those Magistrates, yea, that Commonwealth which makes such Magistrates, must needs have power and authority from Christ Jesus to fit Judge and to determine in all the great controversies concerning doctrine, discipline, government, etc.

And then I ask, whether upon this ground it must not evidently follow, that

Either there is no lawful Commonwealth nor civil State of men in the world, which is not qualified with this spiritual discerning: (and then also that the very Commonweal hath more light concerning the Church of Christ, than the Church itself.)

Or, that the Commonweal and Magistrates thereof must judge and punish as they are persuaded in their own belief and conscience, (be their conscience Paganish, Turkish, or Antichristian) what is this but to confound Heaven and Earth together, and not only to take away the being of Christianity out of the World, but to take away all civility, and the world out of this world, and to lay all upon heaps of confusion? . . .

Since there is so much controversy in the World, where the name of Christ is taken up, concerning the true Church, the Ministry and Worship, and who are those that truly fear God; I ask who shall judge in this case, who be they that fear God?

It must needs be granted, that such as have the power of suffering or not suffering, such Consciences, must judge: and then must it follow (as before I intimated) that the Civil State must judge of the truth of the Spiritual; and then Magistrates fearing or not fearing God, must judge of the fear of God: also that their judgement or sentence must be according to their conscience, of what Religion soever: Or that there is no lawful Magistrate, who is not able to judge in such cases. And lastly, that since the Sovereign power of all Civil Authority is founded in the consent of the People, that every Commonweal hath radically and fundamentally in it a power of true discerning the true fear of God, which they transfer to their Magistrates and Officers: Or else that there are no lawful Kingdoms, Cities, or Towns in the World, in which a man may live, and unto whose Civil Government he may submit: and then (as I said before) there must be no World, nor is it lawful to live in it, because it hath not a true discerning Spirit to judge them that fear or not fear God. . . .

Truth. Alas, who knows not what lamentable differences have been between the same Ministers of the Church of England, some conforming, others leaving their livings, friends, country, life, rather than conform; when others again (of whose personal godliness it is not questioned) have succeeded by conformity into such forsaken (so called) Livings? How great the present differences even amongst them that fear God, concerning Faith, Justification, and the evidence of it? concerning Repentance and godly sorrow, as also and mainly concerning the Church, the Matter, Form, Administrations and Government of it?

Let none now think that the passage to New England by Sea, or the nature of the Country can do what only the Key of David can do, to wit, open and shut the Consciences of men.

Beside, how can this be a faithful and upright acknowledgement of their weakness and imperfection, when they preach, print, and practise such violence to the souls and bodies of others, and by their Rules and Grounds ought to proceed even to the killing of those whom they judge so dear unto them, and in respect of godliness far above themselves? . . .

Truth. From this confession, that the Church or Kingdom of Christ may be set up without prejudice of the Commonweal, according to John 18. 36. My Kingdom is not of this World, etc. I observe that although the Kingdom of Christ, the Church and the Civil Kingdom or Government be not inconsistent, but that both

may stand together; yet that they are independent according to
that Scripture, and that therefore there may be (as formerly I have
proved) flourishing Commonweals and Societies of men where no
Church of Christ abideth; and secondly, the Commonweal may be
in perfect peace and quiet, notwithstanding the Church, the Commonweal of Christ be in distractions, and spiritual oppositions both
against their Religions, and sometimes amongst themselves, as the
Church of Christ in Corinth troubled with divisions, contentions,
etc.

Secondly, I observe it is true the Church helpeth forward the
prosperity of the Commonweal by spiritual means, Jer. 29. 7. The
prayers of God's people procure the peace of the City, where they
abide, yet that Christ's Ordinances and administrations of Worship are appointed and given by Christ to any Civil State, Town or
City as is implied by the instance of Geneva, that I confidently deny.

The Ordinances and Discipline of Christ Jesus, though wrong-
fully and profanely applied to natural and unregenerate men may
cast a blush of civility and morality upon them as in Geneva and
other places (for the shining brightness of the very shadow of
Christ's Ordinances casts a shame upon barbarism and incivility)
yet withal I affirm that the misapplication of Ordinances to unregenerate and unrepentant persons hardens up their souls in a
dreadful sleep and dream of their own blessed estate, and sends
millions of souls to hell in a secure expectation of a false salvation.

However they affirm that persons are not to be compelled to be
members of Churches, nor the Church compelled to receive any:
Yet if persons be compelled to forsake their Religion which their
hearts cleave to, and to come to Church, to the worship of the
Word, Prayers, Psalms, and Contributions, and this all their days:
I ask whether this be not this people's Religion, unto which sub-
mitting, they shall be quiet all their days, without the inforcing
them to the practice of any other Religion? And if this be not so,
then I ask, Will it not inevitably follow, that they (not only permit,
but) enforce people to be of no Religion at all, all their days?

This toleration of Religion, or rather irreligious compulsion, is
above all tolerations, monstrous, to wit, to compel men to be of no
Religion all their days. I desire all men and these worthy Authors
of this Model, to lay their hands upon their heart, and to consider

whether this compulsion of men to hear the Word, (as they say) whether it carries men, to wit, to be of no Religion all their days, worse than the very Indians, who dare not live without Religion according as they are persuaded.

Lastly, I add, from the Ordinances of the Lord Jesus, and practice of the Apostles (Acts 2. 42.) where the Word and Prayer is joined with the exercise of their fellowship, and breaking of Bread; in which Exercises the Church continued constantly: that it is apparent that a Civil State may as lawfully compel men by the civil sword to the breaking of bread, or Lord's Supper, as to the Word or Prayer, or Fellowship.

For first, they are all of the same nature, Ordinances in the Church (I speak of the feeding Ministry in the Church, unto which persons are compelled) and Church Worship. Secondly, every conscience in the World is fearful, at least shy of the Priests and Ministers of other Gods and Worships, and of holding Spiritual fellowship in any of their Services. Which is the case of many a Soul, viz. to question the Ministers themselves, as well as the Supper itself. . . .

It is reasonable to expect and demand of such as live within the State a civil maintenance of their civil officers, and to force it where it is denied. It is reasonable for a School-master to demand his recompence for his labor in his School: but it is not reasonable to expect or force it from strangers, enemies, rebels to that City, from such as come not within, or else would not be received into the School. What is the Church of Christ Jesus, but the City, the School, and Family of Christ? the Officers of this City, School, Family, may reasonable expect maintenance from such [as] they minister unto, but not from strangers, enemies, etc. . . .

Peace. By these weights we may try the weight of that commonly received and not questioned opinion, viz. That the civil state and the spiritual, the Church and Commonweal, they are like Hippocrates' twins, they are born together, grow up together, laugh together, weep together, sicken and die together.

Truth. A witty, yet a most dangerous Fiction of the Father of Lies, who hardened in Rebellion against God, persuades God's people to drink down such a deadly poison, though he knows the truth of these five particulars, which I shall remind you of.

First, many flourishing States in the World have been and are at this day, which hear not of Jesus Christ, and therefore have not the presence and concurrence of a Church of Christ with them.

Secondly, there have been many thousands of God's people, who in their personal estate and life of grace were awake to God, but in respect of Church estate they knew no other than a Church of dead stones, the Parish Church; or though some light be of late come in through some cranny, yet they seek not after, or least of all are joined to any true Church of God, consisting of living and believing stones.

So that by these New English Ministers' principles, not only is the door of calling to Magistracy shut against natural and unregenerate men (though excellently fitted for civil offices) but also against the best and ablest servants of God, except they be entered into Church estate; so that thousands of God's own people (excellently qualified) not knowing, or not entering into such a Church estate, shall not be accounted fit for civil services.

Thirdly, admit that a civil Magistrate be neither a member of a true Church of Christ (if any be in his dominions) nor in his person fear God, yet may he (possibly) give free permission without molestation, yea, and sometimes encouragement and assistance to the service and Church of God. Thus we find Abraham permitted to build and set up an Altar to his God wheresoever he came amongst the idolatrous Nations in the Land of Canaan. Thus Cyrus proclaims liberty to all the people of God in his Dominions, freely to go up and build the Temple of God at Jerusalem, and Artaxerxes after him confirmed it.

Thus the Roman Emperors and Governors under him permitted the Church of God, the Jews in the Lord Christ's time, their Temple and Worship, although in Civil things they were subject to the Romans.

Fourthly, the Scriptures of Truth and the Records of Time concur in this, that the first Churches of Christ Jesus, the lights, patterns, and precedents to all succeeding Ages, were gathered and governed without the aid, assistance, or countenance of any Civil Authority, from which they suffered great persecutions for the name of the Lord Jesus professed amongst them.

The Nations, Rulers, and Kings of the Earth tumultuously rage

against the Lord and his Anointed, Psal. 2. 1.2. Yet vers. 6. it hath
pleased the Father to set the Lord Jesus King upon his holy Hill
of Zion.

Christ Jesus would not be pleased to make use of the Civil
Magistrate to assist him in his Spiritual Kingdom; nor would he yet
be daunted or discouraged in his Servants by all their threats and
terrors: for Love is strong as death, and the coals thereof give a
most vehement flame, and are not quenched by all the waters and
floods of mightiest opposition, Cant. 8.

Christ's Church is like a chaste and loving wife, in whose heart
is fixed her Husband's love, who hath found the tenderness of his
love towards her, and hath been made fruitful by him, and therefore seeks she not the smiles, nor fears the frowns of all the Emperors in the World to bring her Christ unto her, or keep him
from her.

Lastly, we find in the tyrannical usurpations of the Romish Anti-
christ, the 10 horns (which some of good note conceive to be the
10 Kingdoms, into which the Roman Empire was quartered and
divided) are expressly said Revel. 17. 13. to have one mind to
give their power and strength unto the Beast, yea (ver. 17.) their
Kingdom unto the Beast, until the Words of God shall be ful-
filled: whence it follows, that all those Nations that are guilded
over with the name of Christ, have under that mask or vizard (as
some Executioners and Tormentors in the Inquisition use to tor-
ment) persecuted the Lord Jesus Christ, either with a more open,
gross and bloody, or with a more subtle, secret and gentle violence.

Let us cast our eyes about, turn over the Records and examine
the experience of past and present Generations, and see if all particular observations amount not to this sum, viz. that the great
whore hath committed fornication with the Kings of the Earth,
and made drunk thereof Nations with the cup of the wine of her
fornications: In which drunkedness and whoredom (as whores use
to practice) she hath robbed the Kings and Nations of their power
and strength, and (Jezebel-like) having procured the King's names
and seals, she drinks drunk, Revel. 17. with the blood of Naboth,
who (because he dares not part with his rightful inheritance in the
land of Canaan, the blessed land of promise and salvation in
Christ) as a Traitor to the civil State, and Blasphemer against God,

she (under the color of a day of humiliation in Prayer and Fasting) stones to death. . . .

As it is most true that Magistracy in general is of God (Rom. 13) for the preservation of Mankind in civil order and peace, (the World otherwise would be like the Sea, wherein Men, like Fishes would hunt and devour each other, and the greater devour the less:) so also it is true, that Magistracy in special for the several kinds of it is of Man, 1. Pet. 2. 13. Now what kind of Magistrate soever the people shall agree to set up, whether he receive Christianity before he be set in office, or whether he receive Christianity after, he receives no more power of Magistracy, than a Magistrate that hath received no Christianity. For neither of them both can receive more, than the Commonweal, the Body of People and civil State, as men, communicate unto them, and betrust with them.

All lawful Magistrates in the World, both before the coming of Christ Jesus, and since, (excepting those unparalleled typical Magistrates of the Church of Israel) are but Derivatives and Agents immediately derived and employed as eyes and hands, serving for the good of the whole: Hence they have and can have no more Power, than fundamentally lies in the Bodies or Fountains themselves, which Power, Might, or Authority, is not Religious, Christian, etc. but natural, humane and civil.

And hence it is true, that a Christian Captain, Christian Merchant, Physician, Lawyer, Pilot, Father, Master, and (so consequently) Magistrate, etc. is no more a Captain, Merchant, Physician, Lawyer, Pilot, Father, Master, Magistrate, etc. than a Captain, Merchant, etc. of any other Conscience or Religion.

'Tis true, Christianity teacheth all these to act in their several callings, to an higher ultimate end, from higher principles in a more heavenly and spiritual manner, etc. . . .

Truth. In his season God will glorify himself in all his Truths: but to gratify thy desire, thus: A Pagan or Antichristian Pilot may be as skilful to carry the Ship to its desired Port, as any Christian Mariner or Pilot in the World, and may perform that work with as much safety and speed: yet have they not command over the souls and consciences of their passengers or mariners under them, although they may justly see to the labor of the one, and the civil behavior of all in the ship: A Christian Pilot he performs the same work, (as likewise doth the Metaphorical Pilot in the ship of the Commonweal) from a principle of knowledge and experience: but more than this, he acts from a root of the fear of God and love to mankind, in his whole course. Secondly, his aim is more to glorify God than to gain his pay, or make his voyage. Thirdly, he walks heavenly with Men, and God, in a constant observation of God's hand in storms, calms, etc. so that the thread of Navigation being equally spun by a believing or unbelieving Pilot, yet is it drawn over with the gold of Godliness and Christianity by a Christian Pilot, while he is holy in all manner of Christianity, 1 Pet. 1. 15. But lastly, the Christian Pilot's power over the Souls and consciences of his Sailors and Passengers is not greater than that of the Antichristian, otherwise than he can subdue the souls of any by the two-edged sword of the Spirit, the Word of God, and by his holy demeanor in his place, etc. . . .

Peace. Dear Truth, We are now arrived at their last Head: the Title is this, viz.

Their power in the Liberties and Privileges of these Churches.

First, all Magistrates ought to be chosen out of Church-members, Exod. 18. 21. Deut. 17. 15. Prov. 29. 2. When the Righteous rule, the people rejoice. Secondly, that all free men elected, be only Church members.

1. Because if none but Church members should rule, then others should not choose, because they may elect others beside Church members.

2. From the pattern of Israel, where none had power to choose but only Israel, or such as were joined to the people of God.

3. If it shall fall out, that in the Court consisting of Magistrates and Deputies, there be a dissent between them which may hinder the common good, that they now return for ending the same, to their first principles, which are the Free men, and let them be consulted with.

Truth. In this Head are 2 branches: First concerning the choice of Magistrates, that such ought to be chosen as are Church members: for which is quoted, Exod. 18. 21. Deut. 17. 15. Proverbs 19. 29.

Unto which I answer: It were to be wished, that since the point is so weighty, as concerning the Pilots and Steersmen of Kingdoms and Nations, etc., on whose ability, care and faithfulness depends most commonly the peace and safety of the commonweals they sail in: I say it were to be wished that they had more fully explained what they intend by this Affirmative, viz. Magistrates ought to be chosen out of Church members.

For if they intend by this (ought to be chosen) necessity of convenience, viz. that for the greater advancement of common utility and rejoicing of the people, according to the place quoted (Prov. 29.2) it were to be desired, prayed for, and peaceably endeavored, then I readily assent unto them.

But if by this (Ought) they intend such a necessity as those Scriptures quoted imply, viz. that people shall sin by choosing such for Magistrates as are not members of Churches; as the Israelites should have sinned, if they had not (according to Jethro's counsel, Exod. 18. and according to the command of God. Deut. 18.) chosen their Judges and Kings within themselves in Israel: then I propose these necessary Queries.

First, whether those are not lawful Civil combinations, societies, and communions of men, in Towns, Cities, States or Kingdoms, where no Church of Christ is resident, yea, where his name was never yet heard of: I add to this, that Men of no small note, skilful in the state of the World, acknowledge, that the World divided into 30 parts, 25 of that 30 have never yet heard of the name of Christ: If their Civil polities and combinations be not lawful, (because they are not Churches, and their Magistrates Church members) then disorder, confusion, and all unrighteousness is lawful, and pleasing to God.

Secondly, whether in such States or Commonweals, where a Church or Churches of Christ are resident, such persons may not lawfully succeed to the Crown or Government, in whom the fear of God (according to Jethro's counsel) cannot be discerned, nor are brethren of the Church, (according to Deut. 17.) but only are fitted with Civil and Moral abilities, to manage the Civil affairs of the Civil State.

Thirdly, since not many Wise and Noble are called, but the poor receive the Gospel, as God hath chosen the poor of the World to be rich in Faith, 1. Cor. 1. Jam. 2. Whether it may not ordinarily come to pass, that there may not be found in a true Church of

Christ (which sometimes consisteth but of few persons) persons fit to be either Kings or Governors, etc., whose civil office is no less difficult than the office of a Doctor of Physic, a Master or Pilot of a Ship, or a Captain or Commander of a Band or Army of men: for which services, the children of God may be no ways qualified, though otherwise excellent for the fear of God, and the knowledge and Grace of the Lord Jesus.

Fourthly, if Magistrates ought (that is, ought only) to be chosen out of the Church, I demand if they ought not also to be dethroned and deposed, when they cease to be of the Church, either by voluntary departure from it, or by excommunication out of it, according to the bloody tenents and practise of some Papists, with whom the Protestants (according to their principles) although they seem to abhor it, do absolutely agree?

Fifthly, therefore, lastly, I ask if this be not to turn the World upside down, to turn the World out of the World, to pluck up the roots and foundations of all common society in the World? to turn the Garden and Paradise of the Church and Saints into the Field of the Civil State of the World, and to reduce the World to the first chaos or confusion.

William Penn
1670

THE GREAT CASE OF LIBERTY OF CONSCIENCE
ONCE MORE BRIEFLY DEBATED AND DEFENDED BY THE AUTHORITY OF REASON, SCRIPTURE, AND ANTIQUITY

Preface

Were some as Christian as they boast themselves to be, it would save us all the labor we bestow in rendering Persecution so unchristian as it most truly is. Nay, were they those men of reason they character themselves, and what the civil law styles good citizens, it had been needless for us to tell them, that neither can any external coercive power convince the understanding of the poorest idiot, nor fines and prisons be judged fit and adequate penalties for faults purely intellectual; as well as that they are destructive of all civil government.

But we need not run so far as beyond the seas, to fetch the sense of the Codes, Institutes, and Digests, out of the *Corpus Civile,* to adjudge such practices incongruous with the good of civil society; since our own good, old, admirable laws of England have made such excellent provision for its inhabitants, that if they were but thought as fit to be executed by this present age, as they were rightly judged necessary to be made by our careful ancestors, we know how great a stroke they would give such as venture to lead away our property in triumph (as our just forfeiture) for only worshipping our God in a differing way from that which is more generally professed and established.

And indeed it is most truly lamentable, that above others (who have been found in so unnatural and anti-christian an employment) those that by their own frequent practices and voluminous apologies, have defended a separation from the Papacy, should now

52

become such earnest persecutors for it; not considering, that the enaction of such laws as restrain persons from the free exercise of their consciences in matters of religion, is but a knotting whip-cord to lash their own posterity; whom they can never promise to be conformed to a National Religion. Nay, since mankind is subject to such mutability, they cannot ensure themselves from being taken by some persuasions that are esteemed heterodox, and consequently catch themselves in snares of their own providing. And for men thus liable to change, and no ways certain of their own belief to be most infallible, as by their multiplied concessions may appear, to enact any religion, or prohibit persons from the free exercise of theirs, sounds harsh in the ears of all modest and un-biassed men. We are bold to say, our Protestant ancestors thought of nothing less, than to be succeeded by persons vainglorious of their Reformation, and yet adversaries to Liberty of Conscience: For to people in their wits it seems a paradox.

Not that we are so ignorant, as to think it is within the reach of human power to fetter conscience, or to restrain its liberty, strictly taken: but that plain English, of Liberty of Conscience, we would be understood to mean, is this; namely, "The free and uninter-rupted exercise of our consciences, in that way of worship we are most clearly persuaded God requires us to serve him in, without endangering our undoubted birth-right of English freedoms:" Which being matter of FAITH, we sin if we omit; and they cannot do less, that shall endeavor it.

To tell us we are obstinate, and enemies to government, are but those groundless phrases the first reformers were not a little pestered with: but as they said, so say we, The being called this, or that, does not conclude us so: and hitherto we have not been detected of that fact, which only justifies such criminations.

But however free we can approve ourselves of actions prejudicial to the civil government; it is most certain we have not suffered a little, as criminals, and therefore have been far from being free from sufferings; indeed, in some respect, horrid plunders: widows have lost their cows, orphans their beds, and laborers their tools. A tragedy so sad, that methinks it should oblige them to do in England as they did at Athens: when they had sacrificed their divine Socrates to the sottish fury of their lewd and comical multitude, they so regretted their hasty murder, that not only the memorial of Socrates was most venerable with them, but his enemies they esteemed so much theirs, that none would trade or hold the least commerce with them; for which some turned their own executioners, and without any other warrant than their own guilt, hanged themselves. How near akin the wretched mercenary informers of our age are to those, the great resemblance that is betwixt their actions manifestly shows.

And we are bold to say, the grand fomentors of persecution are no better friends to the English state, than were Anytus and Aristophanes of old to that of Athens; the case being so nearly the same, as they did not more bitterly envy the reputation of Socrates amongst the Athenians for his grace and religious lectures (thereby giving the youth a diversion from frequenting their plays) than some now emulate the true dissenter, for his pious life, and great industry.

And as that famous common-wealth was noted to decline, and the most observing persons of it dated its decay from that illegal and ingrateful carriage towards Socrates (witness their dreadful plagues, with other multiplied disasters) so it is not less worthy observation, that heaven hath not been wholly wanting to scourge this land, for, as well their cruelty to the conscientious, as their other multiplied provocations.

And when we seriously consider the dreadful judgments that now impend the nation (by reason of the robbery, violence, unwonted oppression, that almost everywhere have not only been committed upon the poor, the widow, and the fatherless; but most tenaciously justified, and the actors manifestly encouraged) in mere pity and concern for the everlasting welfare of such as have not quite sinned away their visitation (for some have) we once more bring to public view our reasons against persecution, backed with the plainest instances both of Scripture and Antiquity; if but one may be persuaded to desist from making any farther progress in such an anti-protestant, and truly anti-christian path, as that of persecuting honest and virtuous Englishmen, for only worshipping the God that made them in the way they judge most acceptable with him.

But if those who ought to think themselves obliged to weigh

these affairs with the greatest deliberation, will obstinately close their eyes to these last remonstrances, and slightly over-look the pinching case of so many thousand families, that are by these severities exposed for prey to the unsatiable appetites of a villainous crew of broken informers, daubing themselves with that deluding apprehension of pleasing God, or at least of profiting the country; (whilst they greatly displease the one, and evidently ruin the other) as certain as ever the Lord God Almighty destroyed Sodom, and layed waste Gomorrah, by the consuming flame of his just indignation, will he hasten to make desolate this wanton land, and not leave a hiding place for the oppressor.

Let no man therefore think himself too big to be admonished, nor put too slight a value upon the Lives, Liberties, and Properties of so many thousand free-born English families, embarked in that one concern of Liberty of Conscience. It will become him better to reflect upon his own mortality, and not forget his breath is in his nostrils, and that every action of his life the everlasting God will bring to judgment, and him for them.

Chapter I

The great case of Liberty of Conscience, so often debated and defended (however dissatisfactorily to such as have so little conscience as to persecute for it) is once more brought to public view, by a late act against Dissenters, and Bill, or an additional one, that we all hoped the wisdom of our rulers had long since laid aside, as what was fitter to be passed into an act of perpetual oblivion. The kingdoms are alarmed at this procedure, and thousands greatly at a stand, wondering what should be the meaning of such hasty resolutions, that seem as fatal as they were unexpected. Some ask what wrong they have done? Others, what peace they have broken? and all, what plots they have formed to prejudice the present government, or occasions given to hatch new jealousies of them and their proceedings? being not conscious to themselves of guilt in any such respect.

For mine own part, I publicly confess myself to be a very hearty Dissenter from the established worship of these nations, as believing Protestants to have much degenerated from their first principles, and as owning the poor despised Quakers, in life and doctrine, to have espoused the cause of God, and to be the undoubted followers of Jesus Christ, in his most holy, strait, and narrow way, that leads to the eternal rest. In all which I know no treason, nor any principle that would urge me to a thought injurious to the civil peace. If any be defective in this particular, it is equal both individuals and whole societies should answer for their own defaults; but we are clear.

However, all conclude that union very ominous and unhappy, which makes the first discovery of itself "by a John Baptist's head in a charger." They mean that feast which some are designed to make upon the liberties and properties of free-born Englishmen: Since to have the entail of those undoubted hereditary rights cut off, for matters purely relative of another world, is a severe beheading in the law: which must be obvious to all, but such as measure the justice of things only, by that proportion they bear with their own interest. A sort of men that seek themselves, though at the apparent loss of whole societies; like to that barbarous fancy of old, which had rather that Rome should burn, than it be without the satisfaction of a bonfire. And sad it is, when men have so far stupefied their understandings with the strong doses of their private interest, as to become insensible of the public's. Certainly such an over-fondness for self, or that strong inclination to raise themselves in the ruin of what does not so much oppose them, as that they will believe so, because they would be persecuting, is a malignant enemy to that tranquillity, which all dissenting parties seem to believe would be the consequence of a toleration.

In short we say, there can be but two ends in persecution; the one to satisfy (which none can ever do) the insatiable appetites of a decimating clergy (whose best arguments are fines and imprisonments); and the other, as thinking therein they do God good service; but it is so hateful a thing upon any account, that we shall make it appear, by this ensuing discourse, to be a declared enemy to God, religion, and the good of human society.

The whole will be small, since it is but an epitome of no larger a tract than fourteen sheets; yet divides itself into the same particulars, every of which we shall defend against imposition, restraint, and persecution, though not with that scope of reason (nor consequently pleasure to the readers) being by other contingent disappointments limited to a narrow stint.

The terms explained, and the question stated.

First, By Liberty of Conscience, we understand not only a mere Liberty of the Mind, in believing or disbelieving this or that principle or doctrine; but "the exercise of ourselves in a visible way of worship, upon our believing it to be indispensably required at our hands, that if we neglect it for fear or favor of any mortal man, we sin, and incur divine wrath." Yet we would be so understood to extend and justify the lawfulness of our so meeting to worship God, as not to contrive, or abet any contrivance destructive of the government and laws of the land, tending to matters of an external nature, directly or indirectly; but so far only as it may refer to religious matters, and a life to come, and consequently wholly independent of the secular affairs of this, wherein we are supposed to transgress.

Secondly, By imposition, restraint, and persecution, we do not only mean the strict requiring of us to believe this to be true, or that to be false; and upon refusal, to incur the penalties enacted in such cases; but by those terms we mean thus much, "any coercive let or hindrance to us, from meeting together to perform those religious exercises which are according to our faith and persuasion."

The question stated.

For proof of the aforesaid terms thus given, we singly state the question thus;

Whether imposition, restraint, and persecution, upon persons for exercising such a liberty of conscience as is before expressed, and so circumstantiated, be not to impeach the honor of God, the meekness of the Christian religion, the authority of Scripture, the privilege of nature, the principles of common reason, the well being of government, and apprehensions of the greatest personages of former and latter ages?

First, Then we say, that Imposition, Restraint, and Persecution, for matters relating to conscience, directly invade the divine prerogative, and divest the Almighty of a due, proper to none besides himself. And this we prove by these five particulars:

First, If we do allow the honor of our creation due to God only, and that no other besides himself has endowed us with those excellent gifts of Understanding, Reason, Judgment, and Faith, and consequently that he only is the object, as well as the author, both of our Faith, Worship, and Service; then whosoever shall interpose their authority to enact faith and worship in a way that seems not to us congruous with what he has discovered to us to be faith and worship (whose alone property it is to do it) or to restrain us from what we are persuaded is our indispensable duty, they evidently usurp this authority, and invade his incommunicable right of government over conscience: "For the Inspiration of the Almighty gives understanding: and faith is the gift of God," says the divine writ.

Secondly, Such magisterial determinations carry an evident claim to that infallibility, which Protestants have been hitherto so jealous of owning, that, to avoid the Papists, they have denied it to all but God himself.

Either they have forsook their old plea; or if not, we desire to know when, and where, they were invested with that divine excellency; and whether imposition, restraint, and persecution, were ever deemed by God the fruits of his Spirit. However, that itself was not sufficient; for unless it appears as well to us that they have it, as to them who have it, we cannot believe it upon any convincing evidence, but by tradition only, an anti-protestant way of believing.

Thirdly, It enthrones man as king over conscience, the alone just claim and privilege of his Creator; whose thoughts are not as men's thoughts, but has reserved to himself that empire from all the Caesars on earth: For if men, in reference to souls and bodies, things appertaining to this and the other world, shall be subject to their fellow-creatures, what follows, but that Caesar (however he got it) has all, God's share, and his own too? And being Lord of both, both are Caesar's, and not God's.

Fourthly, It defeats God's work of Grace, and the invisible operation of his eternal Spirit, (which can alone beget faith, and is only to be obeyed, in and about religion and worship) and attributes men's conformity to outward force and corporal punishments. A faith subject to as many revolutions as the powers that enact it.

Fifthly and lastly, Such persons assume the judgment of the

great tribunal unto themselves; for to whomsoever men are im-
posedly or restrictively subject and accountable in matters of faith,
worship and conscience; in them alone must the power of judgment
reside; but it is equally true that God shall judge all by Jesus
Christ, and that no man is so accountable to his fellow-creatures,
as to be imposed upon, restrained, or persecuted for any matter of
conscience whatever.

Thus, and in many more particulars, are men accustomed to
intrench upon Divine Property, to gratify particular interests in
the world; and (at best) through a misguided apprehension to
imagine "they do God good service," that where they cannot give
faith, they will use force; which kind of sacrifice is nothing less
unreasonable than the other is abominable: God will not give
his honor to another; and to him only, that searches the heart and
tries the reins, it is our duty to ascribe the gifts of understanding
and faith, without which none can please God.

Chapter II

The next great evil which attends external force in matters of
faith and worship, is no less than the overthrow of the whole
Christian religion; and this we will briefly evidence in these four
particulars, 1. That there can be nothing more remote from the
nature, 2. The practice, 3. The promotion, 4. The rewards of it.

First, It is the privilege of the Christian faith above the dark
suggestions of ancient and modern superstitious traditions, to carry
with it a most self-evidencing verity, which ever was sufficient to
proselyte believers, without the weak auxiliaries of external power.
The Son of God, and great example of the world, was so far from
calling his Father's omnipotency in legions of angels to his defence,
that he at once repealed all acts of force, and defined to us the
nature of his religion in this one great saying of his, MY KINGDOM IS
NOT OF THIS WORLD. It was spiritual, not carnal; accompanied
with weapons as heavenly as its own nature, and designed for the
good and salvation of the soul, and not the injury and destruction
of the body: no gaols, fines, exiles, &c. but "sound Reason, clear
Truth, and strict Life." In short, the Christian religion intreats all,
but compels none.

Secondly, That restraint and persecution overturn the practice of it. I need go no farther than the allowed Martyrologies of several ages, of which the Scriptures claim a share; begin with Abel, go down to Moses, so to the Prophets, and then to the meek example of Jesus Christ himself; how patiently devoted was he to undergo the contradictions of men and so far from persecuting any, that he would not so much as revile his persecutors, but prayed for them. Thus lived his apostles, and the true Christians of the first three hundred years. Nor are the famous stories of our first reformers silent in the matter; witness the Christian practices of the Waldenses, Lollards, Hussites, Lutherans, and our noble martyrs; who, as became the true followers of Jesus Christ, enacted and confirmed their religion with their own blood, and not with the blood of their opposers.

Thirdly, Restraint and persecution obstruct the promotion of the Christian Religion: For if such as restrain, confess themselves "miserable sinners, and altogether imperfect," it either follows, that they never desire to be better, or that they should encourage such as may be capable of farther informing and reforming them: They condemn the Papists for incoffining the Scriptures and their worship in an unknown tongue, and yet are guilty themselves of the same kind of fact.

Fourthly, They prevent many of eternal rewards: For where any are religious for fear, and that of men, it is slavish, and the recompence of such religion is condemnation, not peace: besides, it is man that is served; who having no power but what is temporary, his reward must needs be so too: he that imposes a duty, or restrains from one, must reward; but because no man can reward for such duties, no man can or ought to impose them, or restrain from them. So that we conclude Imposition, Restraint and Persecution, are destructive of the Christian religion, in the Nature, Practice, Promotion and Rewards of it, which are eternal. . . .

Chapter V

We next urge, that force, in matters relating to conscience, carries a plain contradiction to government, in the nature, execution, and end of it.

By government we understand, an external order of justice, or the right and prudent disciplining of any society by just laws, either in the relaxation or execution of them.

First, It carries a contradiction to government in the nature of it, which is justice, and that in three respects.

1. It is the first lesson that great Synteresis, so much renowned by philosophers and civilians, learns mankind, "To do as they would be done to;" since he that gives what he would not take, or takes what he would not give, only shows care for himself, but neither kindness nor justice for another.

2. The just nature of government lies in a fair and equal retribution: but what can be more unequal, than that men should be rated more than their proportion to answer the necessities of government, and yet that they should not only receive no protection from it, but by it be disseised of their dear liberty and properties? We say, to be compelled to pay that power that exerts itself to ruin those that pay it, or that any should be required to enrich those that ruin them, is hard and unequal, and therefore contrary to the just nature of government. If we must be contributaries to the maintenance of it, we are entitled to a protection from it.

3. It is the justice of government to proportion penalties to the crime committed. Now granting our dissent to be a fault, yet the infliction of a corporal or external punishment, for a mere mental error (and that not voluntary) is unreasonable and inadequate, as well as against particular directions of the Scriptures, Tit. iii. 9, 10, 11. For as corporal penalties cannot convince the understanding; so neither can they be commensurate punishments for faults purely intellectual: and for the government of this world to intermeddle with what belongs to the government of another, and which can have no ill aspect or influence upon it, shows more of invasion than right and justice.

Secondly, It carries a contradiction to government in the execution of it, which is prudence, and that in these instances.

1. The state of the case is this, that there is no republic so great, no empire so vast, but the laws of them are resolvable into these two series or heads; "Of laws fundamental, which are indispensable and immutable; and laws superficial, which are temporary and alterable;" and as it is justice and prudence to be punctual in

the execution of the former, so by circumstances, it may be neither to execute the latter, they being suited to the present conveniency and emergency of state; as the prohibiting of cattle out of Ireland was judged by advantage to the farmers of England, yet a murrain would make it the good of the whole that the law should be broke, or at least the execution of it suspended. That the law of restraint, in point of conscience, is of this number, we may further manifest, and the imprudence of thinking otherwise: for first, if the saying were as true as it is false, "No bishop, no king," (which admits of various readings; as "no decimating clergy, or no persecution, no king,") we should be as silent as some would have us; but the confidence of their assertion, and the impolicy of such as believe it, makes us to say, that a greater injury cannot be done to the present government. For if such laws and establishments are fundamental, they are as immutable as mankind itself; but that they are as alterable as the conjectures and opinions of governors have been, is evident; since the same fundamental indispensable laws and policy of these kingdoms have still remained, through all variety of opposite ruling opinions and judgments, and disjoined from them all. Therefore to admit of such a fixation to temporary laws, must needs be highly imprudent, and destructive of the essential parts of the government of these countries.

2. That since there has been a time of connivance, and that with no ill success to public affairs, it cannot be prudence to discontinue it, unless it was imprudence before to give it; and such little deserve it that think so.

3. Dissenters not being conscious to themselves of any just forfeiture of that favor, are as well grieved in their resentments of this alteration, as the contrary did oblige them to very grateful acknowledgments.

4. This must be done to gratify all, or the greatest part, or but some few only; it is a demonstration, all are not pleased with it; that the greatest number is not, the empty public auditories will speak: in short, how should either be, when six parties are sacrificed to the seventh: that this cannot be prudence, common maxims and observations prove.

5. It strikes fatally at Protestant sincerity: for will the Papists say, Did Protestants exclaim against us for persecutors, and are

they now the men themselves? Was it an instance of weakness in our religion, and is it become a demonstration of strength in theirs? Have they transmuted it from antichristian in us, to christian in themselves? let persecutors answer.

6. It is not only an example, but an incentive to the Romanists to persecute the reformed religion abroad: for when they see their actions (once void of all excuse) now defended by the example of Protestants, that once accused them, (but now themselves) doubtless they will revive their cruelty.

7. It overturns the very ground of the Protestants retreat from Rome: for if men must be restrained, upon pretended prudential considerations, from the exercise of their conscience in England; why not the same in France, Holland, Germany, Constantinople, &c. where matters of state may equally be pleaded? This makes religion state-policy; and faith and worship, subservient to the humors and interests of superiors: such doctrine would have prevented our ancestors retreat; and we wish it be not the beginning of a back-march; for some think it shrewdly to be suspected, where religion is suited to the government, and conscience to its conveniency.

8. Vice is encouraged: for if licentious persons see men of virtue molested for assembling with a religious purpose to reverence and worship God, and that are otherwise most serviceable to the commonwealth, they may and will infer, it is better for them to be as they are; since not to be demure, as they call it, is half-way to that kind of accomplishment which procures preferment.

9. For such persons as are so poor-spirited as to truckle under such restraints, what conquest is there over them, that before were conscientious men, and now hypocrites? who so forward to be avenged of them, that brought this guilt upon them, as they themselves? and how can the imposers be secure of their friendship, whom they have taught to change with the times?

10. Such laws are so far from benefiting the country, that the execution of them will be the assured ruin of it, in the revenues, and consequently in the power of it: for where there is a decay of families, there will be of trade; so of wealth, and in the end of strength and power: and if both kinds of relief fail, men, the prop of republicks; money, the stay of monarchies; this, as requiring mer-

cenaries; that, as needing freemen; farewell the interest of England! 'tis true, the priests get (though that is but for a time) but the king and people lose, as the event will show.

11. It ever was the prudence of wise magistrates to oblige their people; but what comes shorter of it than persecution? what dearer to them than the liberty of their conscience? what cannot they better spare than it? their peace consists in the enjoyment of it; and he that by compliance has lost it, carries his penalty with him, and is his own prison. Surely such practices must render the government uneasy, and beget a great disrespect to the governors, in the hearts of the people.

12. But that which concludes our prudential part shall be this, that after all their pains and good-will to stretch men to their measure, they never will be able to accomplish their end: and if he be an unwise man, that provides means where he designs no end, how near is he of kin to him that proposes an end unobtainable. Experience has told us. 1. How invective it has made the imposed-on. 2. What distraction have ensued such attempts. 3. What reproach has followed to the Christian religion, when the professors of it have used a coercive power upon conscience. And lastly, That force never yet made either a good Christian, or a good subject.

Thirdly, and lastly, Since the proceedings we argue against are proved so destructive to the justice and prudence of government, we ought the less to wonder that they should hold the same malignity against the end of it, which is felicity, since the wonder would be to find it otherwise; and this is evident from these three considerations:

1. Peace (the end of war and government, and its great happiness too) has been, is, and yet will be, broken by the frequent tumultuary disturbance that ensue the disquieting our meetings, and the estreating fines upon our goods and estates. And what these things may issue in, concerneth the civil magistrate to consider.

2. Plenty (another great end of government) will be converted into poverty, by the destruction of so many thousand families as refuse compliance and conformity, and that not only to the sufferers, but influentially to all the rest; a demonstration of which

we have in all those places where the late act has been any thing considerably put in execution. Besides, how great provocation such incharity and cruel usage, as stripping widows, fatherless, and poor, of their very necessaries for human life, merely upon an account of faith or worship, must needs be to the just and righteous Lord of heaven and earth, scriptures, and plenty of other histories, plainly shown us.

3. Unity (not the least, but greatest end of government) is lost: for by seeking an unity of opinion, by the ways intended, the unity requisite to uphold us as a civil society, will be quite destroyed. And such as relinquish that, to get the other, besides that they are unwise, will infallibly lose both in the end.

In short, we say that it is unreasonable we should not be entertained as men, because some think we are not as good Christians as they pretend to wish us; or that we should be deprived of our liberties and properties, who never broke the laws that gave them to us: what can be harder, than to take that from us by a law, which the great indulgence and solicitude of our ancestors took so much pains to intail upon us by law. . . .

And we are persuaded, that no temporary subsequential law whatever to our fundamental rights, (as this of force on conscience is) can invalidate so essential a part of the government, as English liberty and property: nor that it is in the power of any on earth to deprive us of them, till we have first done it ourselves, by such enormous facts as those very laws prohibit, and make our forfeiture of that benefit we should otherwise receive by them: for these being such cardinal and fundamental points of English law-doctrine, individually, and by the collective body of the people, agreed to, and on which, as the most solid basis, our secondary legislative power, as well as executive, is built; it seems most rational that the superstructure cannot quarrel or invalidate its own foundation, without manifestly endangering its own security; the effect is ever less noble than the cause; the gift than the giver; and the superstructure than the foundation.

The single question to be resolved in the case, briefly will be this, whether any visible authority (being founded in its primitive institution upon those fundamental laws, that inviolably preserve the people in all their just rights and privileges) may invalidate all, or any, of the said laws, without an implicit shaking of its own foundation, and a clear overthrow of its own constitution of government, and so reduce them to their *Statu quo prius,* or first principles? The resolution is every man's, at his own pleasure. . . .

Those who intend us no share or interest in the laws of England, as they relate to civil matters, unless we correspond with them in points of faith and worship, must do two things, First, it will lie heavy on their parts to prove, that the ancient compact and original of our laws carries that proviso with it; else we are manifestly disseised of our free-customs.

Secondly, They are to prove the reasonableness of such proceedings to our understandings, that we may not be concluded by a law we know not how to understand: for if I take the matter rightly (as I think I do) we must not buy or sell, unless of this or that persuasion in religion; not considering civil society was in the world before the Protestant profession; men, as such, and in affairs peculiarly relative to them in an external and civil capacity, have subsisted many ages under great variety of religious apprehensions, and therefore not so dependent on them as to receive any variation or revolution with them. What shall we say then? but that some will not that we should live, breathe, and commerce as men, because we are not such modelled Christians as they coercively would have us: they might with as much justice and reputation to themselves forbid us to look or see unless our eyes were grey, black, brown, blue, or some one color best suiting theirs: for not to be able to give us faith, or save our consciences harmless, and yet to persecute us for refusing conformity, is intolerable hard measure.

In short, that coercive way of bringing all men to their height of persuasion, must either arise from exorbitant zeal and superstition, or from a consciousness of error and defect, which is unwilling anything more sincere and reformed should take place; being of that cardinal's mind, who therefore would not hearken to a reformation, at the sitting of the council of Trent, because he would not so far approve the reformers judgment (for having once condescended to their apprehensions, he thought it would for ever enslave them to their sense); though otherwise he saw, as much as any man, the grand necessity of a reformation, both of the Roman doctrine and conversation. . . .

To conclude; Liberty of Conscience, as thus stated and defended, we ask, as our undoubted right by the law of God, of nature, and of our own country. It has been often promised; we have long waited for it; we have writ much, and suffered in its defence, and have made many true complaints, but found little or no redress.

However, we take the righteous holy God to record, against all objections that are ignorantly or designedly raised against us, That

1st. We hold no principle destructive of the English government.

2d. That we plead for no such Dissenter (if such a one there be.)

3d. That we desire the temporal and eternal happiness of all persons (in submission to the divine will of God); heartily forgiving our cruel persecutors.

4thly, and lastly, We shall engage, by God's assistance, to lead peaceable, just and industrious lives amongst men, to the good and example of all. But if, after all we have said, this short discourse should not be credited, nor answered in any of its sober reasons and requests, but sufferings should be the present lot of our inheritance from this generation; be it known to them all, that meet we must, and meet we cannot but encourage all to do (whatever we sustain) in God's name and authority, who is Lord of Hosts, and King of Kings; at the revelation of whose righteous judgments, and glorious tribunal, mortal men shall render an account of the deeds done in the body. And whatever the apprehensions of such may be concerning this discourse, it was writ in love, and from a true sense of the present state of things, and time and the event will vindicate it from untruth. In the mean while, it is matter of great satisfaction to the author, that he has so plainly cleared his conscience, in pleading for the "Liberty of other men's," and publicly borne his honest testimony for God, not out of season to his POOR COUNTRY.

3

Building the Wall of Separation

IN AMERICA, in the era of enlightenment — the age of confidence in the power of human reason to unravel the threads of all the difficulties of mankind — men feared but one bogey, absolute power. Only the untrammeled mind — the "free-born mind," as a popular hymn of the late eighteenth century phrased it — could be exercised freely in the solution of human problems. Such freedom could not exist where despotic power reigned. The powerful conservative force of established institutions had to be broken down so that the human mind might be freed from the dominance of the despotisms whose status conservatism maintained. Antimonarchism was not enough; all the props of monarchy had to be torn down. Nothing was to be left standing on which royal power might found itself anew.

Walking always in fear of a re-established tyranny, leaders of the American Revolutionary and post-Revolutionary days were all against monarchy, and most of them were against strong centralized government; with but few exceptions they opposed strong centralized financial institutions and favored free trade against any form of mercantilism; virtually all of them were opposed to a church establishment, while many resented all church influence, and not a few were anticlerical. Not only did they believe that the best government was self-government, and the best principle of economic life was self-interest; they also thought that the best religious life was personal, not institutional. Thomas Paine, phrasemaker extraordinary, gave this theme of the enlightened American mind its tersest expression when he said, "My own mind is my own church."

Fearing strong churches and strong government, and distrusting the clergy who gained influence through the first and support from the second, the men of the age of reason strove mightily to build a wall of separation between the government and the church. It was to be a wall impassable in either direction; religion was to have no influence in the state, to give no support to the institutions of government; the state was to have no part in religious life, to give no support to religious institutions. Such a wall would keep government weak and the citizenry strong, the churches weak and personal religion strong. The ideals of political liberty and religious liberty went hand in hand.

Where there was no established church prior to the Revolution, there was no need to eliminate establishment after the Revolution. But where, as in Virginia, the established church was strong, a struggle for disestablishment had to be waged. Thomas Jefferson regarded his part in leading this struggle as one of the three most memorable actions of his life, on a par with his writing of the Declaration of Independence and his foundation of the University of Virginia — religious liberty, political liberty, and education, without which religious and political liberty could only be temporary. One of his chief associates in the battle for disestablishment was James Madison, who also served political liberty in the Constitutional Convention, and succeeded his older friend as Rector of the University.

Jefferson proposed religious toleration in the Virginia constitutional convention of 1776. Although his proposal was not included in the constitution, it was, thanks to Madison, included in the supplementary bill of rights. The extension of Jefferson's campaign for freedom of religion by the disestablishment of the tax-supported Anglican Church was incorporated into the celebrated but too-little-read "Act for Establishing Religious Freedom." Jefferson presented this bill to the legislature of his state as early as 1779. He found arrayed against him not only the clergy, but also the wealthier landowners, who valued the conservative power of their ecclesiastical ally. Yet seven years later, during Jefferson's absence in France, the act was passed despite this opposition.

The stirring opening clause of the act must be taken as a partial elucidation of that other great Jeffersonian composition, the Declaration of Independence. "Well aware that Almighty God hath created the mind free" is a commentary on "that all men are created equal; that they are endowed by their Creator with certain inalienable rights; that among these are life, liberty and the pursuit of happiness." Consider the two statements together; what do they say? One aspect of the inalienable right of liberty is the free use of the human mind, itself created free. What Jefferson meant by the free use of a free mind becomes clearer when the section of his *Notes on Virginia* dealing with religion is introduced into the picture. "The legitimate powers of government extend to such acts only as are injurious to others. But it does me no injury for my neighbor to say there are twenty gods, or no God." For the government to force outward conformity would tend to make of my neighbor a hypocrite. If he is in error, his conscience is answerable to God and to God alone for his error. Although governmental restraints on religious expression are no help, "reason and free inquiry are the only effectual agents against error." Reason supports truth by challenging error; for Jefferson that could not be true which was not reasonable.

Another commendable aspect of the Jeffersonian position was its assertion of the independence of citizenship and religious ideas. One does not deny a mathematician the right to vote because he differs from the prevailing theorems of geometry; "our civil rights have no dependence on our religious opinions, more than our opinions in physics or geometry." When mathematical, physical, or religious theories lead to overt actions against the public order, then it is time for government to intervene. Until that time, we must hold to our faith "that truth is great and will prevail if left to herself, that she is the proper and sufficient antagonist to error."

These two pillars of separation represented, for Jefferson, the solution to two major problems of the relation of church and state. Disestablishment of the Anglican Church provided, at one and the same time, for a free choice among churches for the individual, and for the elimination of political influence on religion; whereas the principle of the independence of citizenship and religion provided, at one and the same time, for a free choice among political views for the individual, and for the elimination of the formal influence of religious institutions on the state. There is, however, a third problem in this relationship: if religion can make a breach in the wall of separation by gaining a place of dominance and control in an aspect of life which later exerts influence on the state, the indirect influence of the church on the state will be more potent and more insidious than any direct influence. The institution through which such indirect control can most readily be established is education, which was for long the special concern of religious authorities.

To this problem the foundation of the University of Virginia was to provide a solution on the level of higher education; but infiltration on the level of elementary schooling can be just as dangerous to liberty as indoctrination on the more advanced level. Furthermore, if religious teachers of any or all denominations are paid by the state out of tax monies, there has developed a virtual establishment of religion. One of the major blows against establishment was, therefore, struck in Madison's brilliant "Memorial and Remonstrance on the Religious Rights of Man," written during the session of 1784-85 of the Virginia House of Delegates, as an attack upon a bill "establishing a provision for teachers of the Christian religion." The memorial consisted of sixteen arguments to prove that the right to freedom of conscience is one of the inalienable rights of man; that interference in matters of religion violates the principles of equality; that it gives too wide a jurisdiction to the legislature and implies that the civil magistrate is competent to judge of religious truth; that state establishments do not further true religion or strengthen civil government; that generally laws invading the religious rights of free men tend to weaken the tenure of all rights.

This was not a new position for Madison. As a delegate to the Virginia constitutional committee of 1776, he had added to the declaration of rights proposed by George Mason those phrases which included freedom of religion among the natural rights. It is noteworthy that it was not until after his participation in the deliberations of this committee that Madison became intimate with Jefferson. His original belief in the religious rights of man did not, therefore, stem from Jefferson's views, though he may later have been confirmed in these opinions by Jefferson.

Throughout Madison's career he remained faithful to the views expressed in the memorial. In 1822 he condemned heartily the view that church and state needed each other for survival. In a letter to Edward Everett in 1823 he maintained that separation of church and state is more conducive to the spread of true religion than church establishment. He maintained the extreme secularist position that chaplains should not be paid out of the treasury and that the President should not issue executive proclamations of religious fasts and festivals, a position taken only by him and by Jefferson among all our presidents.

Madison's general political philosophy, implicit in the memorial, was, like Jefferson's, that of the social-contract school. Man, in his original state of nature (recognized by Madison as a purely theoretical state as far as our observations are concerned), united for mutual protection with his fellow men. This union was made possible by the surrender of certain sovereign rights; other rights, however, such as those of life, liberty, and property, were "inalienable." Madison believed that the original compact was for the formation of society and that a second, political compact was necessary to form a government. Thus, the government is never a party to the compact, but is its result, its creation. The American Revolution was not followed by a return to a state of nature, since only the political compact, not the underlying social compact, had been dissolved.

Because of Madison's belief that sovereignty is both alienable and divisible, with the exception of the natural rights noted above, he was able to elaborate an extremely complicated account of the relations of the government of the United States to those of the several states (its federal character) and to the people of the country (its national character). The mixed federal and national character of the Union is well defined in *The Federalist*, No. 39, one of the papers contributed by Madison to that series:

The proposed Constitution . . . is, in strictness, neither a national nor a federal Constitution, but a composition of both. In its foundation, it is federal, not national; in the sources from which the ordinary powers of the government are drawn, it is partly federal and partly national; in the operation of these powers, it is national, not federal; in the extent of them, again, it is federal, not national; and finally, in the authoritative mode of introducing amendments, it is neither wholly federal nor wholly national.

In common with many political thinkers of the Enlightenment, Madison was convinced that "the necessity of any government is a misfortune," and that government is "the greatest of all reflections on human nature." To the extent that government is a measure of the weakness of man, its functions are largely negative, concerned with the correction of man's natural propensities to evil. The essence of Madison's views on the functions of government is to be found best expressed in his final message to Congress, December 3, 1816:

A government pursuing the public good as its sole object, and regulating its means by the great principles consecrated in its charter, and by those moral principles to which they are so well allied; a government which watches over the purity of elections, the freedom of speech, and the press, trial by jury, and the equal interdict against encroachments and compacts between religion and state; which maintains inviolably the maxims of public faith, the security of persons and property, and encourages in every authorized mode that general diffusion of knowledge which guarantees to public liberty its permanency and to those who possess the blessing the true enjoyment of it; a government which avoids intrusion on the internal repose of other nations and repels them from its own . . . a government, in a word, whose conduct within and without may bespeak the most noble of all ambitions — that of promoting peace on earth and good will to men.

In statements like these, then, did both Madison and Jefferson show that their first concern and their last was for liberty. To them is in large measure due the credit for building a wall of separation between church and state which still stands, and still serves as a fundamental guarantee of the liberty of the American people. Attempts have been made to break down the separating wall in the century and half that have passed since its building. But the wall was well and truly built and has never lacked defenders. These cornerstones have been collected to do honor to those who built and those who maintained.

Thomas Jefferson

1779

AN ACT FOR ESTABLISHING
RELIGIOUS FREEDOM

Well aware that Almighty God hath created the mind free; that all attempts to influence it by temporal punishments or burdens, or by civil incapacitations, tend only to beget habits of hypocrisy and meanness, and are a departure from the plan of the Holy Author of our religion, who being Lord both of body and mind, yet chose not to propagate it by coercions on either, as was in his Almighty power to do; that the impious presumption of legislators and rulers, civil as well as ecclesiastical, who, being themselves but fallible and uninspired men have assumed dominion over the faith of others, setting up their own opinions and modes of thinking as the only true and infallible, and as such endeavoring to impose them on others, hath established and maintained false religions over the greatest part of the world, and through all time; that to compel a man to furnish contributions of money for the propagation of opinions which he disbelieves, is sinful and tyrannical; that even the forcing him to support this or that teacher of his own religious persuasion, is depriving him of the comfortable liberty of giving his contributions to the particular pastor whose morals he would make his pattern, and whose power he feels most persuasive to righteousness, and is withdrawing from the ministry those temporal rewards, which proceeding from an approbation of their personal conduct, are an additional incitement to earnest and unremitting labors for the instruction of mankind; that our civil rights have no dependence on our religious opinions, more than our opinions in physics or geometry; that, therefore, the proscribing any citizen as unworthy the public confidence by laying upon him an incapacity of being called to the offices of trust and emolument, unless he profess or renounce this or that religious opinion, is depriving him injuriously of those privileges and advantages to which in common with his fellow citizens he has a natural right; that it tends also to corrupt the principles of that very religion it is meant to encourage, by bribing, with a monopoly of worldly honors and emoluments, those who will externally profess and conform to it; that though indeed these are criminal who do not withstand such temptation, yet neither are those innocent who lay the bait in their way; that to suffer the civil magistrate to intrude his powers into the field of opinion and to restrain the profession or propagation of principles, on the supposition of their ill tendency, is a dangerous fallacy, which at once destroys all religious liberty, because he being of course judge of that tendency, will make his opinions the rule of judgment, and approve or condemn the sentiments of others only as they shall square with or differ from his own; that it is time enough for the rightful purposes of civil government, for its officers to interfere when principles break out into overt acts against peace and good order; and finally, that truth is great and will prevail if left to herself, that she is the proper and sufficient antagonist to error, and has nothing to fear from the conflict, unless by human interposition disarmed of her natural weapons, free argument and debate, errors ceasing to be dangerous when it is permitted freely to contradict them.

Be it therefore enacted by the General Assembly. That no man shall be compelled to frequent or support any religious worship, place or ministry whatsoever, nor shall be enforced, restrained, molested, or burthened in his body or goods, nor shall otherwise suffer on account of his religious opinions or belief; but that all men shall be free to profess, and by argument to maintain, their opinions in matters of religion, and that the same shall in nowise diminish, enlarge, or affect their civil capacities.

And though we well know this Assembly, elected by the people for the ordinary purposes of legislation only, have no power to restrain the acts of succeeding assemblies, constituted with the powers equal to our own, and that therefore to declare this act irrevocable, would be of no effect in law, yet we are free to declare, and do declare, that the rights hereby asserted are of the natural rights of mankind, and that if any act shall be hereafter passed to repeal the present or to narrow its operation, such act will be an infringement of natural right.

Thomas Jefferson
1781-82

NOTES ON VIRGINIA

QUERY XVII
THE DIFFERENT RELIGIONS RECEIVED INTO THAT STATE

The first settlers in this country were emigrants from England, of the English Church, just at a point of time when it was flushed with complete victory over the religious of all other persuasions. Possessed, as they became, of the powers of making, administering, and executing the laws, they showed equal intolerance in this country with their Presbyterian brethren, who had emigrated to the northern government. The poor Quakers were flying from persecution in England. They cast their eyes on these new countries as asylums of civil and religious freedom; but they found them free only for the reigning sect. Several acts of the Virginia assembly of 1659, 1662, and 1693, had made it penal in parents to refuse to have their children baptized; had prohibited the unlawful assembling of Quakers; had made it penal for any master of a vessel to bring a Quaker into the State; had ordered those already here, and such as should come thereafter, to be imprisoned till they should abjure the country; provided a milder punishment for their first and second return, but death for their third; had inhibited all persons from suffering their meetings in or near their houses, entertaining them individually, or disposing of books which supported their tenets. If no execution took place here, as did in New England, it was not owing to the moderation of the church, or spirit of the legislature, as may be inferred from the law itself; but to historical circumstances which have been handed down to us. The Anglicans retained full possession of the country about a century. Other opinions began to creep in, and the great care of the government to support their own church, having begotten an equal degree

76

of indolence in its clergy, two-thirds of the people had become dissenters at the commencement of the present revolution. The laws, indeed, were still oppressive on them, but the spirit of the one party had subsided into moderation, and of the other had risen to a degree of determination which commanded respect.

The present state of our laws on the subject of religion is this. The convention of May, 1776, in their declaration of rights, declared it to be a truth, and a natural right, that the exercise of religion should be free; but when they proceeded to form on that declaration the ordinance of government, instead of taking up every principle declared in the bill of rights, and guarding it by legislative sanction, they passed over that which asserted our religious rights, leaving them as they found them. The same convention, however, when they met as a member of the general assembly in October, 1776, repealed all *acts of Parliament* which had rendered criminal the maintaining any opinions in matters of religion, the forbearing to repair to church, and the exercising any mode of worship, and suspended the laws giving salaries to the clergy, which suspension was made perpetual in October, 1779. Statutory oppressions in religion being thus wiped away, we remain at present under those only imposed by the common law, or by our own acts of assembly. At the common law, *heresy* was a capital offence, punishable by burning. Its definition was left to the ecclesiastical judges, before whom the conviction was, till the statute of the I El. c. I circumscribed it, by declaring, that nothing should be deemed heresy, but what had been so determined by authority of the canonical scriptures, or by one of the four first general councils, or by other council, having for the grounds of their declaration the express and plain words of the scriptures. Heresy, thus circumscribed, being an offence against the common law, our act of assembly of October, 1777, c. 17, gives cognizance of it to the general court, by declaring that the jurisdiction of that court shall be general in all matters at the common law. The execution is by the writ *De haeretico comburendo*. By our own act of assembly of 1705, c. 30, if a person brought up in the Christian religion denies the being of a God, or the Trinity, or asserts there are more gods than one, or denies the Christian religion to be true, or the scriptures to be of divine authority, he is punishable on the first offence by incapacity to hold any office or employment ecclesiastical, civil, or military; on the second by disability to sue, to take any gift or legacy, to be guardian, executor, or administrator, and by three years' imprisonment without bail. A father's right to the custody of his own children being founded in law on his right of guardianship, this being taken away, they may of course be severed from him, and put by the authority of a court into more orthodox hands. This is a summary view of that religious slavery under which a people have been willing to remain, who have lavished their lives and fortunes for the establishment of their civil freedom. The error seems not sufficiently eradicated, that the operations of the mind, as well as the acts of the body, are subject to the coercion of the laws. But our rulers can have no authority over such natural rights, only as we have submitted to them. The rights of conscience we never submitted, we could not submit. We are answerable for them to our God. The legitimate powers of government extend to such acts only as are injurious to others. But it does me no injury for my neighbor to say there are twenty gods, or no God. It neither picks my pocket nor breaks my leg. If it be said, his testimony in a court of justice cannot be relied on, reject it then, and be the stigma on him. Constraint may make him worse by making him a hypocrite, but it will never make him a truer man. It may fix him obstinately in his errors, but will not cure them. Reason and free inquiry are the only effectual agents against error. Give a loose to them, they will support the true religion by bringing every false one to their tribunal, to the test of their investigation. They are the natural enemies of error, and of error only. Had not the Roman government permitted free inquiry, Christianity could never have been introduced. Had not free inquiry been indulged at the era of the Reformation, the corruptions of Christianity could not have been purged away. If it be restrained now, the present corruptions will be protected, and new ones encouraged. Was the government to prescribe to us our medicine and diet, our bodies would be in such keeping as our souls are now. Thus in France the emetic was once forbidden as a medicine, the potato as an article of food. Government is just as infallible, too, when it fixes systems in physics. Galileo was sent to the Inquisition for affirming that the earth was a sphere;

the government had declared it to be as flat as a trencher, and Galileo was obliged to abjure his error. This error, however, at length prevailed, the earth became a globe, and Descartes declared it was whirled round its axis by a vortex. The government in which he lived was wise enough to see that this was no question of civil jurisdiction, or we should all have been involved by authority in vortices. In fact, the vortices have been exploded, and the Newtonian principle of gravitation is now more firmly established, on the basis of reason, than it would be were the government to step in, and to make it an article of necessary faith. Reason and experiment have been indulged, and error has fled before them. It is error alone which needs the support of government. Truth can stand by itself. Subject opinions to coercion: whom will you make your inquisitors? Fallible men; men governed by bad passions, by private as well as public reasons. And why subject it to coercion? To produce uniformity. But is uniformity of opinion desirable? No more than of face and stature. Introduce the bed of Procrustes then, as there is danger that the large men may beat the small, make us all of a size, by lopping the former and stretching the latter. Difference of opinion is advantageous in religion. The several sects perform the office of a *censor morum* over each other. Is uniformity attainable? Millions of innocent men, women, and children, since the introduction of Christianity, have been burnt, tortured, fined, imprisoned; yet we have not advanced one inch towards uniformity. What has been the effect of coercion? To make one half the world fools, and the other half hypocrites. To support roguery and error all over the earth. Let us reflect that it is inhabited by a thousand millions of people. That these profess probably a thousand different systems of religion. That ours is but one of that thousand. That if there be but one right, and ours that one, we should wish to see the nine hundred and ninety-nine wandering sects gathered into the fold of truth. But against such a majority we cannot effect this by force. Reason and persuasion are the only practicable instruments. To make way for these, free inquiry must be indulged; and how can we wish others to indulge it while we refuse it ourselves. But every State, says an inquisitor, has established some religion. No two, say I, have established the same. Is this a proof of the infallibility of establishments? Our sister States of Pennsylvania and New York, however, have long subsisted without any establishment at all. The experiment was new and doubtful when they made it. It has answered beyond conception. They flourish infinitely. Religion is well supported; of various kinds, indeed, but all good enough; all sufficient to preserve peace and order; or if a sect arises, whose tenets would subvert morals, good sense has fair play, and reasons and laughs it out of doors, without suffering the State to be troubled with it. They do not hang more malefactors than we do. They are not more disturbed with religious dissensions. On the contrary, their harmony is unparalleled, and can be ascribed to nothing but their unbounded tolerance, because there is no other circumstance in which they differ from every nation on earth. They have made the happy discovery, that the way to silence religious disputes, is to take no notice of them. Let us too give this experiment fair play, and get rid, while we may, of those tyrannical laws. It is true, we are as yet secured against them by the spirit of the times. I doubt whether the people of this country would suffer an execution for heresy, or a three years' imprisonment for not comprehending the mysteries of the Trinity. But is the spirit of the people an infallible, a permanent reliance? Is it government? Is this the kind of protection we receive in return for the rights we give up? Besides, the spirit of the times may alter, will alter. Our rulers will become corrupt, our people careless. A single zealot may commence persecutor, and better men be his victims. It can never be too often repeated, that the time for fixing every essential right on a legal basis is while our rulers are honest, and ourselves united. From the conclusion of this war we shall be going down hill. It will not then be necessary to resort every moment to the people for support. They will be forgotten, therefore, and their rights disregarded. They will forget themselves, but in the sole faculty of making money, and will never think of uniting to effect a due respect for their rights. The shackles, therefore, which shall not be knocked off at the conclusion of this war, will remain on us long, will be made heavier and heavier, till our rights shall revive or expire in a convulsion.

James Madison

1784

A MEMORIAL AND REMONSTRANCE ON THE RELIGIOUS RIGHTS OF MAN

To the Honorable the General Assembly of the State of Virginia.

We, the subscribers, citizens of the said commonwealth, having taken into serious consideration a bill printed by order of the last session of the general assembly, entitled "A bill for establishing a provision for teachers of the Christian religion," and conceiving that the same, if finally armed with the sanctions of a law, will be a dangerous abuse of power, are bound, as faithful members of a free state, to remonstrate against the said bill —

Because we hold it for a "fundamental and undeniable truth," that religion, or the duty which we owe to our creator, and the manner of discharging it, can be directed only by reason and conviction, not by force or violence. The religion, then, of every man, must be left to the conviction and conscience of every man; and it is the right of every man to exercise it as these may dictate. This right is, in its nature, an unalienable right. It is unalienable, because the opinions of men, depending only on the evidence contemplated in their own minds, cannot follow the dictates of other men; it is unalienable, also, because what is here a right towards men, is a duty towards the creator. It is the duty of every man to render the creator such homage, and *such only,* as he believes to be acceptable to him; this duty is precedent, both in order of time and degree of obligation, to the claims of civil society. Before any man can be considered as a member of civil society, he must be considered as a subject of the governor of the universe; and if a member of civil society, who enters into any subordinate association, must always do it with a reservation of his duty to the general

81

authority, much more must every man who becomes a member of any particular civil society do it *with the saving his allegiance to the universal sovereign.* We maintain, therefore, that in matters of religion no man's right is abridged by the institution of civil society; and that religion is wholly exempt from its cognizance. True it is, that no other rule exists, by which any question which may divide society can be ultimately determined, but the will of the majority; but it is also true, that the majority may trespass on the rights of the minority.

Because, if religion be exempt from the authority of the society at large, still less can it be subject to that of the legislative body. The latter are but the creatures and vicegerents of the former. Their jurisdiction is both derivative and limited. It is limited with regard to the coordinate departments; more necessarily is it limited with regard to the constituents. The preservation of a free government requires not merely that the metes and bounds which separate each department of power be universally maintained; but more especially, that neither of them be suffered to overleap the great barrier which defends the rights of the people. The rulers who are guilty of such an encroachment, exceed the commission from which they derive their authority, and are tyrants. The people who submit to it are governed by laws made neither by themselves, nor by an authority derived from them, and are slaves.

Because it is proper to take alarm at the first experiment on our liberties. We hold this prudent jealousy to be the first duty of citizens, and one of the noblest characteristics of the late revolution. The freemen of America did not wait till usurped power had strengthened itself by exercise, and entangled the question in precedents. They saw all the consequences by denying the principle. We revere this lesson too much soon to forget it. Who does not see that the same authority which can establish Christianity, in exclusion of all other religions, may establish, with the same ease, any particular sect of Christians, in exclusion of all other sects? That the same authority that can call for each citizen to contribute three pence only of his property for the support of only one establishment, may force him to conform to any one establishment, in all cases whatsoever?

Because the bill violates that equality which ought to be the basis of every law, and which is more indispensable in proportion as the validity or expediency of any law is more liable to be impeached. If "all men by nature are equally free and independent," all men are to be considered as entering into society on equal conditions, as relinquishing no more, and, therefore, retaining no less, one than another, of their rights. Above all, they are to be considered as retaining an "equal right to the free exercise of religion, according to the dictates of conscience." While we assert for ourselves a freedom to embrace, to profess, and to observe, the religion which we believe to be of divine origin, we cannot deny an equal freedom to those whose minds have not yet yielded to the evidence which has convinced us. If this freedom be abused, it is an offence against God, *not against man:* to God, therefore, *not to man,* must an account of it be rendered. As the bill violates equality by subjecting some to peculiar burdens, so it violates the same principle by granting to others peculiar exemptions. Are the Quakers and Menonists the only sects who think compulsive support of their religions unnecessary and unwarrantable? Can their piety alone be entrusted with the care of public worship? Ought their religions to be endowed, above all others, with extraordinary privileges, by which proselytes may be enticed from all others? We think too favorably of the justice and good sense of these denominations to believe that they either covet preeminence over their fellow citizens, or that they will be seduced by them from the common opposition to the measure.

Because the bill implies, either that the civil magistrate is a competent judge of truth, or that he may employ religion as an engine of civil policy. The first is an arrogant pretension, falsified by the contradictory opinions of rulers in all ages, and throughout the world: the second is an unhallowed perversion of the means of salvation.

Because the establishment proposed by the bill is not requisite for the support of the Christian religion. To say that it is, is a contradiction to the Christian religion itself; for every page of it disavows a dependence on the powers of this world: it is a contradiction to fact; for it is known that this religion both existed and flourished, not only without the support of human laws, but in spite of every opposition from them; and not only during the period of miraculous aid, but long after it had been left to its own evidence, and the ordinary care of Providence. Nay, it is a contradiction in terms; for a religion not invented by human policy must have pre-existed and been supported before it was established by human policy. It is, moreover, to weaken in those who profess this religion a pious confidence in its innate excellence, and the patronage of its author; and to foster in those who still reject it, a suspicion that its friends are too conscious of its fallacies to trust it to its own merits.

Because experience witnesseth that ecclesiastical establishments, instead of maintaining the purity and efficacy of religion, have had a contrary operation. During almost fifteen centuries has the legal establishment of Christianity been on trial. What have been its fruits? More or less, in all places, pride and indolence in the clergy; ignorance and servility in the laity; in both, superstition, bigotry, and persecution. Enquire of the teachers of Christianity for the ages in which it appeared in its greatest lustre; those of every sect point to the ages prior to its incorporation with civil policy. Propose a restoration of this primitive state, in which its teachers depended on the voluntary rewards of their flocks; many of them predict its downfall. On which side ought their testimony to have the greatest weight, when for, or when against, their interest?

Because the establishment in question is not necessary for the support of civil government. If it be urged as necessary for the support of civil government only as it is a means of supporting religion, and if it be not necessary for the latter purpose, it cannot be necessary for the former. If religion be not within the cognizance of civil government, how can its legal establishment be said to be necessary to civil government? What influences, in fact, have ecclesiastical establishments had on civil society? In some instances they have been seen to erect a spiritual tyranny on the ruins of civil authority; in many instances they have been seen upholding the thrones of political tyranny; in no instance have they been seen the guardians of the liberties of the people. Rulers who wished to subvert the public liberty may have found an established clergy convenient auxiliaries. A just government, instituted to secure and perpetuate it, needs them not. Such a government will be best supported by protecting every citizen in the enjoyment of his religion with the same equal hand that protects his person and property; by neither invading the equal rights of any sect, nor suffering any sect to invade those of another.

Because the proposed establishment is a departure from that generous policy which, offering an asylum to the persecuted and oppressed of every nation and religion, promised a lustre to our country, and an accession to the number of its citizens. What a melancholy mark is the bill, of sudden degeneracy. Instead of holding forth an asylum to the persecuted, it is itself a signal of persecution. It degrades from the equal rank of citizens all those whose opinions in religion do not bend to those of the legislative authority. Distant as it may be, in its present form, from the inquisition, it differs only in degree. The one is the *first* step, the other the *last,* in the *career of intolerance.* The magnanimous sufferer under this cruel scourge in foreign regions, must view the bill as a beacon on our coast, warning him to seek some other haven, where liberty and philanthropy, in their due extent, may offer a more certain repose from his troubles.

Because it will have a like tendency to banish our citizens. The allurements presented by other situations are every day thinning their numbers. To superadd a fresh motive to emigration, by revoking the liberty which they now enjoy, would be the same species of folly which has dishonored and depopulated flourishing kingdoms.

Because it will destroy the moderation and harmony which the forbearance of our laws to intermeddle with religion has produced among its several sects. Torrents of blood have been spilt in the world in vain attempts of the secular arm to extinguish religious discord, by proscribing all differences in religious opinions. Time, at length, has revealed the true remedy. Every relaxation of narrow and rigorous policy, wherever it has been tried, has been found to assuage the disease. The American theatre has exhibited proofs, that equal and complete liberty, if it does not wholly eradicate it, sufficiently destroys its malignant influence on the health and prosperity of the state. If, with the salutary effects of this system under our own eyes, we begin to contract the bounds of religious freedom, we know no name that will too severely reproach our folly. At least, let warning be taken at the first fruits of the threatened innovation. The very appearance of the bill has transformed that "Christian forbearance, love, and charity," which of late mutually prevailed, into animosities and jealousies, which may not soon be appeased. What mischiefs may not be dreaded, should this enemy to the public quiet be armed with the force of a law!

Because the policy of the bill is adverse to the diffusion of the light of Christianity. The first wish of those who enjoy this precious gift ought to be, that it may be imparted to the whole race of mankind. Compare the number of those who have as yet received it, with the number still remaining under the dominion of false religions, and how small is the former! Does the policy of the bill tend to lessen the disproportion? No: it at once discourages those who are strangers to the light of revelation from coming into the region of it: countenances, by example, the nations who continue in darkness, in shutting out those who might convey it to them. Instead of levelling, as far as possible, every obstacle to the victorious progress of truth, the bill, with an ignoble and unchristian timidity, would circumscribe it with a wall of defence against the encroachments of error.

Because attempts to enforce by legal sanctions acts obnoxious to so great a proportion of citizens, tend to enervate the laws in general, and to slacken the bands of society. If it be difficult to execute any law which is not generally deemed necessary or salutary, what must be the case where it is deemed invalid and dangerous? And what may be the effect of so striking an example of impotency in the government on its general authority?

Because a measure of such general magnitude and delicacy ought not to be imposed, without the clearest evidence that it is called for by a majority of citizens: and no satisfactory method is yet proposed, by which the voice of the majority in this case may be determined, or its influence secured. "The people of the respective counties are, indeed, requested to signify their opinion, respecting the adoption of the bill, to the next sessions of assembly;" but the representation must be made equal before the voice either of the representatives or the counties will be that of the people. Our hope is, that neither of the former will, after due consideration, espouse the dangerous principle of the bill. Should the event disappoint us, it will still leave us in full confidence that a fair appeal to the latter will reverse the sentence against our liberties.

Because, finally, "the equal right of every citizen to the free exercise of his religion, according to the dictates of conscience," is held by the same tenure with all our other rights. If we recur to its origin, it is equally the gift of nature; if we weigh its importance, it cannot be less dear to us; if we consult the "declaration of those rights which pertain to the good people of Virginia, as the basis and foundation of government," it is enumerated with equal solemnity, or, rather, studied emphasis.

Either, then, we must say that the will of the legislature is the only measure of their authority, and that, in the plenitude of this authority, they may sweep away all our fundamental rights; or, that they are bound to leave this particular right untouched and sacred: either we must say that they may control the freedom of the press, may abolish the trial by jury, may swallow up the executive and judiciary powers of the state; nay, that they may despoil us of our right of suffrage, and erect themselves into an independent and hereditary assembly: or, we must say, that they have no authority to enact into law the bill under consideration. We, the subscribers, say, that the general assembly of this commonwealth have no such authority; and that no effort may be omitted, on our part, against so dangerous an usurpation, we oppose to it in this remonstrance — earnestly praying, as we are in duty bound, that the SUPREME LAWGIVER OF THE UNIVERSE, by illuminating those to whom it is addressed, may, on the one hand, turn their councils from every act which affronts his holy prerogative, or violates the trust committed to them; and, on the other, guide them into every measure that may be worthy of his blessing, may redound to their own praise, and may establish more firmly the liberties of the people, and the prosperity and happiness of the commonwealth.

4

The Affirmation of Civil Rights for Religious Minorities

IN JEFFERSON'S "Act for Establishing Religious Freedom," the principle that a man's religious professions should in no way affect his civil status was given explicit statement. The same principle was enacted into the Constitution of the United States (Article VI, section 3), which declares that "no religious Test shall ever be required as a Qualification to any Office or public Trust under the United States." Thus it became impossible, in theory at least, for the participation of non-Protestants in civil government to be challenged on religious grounds. No Unitarian could be refused full civil status because he rejected the doctrine of the trinity; no Universalist could be denied the right to vote and to hold office because of his unorthodox views of salvation and damnation; no Roman Catholic could be kept from full participation in government because of his refusal to accept the English Bible; no Jew could be excluded from "those privileges and advantages to which in common with his fellow citizens he has a natural right."

Before this principle was fully accepted, it had to be tried by the ordeal of battle, and triumphantly, if somewhat belatedly, affirmed. It happened, in two cases of more than passing interest, that the testing of the test acts centered in the issue of civil rights for America's Jews. Perhaps by historical accident, but unquestionably with remarkable appropriateness, the earlier of these two cases affirmed the civil rights of a single individual, while the latter involved a general verdict on the "no-test" principle.

The cases are alike in this respect, that both took place in states whose constitutions antedated the Federal Constitution. They are most unlike in that, in one, the issue raised was rapidly, almost immediately, settled, whereas, in the other, the question was agitated and discussed for thirty years before a decision was reached. This prolonged discussion was the reason for the historical accident mentioned earlier. The full civil right of the Jews of Maryland was urged more than ten years before the right of Jacob Henry to a seat in the North Carolina legislature — but granted nearly twenty years later.

North Carolina, whose constitution required its officials to accept the divine authority of the New Testament, but whose declaration of rights granted religious freedom, was faced with the necessity, in 1809, of deciding between these two instruments. Jacob Henry, a Jew, was elected to the House of Commons by the voters of Carteret County. It was, of course, impossible for Mr. Henry to affirm the divine authority of the New Testament. His right to his seat was, therefore, challenged. Mr. Henry was granted the privilege of speaking in defense of his right to retain the seat, and did so in a brief speech which was long considered one of the gems of American oratory. There has been some question raised as to his authorship of the speech; it is reported by one of the historians of North Carolina to have been written for him by Chief Justice Taylor of the State Supreme Court. This attribution was solely on the basis of hearsay, and we are justified in attaching the name of Jacob Henry to this speech until trustworthy evidence of other authorship is furnished.

The speech itself, though brief, is a ringing reiteration of the view that religion is a personal matter between the individual and his Maker, and that no one has the right to challenge or question this personal relation. As long as one does not hold religious opinions dangerous to the state, the state has no power to exclude him from any privilege or obligation of citizenship. The statement was clear-cut and incisive — and it is a pleasure to report that it was decisive. Mr. Henry was overwhelmingly granted the right to his seat in the Commons, and, some years later, the constitutional provisions were changed.

Meantime, as early as 1797, Solomon Etting, a Baltimorean,

petitioned the Maryland House of Delegates to repeal their test act, which was so worded as to prevent Jews from entering the legal profession as well as public office. Thus it was with full justice that Etting's petition claimed that the test act deprived the Jews of Maryland "of many of the invaluable rights of citizenship." This petition was shelved in 1801, but Etting, undiscouraged, continued to submit petitions and memorials. By 1804 his exertions had mustered a group of supporters in the House of Delegates large enough to demand an open vote on the disposition of Etting's current petition, but not large enough to prevent a defeat in the vote. So decisive was this defeat that even Etting himself lost heart, and the question of full civil rights for the Jews of Maryland was permitted to slumber for more than a decade.

When the issue was revived in 1818, it attracted the support of a freshman legislator, Thomas Kennedy of Washington County, in the Maryland Piedmont. Kennedy was an ardent Jeffersonian and a persistent fighter. Despite initial lack of success, he kept the issue before the delegates for eight years, and finally carried through triumphantly the repeal of the test act. This persistence is especially noteworthy when it is remembered that at this time there was probably not a single Jew in Washington County. Kennedy had nothing to gain from his constituents by his espousal of the unpopular cause of Jewish rights. That he had much to lose was made clear in 1823, when a united effort was made by opponents of the repeal of the test act to prevent the re-election of its supporters. The "Christian" opponents of the "Jew ticket" were successful in defeating sixteen incumbents, including Kennedy himself.

Others took up the battle, including Colonel W. G. D. Worthington and H. M. Brackenridge. The repeal was not carried through under their leadership, however, but had to await the return of Kennedy. Re-elected in 1824, he succeeded in pushing his "Jew bill" through the House of Delegates on February 26, 1825, the last day of the session; as required by law, it was confirmed in the following session. The date of its final passage was January 5, 1826. The Jeffersonian principle was vindicated and sustained in Maryland just six months before the death of Jefferson himself.

In this long and exciting struggle in the Maryland House of

Delegates, many fine defenses of the principle of religious freedom were presented by Thomas Kennedy and by those who supported him in his uphill fight for justice to the Jews. Interesting petitions and memorials were submitted by Solomon Etting, Dr. Joshua I. Cohen, and Jacob I. Cohen, Jr. Of all these, the speech of Judge H. M. Brackenridge in January, 1819, is the best statement of the theoretical position of the supporters of freedom of religion in Maryland; because of this excellence it is placed here in abridged form among the great documents which are the cornerstones of religious liberty in America.

Jacob Henry

1809

SPEECH IN THE NORTH CAROLINA
HOUSE OF DELEGATES

I certainly, Mr. Speaker, know not the design of the Declara-
ration of Rights made by the people of this State in the year
1776, if it was not to consecrate certain great and fundamental
rights and principles which even the Constitution cannot impair;
for the 44th section of the latter instrument declares that the
Declaration of Rights ought never to be violated, on any pretence
whatever; if there is any apparent difference between the two
instruments, they ought, if possible, to be reconciled; but if there
is a final repugnance between them, the Declaration of Rights
must be considered paramount; for I believe it is to the Constitution, as the Constitution is to law; it controls and directs it absolutely and conclusively. If, then, a belief in the Protestant religion
is required by the Constitution, to qualify a man for a seat in this
house, and such qualification is dispensed with by the Declaration
of Rights, the provision of the Constitution must be altogether
inoperative; as the language of the Bill of Rights is, "that all men
have a natural and inalienable right to worship ALMIGHTY GOD
according to the dictates of their own consciences." It is undoubtedly a natural right, and when it is declared to be an inalienable
one by the people in their sovereign and original capacity, any attempt to alienate either by the Constitution or by law, must be
vain and fruitless.

It is difficult to conceive how such a provision crept into the
Constitution, unless it is from the difficulty the human mind feels
in suddenly emancipating itself from fetters by which it has long
been enchained: and how adverse it is to the feelings and manners
of the people of the present day every gentleman may satisfy him-

92

self by glancing at the religious belief of the persons who fill the various offices in this State: there are Presbyterians, Lutherans, Calvinists, Mennonists, Baptists, Trinitarians, and Unitarians. But, as far as my observation extends, there are fewer Protestants, in the strict sense of the word, used by the Constitution, than of any other persuasion; for I suppose that they meant by it, the Protestant religion as established by the law in England. For other persuasions we see houses of worship in almost every part of the State, but very few of the Protestant; so few, that indeed I fear that the people of this State would for some time remain unrepresented in this House, if that clause of the Constitution is supposed to be in force. So far from believing in the Thirty-nine Articles, I will venture to assert that a majority of the people never have read them.

If a man should hold religious principles incompatible with the freedom and safety of the State, I do not hesitate to pronounce that he should be excluded from the public councils of the same; and I trust if I know myself, no one would be more ready to aid and assist than myself. But I should really be at a loss to specify any known religious principles which are thus dangerous. It is surely a question between a man and his Maker, and requires more than human attributes to pronounce which of the numerous sects prevailing in the world is most acceptable to the Deity. If a man fulfills the duties of that religion, which his education or his conscience has pointed to him as the true one, no person, I hold, in this our land of liberty, has a right to arraign him at the bar of any inquisition: and the day, I trust, has long passed, when principles merely speculative were propagated by force; when the sincere and pious were made victims, and the light-minded bribed into hypocrites.

The purest homage man could render to the Almighty was the sacrifice of his passions and the performance of his duties. That the ruler of the universe would receive with equal benignity the various offerings of man's adoration, if they proceeded from the heart. Governments only concern the actions and conduct of man, and not his speculative notions. Who among us feels himself so exalted above his fellows as to have a right to dictate to them any mode of belief? Will you bind the conscience in chains, and fasten conviction upon the mind in spite of the conclusions of reason and of those ties and habitudes which are blended with every pulsation of the heart? Are you prepared to plunge at once from the sublime heights of moral legislation into the dark and gloomy caverns of superstitious ignorance? Will you drive from your shores and from the shelter of your constitution, all who do not lay their oblations on the same altar, observe the same ritual, and subscribe to the same dogmas? If so, which, among the various sects into which we are divided, shall be the favored one?

I should insult the understanding of this House to suppose it possible that they could ever assent to such absurdities; for all know that persecution in all its shapes and modifications, is contrary to the genius of our government and the spirit of our laws, and that it can never produce any other effect than to render men hypocrites or martyrs.

When Charles V., Emperor of Germany, tired of the cares of government, resigned his crown to his son, he retired to a monastery, where he amused the evening of his life in regulating the movements of watches, endeavoring to make a number keep the same time; but, not being able to make any two go exactly alike, it led him to reflect upon the folly and crimes he had committed, in attempting the impossibility of making men think alike!!

Nothing is more easily demonstrated than that the conduct alone is the subject of human laws, and that man ought to suffer civil disqualification for what he does, and not for what he thinks. The mind can receive laws only from Him, of whose Divine essence it is a portion; He alone can punish disobedience; for who else can know its movements, or estimate their merits? The religion I profess, inculcates every duty which man owes to his fellow men; it enjoins upon its votaries the practice of every virtue, and the detestation of every vice; it teaches them to hope for the favor of heaven exactly in proportion as their lives have been directed by just, honorable, and beneficent maxims. This, then, gentlemen, is my creed, — it was impressed upon my infant mind; it has been the director of my youth, the monitor of my manhood, and will, I trust, be the consolation of my old age. At any rate, Mr. Speaker, I am sure that you cannot see anything in this Religion, to deprive me of my seat in this house. So far as relates to my life and conduct, the examination of these I submit with cheerfulness to your candid and liberal construction. What may be the religion of him who made this objection against me, or whether he has any religion or not I am unable to say. I have never considered it my duty to pry into the belief of other members of this house. If their actions are upright and conduct just, the rest is for their own consideration, not for mine. I do not seek to make converts to my faith, whatever it may be esteemed in the eyes of my officious friend, nor do I exclude any one from my esteem or friendship, because he and I differ in that respect. The same charity, therefore, it is not unreasonable to expect, will be extended to myself, because in all things that relate to the State and to the duties of civil life, I am bound by the same obligations with my fellow-citizens, nor does any man subscribe more sincerely than myself to the maxim, "whatever ye would that men should do unto you do ye so even unto them, for such is the law and the prophets."

H. M. Brackenridge

1819

SPEECH ON THE MARYLAND "JEW BILL"

Could I, for a moment, suppose it possible for the bill on your table, to lessen, in the slightest degree, by its passage, the attachment we all profess, for the religion in which we have been educated; or could I bring myself to believe, that even those innocent and harmless prejudices, which more or less influence the opinions of the most liberal, are treated with disrespect by bringing the subject before this house, I should be the last person to urge it on your consideration.

But, sir, I feel a firm conviction, that there is no room for any such apprehensions. The known public and private worth, (if I may be allowed thus to express myself in this place,) as well as the firm and fixed religious principles of the gentleman, with whom the bill was originated, and who has supported it in a manner so becoming the enlightened American statesman, and the tolerant Christian, must necessarily repel the suspicion of any but the most generous, disinterested, and philanthropic motives. In the theological view he has just taken of this interesting subject, he has most satisfactorily proved to my mind, that there is nothing in the religious faith which we profess, that enjoins us, to hold to the arbitrary test engrafted as a principle on the constitution of this state, at this day, when it is converted into a stain, by the progressive wisdom of the political world. To the test of that wisdom, I will, nevertheless, endeavor to bring the question now before the house. I will endeavor to show, that the objectionable provision in our own constitution, is at variance with all the sound, and well established political creed of the present enlightened age. For this, I will refer to the opinions publicly avowed, and successfully maintained, by every distinguished statesman, not only of America, but throughout the civilized world. In addition to this, I will show,

96

that the principles for which I this day contend, have received the unequivocal sanction of the most enlightened and respectable political bodies of our country. The subject, although of a most fruitful nature, properly resolves itself into three questions. 1. Have the Jews a *right* to be placed on a footing with other citizens? 2. Is there any urgent reason of state policy, which requires that they should be made an exception? 3. Is there anything incompatible with the respect we owe to the Christian religion, in allowing them a participation in civil offices and employments?

In ascending to first principles, (and in examining institutions supposed to be founded upon them, we must often do so,) I find that we have duties to perform to our Creator, as well as to society, but which are so distinct in their nature, that unless their corresponding obligations be clearly understood, we shall in vain attempt to lay the foundation of a solid and satisfactory argument. It is unquestionably the right of society to compel every one who enjoys its protection, to conform to its ordinances and laws. It is its right so to restrain his *actions,* as to conduce to the general happiness and prosperity. But I contend, that after having exercised this control over his actions, the temporal power has reached its limit; and when it dares to pass that limit, it opens the way to oppression, persecution, and cruelty, such as the history of the world has furnished but too many melancholy examples — not for our imitation, but abhorrence. Opinion, when merely such, when prompting to no act inconsistent with the laws and peace of society, should be encountered only by opinion; and on such occasions the interposition of the temporal arm is improper, however mildly interposed. For it is not the extent, or degree, of compulsion, which renders it improper, but the unjust and arbitrary interference itself. If, as members of society, we have duties whose performance the temporal power may justly enforce, we have, as rational beings, other duties of a much higher nature, to our Creator, of which he is the judge, and to whom, alone, should be referred the punishment, or reward, of their fulfilment or neglect. Religion, therefore, merely as such, is a matter entirely between man and his God. If my position, then, be correct, if will follow, that it must be left to every citizen, as he is to stand or fall by his own merits, or demerits, to entertain that belief, or offer that worship, which in his conscience he thinks most acceptable; and should any of his fellow-citizens desire to release him from what he conceives to be the bondage of error, let it be by an appeal to the reason, and not by a resort to coercion — a coercion which can only affect outward actions, and serve to exhibit power on the one side, and feebleness on the other. He that is thus convinced, will be of the same opinion still. The human frame may be bound in chains; it may be imprisoned and enslaved; it may yield to the dagger of the assassin, or the murderer's bowl; but the immortal mind soars beyond the reach of earthly violence. Upon the self-evident truths which I have spoken, (and on no others can they safely rest,) are built the RIGHTS OF CONSCIENCE, so little understood, or at least respected, in most countries, not so well, I confess it with regret, in Maryland, as they ought to be, but perfectly so in the constitution of the United States; an instrument for which we are indebted as a nation, to the high estimation of enlightened men, and which has conferred on our country, the reputation of being the land of freedom and toleration.

And here, I find it necessary to encounter an argument of those gentlemen who oppose the passage of the bill; they tell us, that no *force,* or coercion, is resorted to by the constitution of Maryland, in consequence of religious faith — that every one is secured in his civil rights, no matter what religion he may profess — that no one can be molested on account of his religious belief — that no one has a right to complain of being denied some common benefit, or being excluded from holding offices, when he does not think proper to conform to the prevailing religious tenets of the community of which he is admitted a member. Sir, I contend, that in conformity to the reasons I have advanced, *every* citizen is entitled to *all* the privileges of citizenship; that the religious opinions of no one can be justly visited upon him, either directly or indirectly, as the immediate or remote consequence of that opinion. If, on account of my religious faith, I am subjected to disqualifications, from which others are free, while there is no paramount reason drawn from a regard to the safety of society, why I should be thus excepted, I cannot but consider myself a persecuted man. The persecution may be but slight in its character, but still it must bear the detested name of persecution. It is true, it is not the fagot, or the wheel, but it is applied for the same reason — because my opinions do not conform to those of the more numerous, or the more powerful.

An odious exclusion from any of the benefits common to the rest of my fellow-citizens, is a persecution, differing only in degree, but of a nature equally unjustifiable with that, whose instruments are chains and torture. In our land of equal rights and equal pretensions to the dignity and emolument of office, to be subjected to a degrading exception, is by no means a nominal punishment.

Sir, in the sentiments which I have uttered on this occasion, I have done nothing more than repeat what has already been so often and so much better expressed, by the enlightened statesmen of our country. There is hardly a distinguished American who has not in some mode or other, given to these ideas his decided approbation. They are deeply engraven on the tablets of those political doctrines which are considered as eternal and immutable. They are among the first lessons inculcated on our youthful minds; they are interwoven in the texture of our political constitutions; and so deeply are we impressed with their truth, that every American who aspires to the character of liberality, as well as to a proper knowledge of the spirit of our institutions, must subscribe to this proposition, as the test of the progress of his attainments — THAT RELIGION IS A MATTER BETWEEN MAN AND HIS GOD — THAT THE TEMPORAL ARM SHOULD BE INTERPOSED TO DIRECT THE ACTIONS OF MEN, AND NOT THEIR THOUGHTS. . . .

I have hitherto, Mr. Speaker, considered rather what ought to be the right of the citizen, than what it really is, as guaranteed by the recorded monument of his liberties; for it is our pride, that for these, we are not indebted to the charter of a sovereign. And here, I do not hesitate to assert, that could this question be brought before some tribunal competent to decide, I would undertake to maintain, that the right which this bill professes to give, is already *secured* by our national compact; I would boldly contend, that the state of Maryland has deprived, and still continues to deprive, American citizens of their just political rights. If we cannot find it in the express letter of the instrument, can we hesitate for a moment, in believing, that it has at least virtually abrogated every part of state laws or constitutions, whose tendency is to infringe the RIGHTS OF CONSCIENCE? But first, let me ask, what says your own declaration of rights on this subject? — It emphatically declares, not merely that it is the right, but that it is the *duty of every man to worship God, in such a manner, as he thinks most acceptable to him.* It is true, this is narrowed by the subsequent clause of the sentence, which would seem to confine that worship to the professors of Christianity; and I will not trouble you with a vindication of the enlightened men who drew up that declaration, from the charge of narrowness of mind, in supposing it impossible for any one, conscientiously to worship God, excepting through the medium of Christianity. I firmly believe, that the subsequent expressions were intended to apply to all who *worship the Deity,* and that it was not the intention to discriminate as to the mode; wherefore, *no person ought by any law to be molested in his person or estate, on account of his religious persuasion or profession, or for his religious practice, unless, under color of religion, any man shall disturb the good order, peace, or safety of the state, or shall infringe the laws of morality, or injure others in their natural, civil, or religious rights.* I will ask, whether the religious test in the constitution of this state, can stand for a moment, when construed by the spirit of this declaration? No, sir, they are utterly incompatible. Let us now turn to the first amendment of the constitution of the United States; we find that congress is expressly forbidden, *to pass any law respecting an establishment of religion.* Does not this speak volumes? And is it not morally certain, that if a declaration of rights had preceded that instrument, the right to worship God free from all human control, or reflection, would have been unequivocally declared? No test-oath is required in that instrument; and can there be a clearer, although but a negative exposition? . . .

Were it necessary for the support of this bill, I would undertake to vindicate the Jewish character from its commonly imputed vices and defects. But the question before the house, has nothing to do with these considerations. I will ask those Christians who now hear me, candidly and dispassionately to examine their own minds, and to say how much of their opinions on the subject of the Jewish character, is the offspring of prejudice? Most of us have been taught from earliest infancy to look upon them as a depraved and wicked people. The books put into our hands, and even the immortal Shakespeare himself, have contributed to fix in our minds this unchristian hatred to a portion of our fellow men. It is true, we have witnessed some honorable exceptions; a modern character (I rejoice to say it for the honor of Christendom,) ventured to be their advocate, and what is more, with success. We have seen, sir, that, in the same country, in proportion as science and civilization have advanced, the condition of the Jew has improved, while his moral character has as uniformly risen to the level of that condition. Will any one seriously compare the Jews of England, of the present day, with the same people a few centuries ago, when degraded and oppressed by the British kings? Will the Jews of Portugal or Turkey, bear a comparison with those of the more liberal governments of Europe? To come nearer home, I will ask whether the American Jew is distinguished by those characteristics so invidiously ascribed to his race, by its enemies? Sir, I have had the honor of being acquainted with a number of American Jews, and do not hesitate to say, that I have found at least an equal proportion of estimable individuals, to that which might be expected in any other class of men. None, sir, appeared to me, more zealously attached to the interests and happiness of our common country; the more so, as it is the only one on earth, they can call by that endearing name. None have more gallantly espoused its cause, both in the late and revolutionary war; none feel a livelier sense of gratitude and affection for the mild and liberal institutions of this country, which not only allow them, publicly and freely, the enjoyment and exercise of their religion, but also, with the exception of the state of Maryland, have done away all those odious civil and political discriminations, by which they are elsewhere thrown into an inferior and degraded caste. In the city which I have the honor to represent, there are Jewish families, which, in point of estimation and worth, stand in the first rank of respectability — who are scarcely remarked as differing from their Christian brethren in their religious tenets, and whose children are educated in the same schools with our youth, AND, LIKE THEM, GLORY IN BEING AMERICANS AND FREEMEN. Have we hitherto had any cause to repent of our liberality — rather of our justice? Sir, I abhor intolerance, *whether it be political or religious;* and yet, I can scarcely regard *religious tolerance* as a virtue. What! has weak and erring man, a right to give *permission* to his fellow mortal, to offer his adorations to the Supreme Being, after his own manner? Did I not feel myself somehow restrained from pursuing this subject, I would endeavor to demonstrate, that the idea of such permission, or toleration, is not better than impiety. But I content myself, with calling your attention to what has been the effect, in this country, at least, of leaving religion to be taught from the pulpit, or to be instilled by early education. Is there, let me ask, less genuine Christianity in America than in any other Christian country? For, if the interference of government be necessary to uphold it, such ought to be the natural consequence. Certainly we are not disposed to confess an inferiority in this particular — Sir, I believe there is MORE. And I am well convinced, that if the success of true religion, were the only end in view, other nations would follow our example of universal toleration. I believe, that in no countries, are there more atheists and deists, than in those where but one mode of worship is sanctioned, or permitted. In my opinion, it is the natural inclination of man, to seek support and refuge in religious feelings; and if he find a religion which his judgment approves, or to which his affections attach him, he will cling to it, as his brightest hope. The man who cannot subscribe to all the doctrines and discipline of catholicism, may still be a protestant — the protestant may be a churchman, a presbyterian, a friend, or a methodist. But the inquisition allows him no choice; he must either embrace that which is tendered him, or be nothing. No, sir, it does not enter into the duties of this body, to guard and preserve the religious faith of Maryland, from schism, and innovation; otherwise, we have been grossly remiss in the performance of that duty. I do not recollect a single statute, or resolution, on the records of this house, for this purpose. Sir, the propagation of error, has never been prevented by force; but force has sometimes given permanence, to what would otherwise have been ephemeral.

Were we about to attempt the conversion of the Jews to Christianity, the true mode, in my opinion, would be, to treat them with kindness, and to allow them a full participation of political and social rights. When men are proscribed for their opinions, those opinions become dear to them; like the traveller in the storm, they draw the mantle closer about them, but on the return of the warm and genial sun, they cast it carelessly away. . . .

There is but one remaining objection to the passage of the bill, and this I will endeavor also to meet, and yet, it is not without reluctance. It has been repeated, that the passage of the bill, is incompatible with the respect we owe to the Christian religion; that this a *Christian land* — that the Christian religion ought here to be, at least, legally avowed, and acknowledged; and that the respect which is due to that institution, may be weakened by abolishing the test. Sir, I can see no disrespect, offered to any system of religion, where the government simply declares, that every man may enjoy his own, provided he discharges his social duties; and that the only support of religion, should be derived from the zeal, affection and faith of those who profess it. Sir, I do firmly believe that it is an insult to the Christian religion, to suppose, that it needs the temporal arm for its support. It has flourished in despite of temporal power — by the interference of temporal power in its behalf, has its progress ever been retarded, or its principles perverted.

But, we are told, that this is a *Christian land,* and that we are Christians! I rejoice to hear it, and I hope we will prove ourselves worthy of the name, by acting on this, and on every other occasion, with Christian spirit. The great author of that sublime religion, teaches us charity and forbearance, to the errors and failings of our fellow men. To his followers, he promised no *worldly benefits,* but crowns of glory in heaven; for he emphatically declared, that *his kingdom was not of this world.* Far from inculcating unkindness and resentment, to those of the Jews who did not believe in him, he even forgave those among them, who were his persecutors, and enemies. Do we find any injunction bequeathed to his followers, to pursue those enemies with vengeance? No — his last words was a prayer for their forgiveness; and shall we dare to punish where he has been pleased to forgive?

But this is a *Christian land!* And let me inquire of the page of history, by what means it became so? Was it through the instrumentality of peace and good will to our fellow men? Perhaps we may say with a clear conscience, that we violated no principle of justice, or Christianity, in our dealings with the poor heathen, whom we found in possession of the soil. But if there is a beam in our own eye, at least we can see the mote in the eye of our Christian brethren of the south. Let us cast a glance towards the bloody Christian conquests of Cortes and Pizarro — they are now *Christian lands,* and by what means did they become so? I can fancy to myself the wretched Guatimozin, stretched on burning coals, his only crime that of *being suspected of unrevealed treasures,* and I hear him rebuke his less patient companion in misery, by the simple, but heroic question, *Am I on a bed of roses?* Who was the Christian on that occasion? No, sir, the soil we inhabit yields its fruit to the just and to the unjust; the sun which gives us life, sheds his glorious beams impartially on all. But the great majority of the dwellers in this land are Christians; therefore is it a *Christian land!* For the same reason, it might be a catholic, episcopal, or presbyterian land. Our political compacts are not entered into as brethren of the Christian faith — but as men, as members of a civilized society. In looking back to our struggle for independence, I find that we engaged in that bloody conflict, for the RIGHTS OF MAN, and not for the purpose of enforcing or defending any particular religious creed. If the accidental circumstance, of our being for the greater part Christians, could justify us in proscribing other religions, the same reason would justify any one of the sects of Christianity, in persecuting the rest. But, sir, all persecution for the sake of opinions, is tyranny — and the first speck of it that may appear, should be eradicated, as the commencement of a deadly gangrene, whose ultimate tendency, is, to convert the body politic, into a corrupt and putrid mass.

Mr. Speaker, if I were required to assign a reason, why, in the course of events, it was permitted by Providence, that this continent should have become known to Europe, the first, and most striking, according to my understanding, would be, *that it was the will of heaven to open here,* AN ASYLUM TO THE PERSECUTED OF EVERY NATION! We are placed here to officiate in that magnificent temple; to us is assigned the noble task of stretching forth the hand of charity, to all those unfortunate men, whom the political tempests of the world may have cast upon our shores. We, as Americans, should feel a generous exultation, when we behold even the JEW, to whom the rest of the world is dark and cheerless, overjoyed to find a HOME in this *Christian land,* in finding here, one sunny spot at last! In perusing an elegant pamphlet, from the pen of an American Jew, and lately published in New York, I felt proud to find myself the citizen of a republic, whose benevolent conduct deserved such an eulogium. "Let us turn, then," says he, "from Europe, and her errors of opinion, on points of faith, to contemplate a more noble prospect — OUR COUNTRY, the bright example of universal tolerance, or liberality, true religion, and good faith. In the formation and arrangement of our civil code, the sages and patriots, whose collected wisdom adopted them, closed the doors upon that great evil, which has shaken the world to its centre. They proclaimed freedom of conscience, and left the errors of the heart to be judged at that tribunal, whose rights should never have been usurped. Here no inquiry of privileges, no asperity of opinion, no invidious distinctions, exist; dignity is blended with equality; justice administered impartially; merit alone has a fixed value, and each man is stimulated by the same laudable ambition — an ambition of doing his duty, and meriting the good will of his fellow men. Until the Jews can recover their ancient rights and dominions, and take their rank among the governments of the earth, THIS IS THEIR CHOSEN COUNTRY; here they can rest with the persecuted from every clime, secure in their persons and property, protected from tyranny and oppression, and participating of equal rights and immunities."

Sir, I have done. I trust I have satisfied every member of this house, of the positions I have undertaken to maintain. I hope we shall no longer persevere in withholding from the Jews, privileges to which they are constitutionally entitled, and which are not controlled by any paramount reason of state policy, arising from a regard to our own safety and welfare. We surely run into no danger, by following the example of the enlightened framers of the federal compact with the great WASHINGTON at their head. Let us boldly, then, adopt that course, the only one which can steer clear of error and inconsistency, and enable us to square our conduct by the immutable rules of justice. Let us sever at once, and for ever, the unnatural union between force and opinion — between temporal power and religious faith. Let us GIVE UNTO CESAR, THOSE THINGS THAT ARE CESAR'S, AND UNTO GOD, THOSE THINGS THAT ARE GOD'S.

5

Resistance to Enforced Sabbath Observance

DURING THE FIRST decade of the nineteenth century, several Christian denominations organized on a national scale. During the second decade, several interdenominational organizations like the American Sunday School Union were formed. The third decade saw the rise of sporadic but nonetheless serious attempts to weaken the separateness of state and church which is the foundation of religious freedom in America. One such attempt, more pretentious, and perhaps for that very reason more widely opposed than the rest, was the attempt of Ezra Stiles Ely of Philadelphia to induce trinitarian Christians to unite politically to defeat candidates for public office who were "infidels, Socinians, or Jews." The spark which Ely tried to blow into the flame of his "Christian party in politics" was resentment that not one of the first six presidents of the United States was an orthodox trinitarian.

Attempts of this sort were generally based upon the sophistical argument that disestablishment and the prohibition of future establishments in the Federal and state constitutions were directed not at the Christian religion but only at public preference given to one Christian denomination over all others. An excellent statement of this argument was given by Dr. Jasper Adams, president of the College of Charleston, South Carolina, in a sermon preached before the convention of the Protestant Episcopal Church of the Diocese of South Carolina in 1833. In this sermon, entitled "The Relation of Christianity to Civil Government in the United States," Adams began with a summary review of the history of church establishments, ending with the assertion that, by the time of the Revolution, the American states had become convinced of the "impolicy of a further union of Church and State according to the ancient mode," and that they had, therefore, "discontinued the ancient connexion." He then raised the question whether the states intended to "abolish Christianity itself within their jurisdictions," or whether they intended only to abandon the preference given to one sect over another, "while they still retained the Christian religion as the foundation-stone of all their social, civil and political institutions."

Adams took the second alternative, asserting that Christianity is recognized in "more or less distinct" terms in Federal and state constitutions. "The reason why any degree of indistinctness exists in any of them unquestionably is that at their formation, it never came into the minds of the framers to suppose, that the existence of Christianity as the religion of their communities, could ever admit of a question." He conceded that the Federal Constitution has little to say about religion, yet found in it justification for the assertion that "the people of the United States profess themselves to be a great Christian nation." His justification of this remarkable assertion must be read in full to be properly appreciated:

In Art. 7th of the Constitution of the United States, that instrument is said to have been framed, "by the unanimous consent of the States present, the seventeenth day of September, *in the year of our Lord* 1787, and of the Independence of the United States of America, the twelfth." In the clause printed in Italic letters, the word *Lord* means the Lord Jesus Christ, and the word *our* preceding it, refers back to the commencing words of the Constitution; to wit, "We the people of the United States." The phrase, then, *our Lord,* making a part of the dating of the Constitution when compared with the commencing clause, contains a distinct recognition of the authority of Christ, and of course, of his religion by the people of the United States. This conclusion is sound, whatever theory we may embrace in regard to the Constitution; — whether we consider it as having been ratified by the people of the United States in the aggregate, or by States, and whether we look upon the Union in the nature of a government, a compact or a league. The date of the Constitution is twofold; — it is first dated by the birth of our Lord Jesus Christ; and then by the Independence of the United States of America. Any argument which should be supposed to prove, that the authority of Christianity is not recognized by the people of the United States in the first mode, would equally prove that the Independence of the United States is not recognized by them in the second mode. The fact is, that the advent of Christ and the Independence of the country, are the two events in which of all others, we are most interested; the former in common with all mankind, and the latter as the Birth of our Nation. This twofold mode, therefore, of dating so solemn an instrument, was singularly appropriate and becoming.

Adams' second argument to prove that the Constitution of the United States of America implicitly established Christianity as the religion of the country is very simple. He argues from the second article of Section 7 — "if any bill shall not be returned by the President within ten days (Sundays excepted) after it shall have been presented to him, the same shall be a law in like manner as if he had signed it . . ." — that there is official recognition of the Christian day of worship; this implies the recognition of the Christian religion in the law of the land. There were enough people who took this sort of argument seriously to lead to a deluge of petitions and memorials to Congress urging the stopping of all transportation of the mails from midnight on Saturday to one minute past midnight on Monday morning.

This "Sabbath Mail" question, trivial as it may seem in retrospect, began to take on the aspect of a major crusade in 1828. The question was debated in the Senate and in the House of Representatives; the petitions that came to the House were referred to the Committee on Post Offices and Post Roads, of which Congressman Richard M. Johnson of Kentucky was chairman. Johnson's report denying the validity of the petitions for halting the mails on Sunday is one of the finest defenses of the principle of religious freedom in the United States. The free-thought wing of the Jacksonian movement greeted it as a masterpiece, and it was one of the few American documents of its period to be reprinted in England. The report deserves the praise it received in its day, and it merits careful reading and consideration today.

In it Johnson denies the justice of the type of argument which was presented above for an implicitly established Christianity. He asserts that "the Constitution regards the conscience of the Jew as sacred as that of the Christian," and that protection is given by the Constitution to the conscientious scruples of the single individual as much as to those of a whole community. The function and duty of the government is to extend to all, regardless of creed, seven days a week, the "protection and the advantages of our benignant institutions." This is the limit of the powers delegated under the Constitution. Nowhere does that instrument authorize Congress "to inquire and determine what part of time, or whether any, has been set apart by the Almighty for religious exercises."

Here, in this Jeffersonian-Jacksonian belief in the restricted power of government, lies the heart of Johnson's argument. In the report, however, he goes farther to proclaim the important American belief that there can be unity in diversity, that regardless of the varieties of religious belief and practice in our country, "we all harmonize as citizens while each is willing that the other shall enjoy the same liberty which he claims for himself."

Richard M. Johnson

1830

SUNDAY OBSERVANCE AND THE MAIL
REPORT OF THE COMMITTEE ON POST OFFICES AND POST ROADS OF THE UNITED STATES HOUSE OF REPRESENTATIVES

The Committee on Post Offices and Post Roads, to whom the memorials were referred, for prohibiting the transportation of mails, and the opening of Post Offices on Sunday, report:—

That the memorialists regard the first day of the week as a day set apart by the Creator for religious exercises, and consider the transportation of the mail and the opening of the post offices on that day the violation of a religious duty, and call for a suppression of the practice. Others, by counter memorials, are known to entertain a different sentiment, believing that no one day of the week is holier than another. Others, holding the universality and immutability of the Jewish decalogue, believe in the sanctity of the seventh day of the week as a day of religious devotion; and, by their memorial now before the committee, they also request that it may be set apart for religious purposes. Each has hitherto been left to the exercise of his own opinion; and it has been regarded as the proper business of government to protect all, and determine for none. But the attempt is now made to bring about a greater uniformity, at least in practice; and, as argument has failed, the government has been called upon to interpose its authority to settle the controversy.

Congress acts under a constitution of delegated and limited powers. The Committee look in vain to that instrument for a delegation of power authorizing this body to inquire and determine what part of time, or whether any, has been set apart by the Almighty for religious exercises. On the contrary, among the few prohibitions which it contains is one that prohibits a religious test;

and another which declares that Congress shall pass no law respecting an establishment of religion, or prohibiting the free exercise thereof. The Committee might here rest the argument, upon the ground that the question referred to them does not come within the cognizance of Congress; but the perseverance and zeal with which the memorialists pursue their object seems to require further elucidation of the subject. And, as the opposers of Sunday mails disclaim all intention to unite church and state, the committee do not feel disposed to impugn their motives; and whatever may be advanced in opposition to the measure will arise from the fears entertained of its fatal tendency to the peace and happiness of the nation. The catastrophe of other nations furnished the framers of the constitution a beacon of awful warning, and they have evinced the greatest possible care in guarding against the same evil.

The law, as it now exists, makes no distinction as to the days of the week, but is imperative, that the Postmasters shall attend at all reasonable hours in every day to perform the duties of their offices; and the Postmaster General has given his instructions to all Postmasters, that, at post offices where the mail arrives on Sunday, the office is to be kept open one hour or more after the arrival and assorting of the mail. But, in case that would interfere with the hours of public worship, the office is to be kept open for one hour after the usual time of dissolving the meeting. This liberal construction of the law does not satisfy the memorialists. But the committee believe that there is no just ground of complaint, unless it be conceded that they have a controlling power over the consciences of others. If Congress shall by the authority of the law sanction the measure recommended, it would constitute a legislative decision of a religious controversy in which even Christians themselves are at issue. However suited such a decision may be to an ecclesiastical council, it is incompatible with a republican legislature, which is purely for political, and not religious purposes.

In our individual character we all entertain opinions and pursue a corresponding practice upon the subject of religion. However diversified these may be, we all harmonize as citizens while each is willing that the other shall enjoy the same liberty which he claims for himself. But in our representative character our individual character is lost. The individual acts for himself; the representative acts for his constituents. He is chosen to represent their *political,* and not their *religious* views — to guard the rights of man; not to restrict the rights of conscience. Despots may regard their subjects as their property and usurp the divine prerogative of prescribing their religious faith; but the history of the world furnishes the melancholy demonstration that the disposition of one man to coerce the religious homage of another springs from an unchastened ambition rather than a sincere devotion to any religion. The principles of our Government do not recognize in the majority any authority over the minority, except in matters which regard the conduct of man to his fellow man. A Jewish monarch, by grasping the holy censer, lost both his sceptre and his freedom. A destiny as little to be envied may be the lot of the American people who hold the sovereignty of power, if they, in the person of their representatives, shall attempt to unite, in the remotest degree, Church and State.

From the earliest period of time religious teachers have attained great ascendancy over the minds of the people; and in every nation, ancient or modern, whether Pagan, Mohammedan, or Christian, have succeeded in the incorporation of their religious tenets with the political institutions of their country. The Persian idols, the Grecian oracles, the Roman auguries, and the modern priesthood of Europe have all in their turn been the subject of popular adulation and the agents of political deception. If the measure recommended should be adopted, it would be difficult for human sagacity to foresee how rapid would be the succession, or how numerous the train of measures which might follow, involving the dearest rights of all — the rights of conscience. It is perhaps fortunate for our country that the proposition should have been made at this early period, while the spirit of the Revolution yet exists in full vigor. Religious zeal enlists the strongest prejudices of the human mind; and, when misdirected, excites the worst passions of our nature under the delusive pretext of doing God service. Nothing so infuriates the heart to deeds of rapine and blood; nothing is so incessant in its toils, so persevering in its determination, so appalling in its course, or so dangerous in its consequences. The equality of right secured by the constitution may bid defiance to mere political tyrants, but the robe of sanctity too often glitters to deceive. The constitution regards the conscience of the Jew as sacred as that of the Christian, and gives no more authority to adopt a measure affecting the conscience of a solitary individual than that of a whole community. That representative who would violate this principle would lose his delegated character and forfeit the confidence of his constituents. If Congress shall declare the first day of the week holy, it will not convince the Jew nor the Sabbatarian. It will dissatisfy both and, consequently, convert neither. Human power may extort vain sacrifices, but Deity alone can command the affections of the heart. It must be recollected that, in the earliest settlement of this country, the spirit of persecution, which drove the pilgrims from their native home, was brought with them to their new habitations; and that some Christians were scourged and others put to death for no other crime than dissenting from the dogmas of their rulers.

With these facts before us, it must be a subject of deep regret that a question should be brought before Congress which involves the dearest privileges of the constitution, and even by those who enjoy its choicest blessings. We should all recollect that Catiline, a professed patriot, was a traitor to Rome; Arnold, a professed whig, was a traitor to America; and Judas, a professed disciple, was a traitor to his Divine Master.

With the exception of the United States, the whole human race, consisting, it is supposed, of eight hundred millions of rational beings, is in religious bondage; and in reviewing the scenes of persecution which history every where presents, unless the committee could believe that the cries of the burning victim and the flames by which he is consumed bear to Heaven a grateful incense, the conclusion is inevitable, that the line cannot be too strongly drawn between Church and State. If a solemn act of legislation shall in *one* point define the God or point out to the citizen one religious duty, it may with equal propriety define *every* part of divine revelation and enforce *every* religious obligation, even to the forms and ceremonies of worship, the endowment of the church, and the support of the clergy.

It was with a kiss that Judas betrayed his Divine Master, and we should all be admonished, no matter what our faith may be, that the rights of conscience cannot be so successfully assailed as under the pretext of holiness. The Christian religion made its way into the world in opposition to all human Governments. Banishment, torture, and death were inflicted in vain to stop its progress. But many of its professors, as soon as clothed in political power, lost the meek spirit which their creed inculcated, and began to inflict on other religions and on dissenting sects of their own religion persecutions more aggravated than those which their own apostles had endured. The ten persecutions of Pagan Emperors were exceeded in atrocity by the massacres and murders perpetrated by Christian hands; and in vain shall we examine the records of Imperial tyranny for an engine of cruelty equal to the *Holy Inquisition.* Every religious sect, however meek in its origin, commenced the work of persecution as soon as it acquired political power. The framers of the constitution recognized the eternal principle that man's relation with God is above human legislation and his rights of conscience inalienable. Reasoning was not necessary to establish this truth; we are conscious of it in our own bosoms. It is this consciousness which, in defiance of human laws, has sustained so many martyrs in tortures and in flames. They *felt* that their duty to God was superior to human enactments and that man could exercise no authority over their consciences; it is an inborn principle which nothing can eradicate.

The bigot in the pride of his authority may lose sight of it; but strip him of his power; prescribe a faith to him which his conscience rejects; threaten him in turn with the dungeon and the faggot; and the spirit which God has implanted in him rises up in rebellion and defies you. Did the primitive Christians ask that Government should recognize and observe their religious institutions? All they asked was *toleration;* all they complained of was persecution. What did the Protestants of Germany and the Huguenots of France ask of their Catholic superiors? *Toleration.* What do the persecuted Catholics of Ireland ask of their oppressors? *Toleration.*

Do not all men in this country enjoy every religious right which martyrs and saints ever asked? Whence, then, the voice of complaint? Who is it that, in the full enjoyment of every principle which human laws can secure, wishes to wrest a portion of these principles from his neighbor? Do the petitioners allege that they cannot conscientiously participate in the profits of the mail contracts and post offices because the mail is carried on Sunday? If this be their motive, then it is worldly gain which stimulates to action and not virtue and religion. Do they complain that men, less conscientious in relation to the Sabbath, obtain advantages over them by receiving their letters and attending to their contents? Still their motive is worldly and selfish. But if their motive be to make Congress to sanction by law their *religious opinions* and *observances,* then their efforts are to be resisted as in their tendency fatal both to religious and political freedom. Why have the petitioners confined their prayer to the mails? Why have they not requested that the Government be required to suspend *all* its executive functions on that day? Why do they not require us to exact that our ships shall not sail, that our armies shall not march, that officers of justice shall not seize the suspected, or guard the convicted? The spirit of evil does not rest on that day. They seem to forget that government is as necessary on Sunday as on any other day of the week. It is the Government ever active in its functions which enables us all, even the petitioners, to worship in our churches in peace. Our Government furnishes very few blessings like our mails. They bear, from the centre of our Republic to its distant extremes, the acts of our legislative bodies, the decisions of the justiciary, and the orders of the Executive. Their speed is often essential to the defense of the country, the suppression of crime, and the dearest interests of the people. Were they suppressed one day of the week, their absence must often be supplied by public expresses, and, besides, while the mail bags might rest, the mail coaches would pursue their journey with the passengers. The mail bears, from one extreme of the Union to the other, letters of relatives and friends, preserving a communion of heart between those far separated and increasing the most pure and refined pleasures of our existence; also, the letters of commercial men convey the state of markets, prevent ruinous speculations, and promote general as well as individual interest; they bear innumerable religious letters, newspapers, magazines, and tracts, which reach almost every house throughout this wide Republic. Is the conveyance of these a violation of the Sabbath? The advance of the human race in intelligence, in virtue and religion itself, depends, in part, upon the speed with which a knowledge of the past is disseminated. Without an interchange between one country and another and between different sections of the same country, every improvement in moral or political science, and the arts of life, would be confined to the neighborhood where it originated. The more rapid and the more frequent this interchange, the more rapid will be the march of intellect and the progress of improvement. The mail is the chief means by which intellectual light irradiates to the extremes of the Republic. Stop it one day in seven, and you retard one seventh the improvement of our country. So far from stopping the mail on Sunday, the committee would recommend the use of all reasonable means to give it a greater expedition and a greater extension. What would be the elevation of our country if every new conception could be made to strike every mind in the Union at the same time! It is not the distance of a Province or State from the seat of Government which endangers its separation, but it is the difficulty and unfrequency of intercourse between them. Our mails reach Missouri and Arkansas in less time than they reached Kentucky and Ohio in the infancy of their settlements; and now, when there are three millions of people, extending a thousand miles west of the Alleghany, we hear less of discontent than when there were a few thousand scattered along their Western base.

To stop the mails one day in seven would be to thrust the whole Western country and other distant parts of this Republic one day's journey from the seat of Government. But were it expedient to put an end to the transmission of letters and newspapers on Sunday because it violates the law of God, have not the petitioners begun wrong in their efforts? If the arm of Government be necessary to compel men to respect and obey the laws of God, do not the State Governments possess infinitely more power in this respect? Let the petitioners turn to *them,* and see if they can induce the passage of laws to respect the observance of the Sabbath; for if it be sinful for the mail to carry letters on Sunday, it must be equally sinful for individuals to write, carry, receive, or read them. It would seem to require that these acts should be made penal to complete the system. Travelling on business or recreation, except to and from church; all printing, carrying, receiving, and reading of newspapers; all conversations and social intercourse, except upon religious subjects, must necessarily be punished to suppress the evil. Would it not also follow, as an inevitable consequence, that every man, woman, and child should be compelled to attend meeting; and, as only one sect, in the opinion of some, can be deemed orthodox, must the law not determine which *that* is, and compel all to hear these teachers and contribute to their support? If minor punishments would not restrain the Jew or the Sabbatarian or the Infidel, who believes Saturday to be the Sabbath, or disbelieves the whole, would not the same system require that we resort to imprisonment, banishment, the rack, and the faggot to force men to violate their own consciences, or compel them to listen to doctrines which they abhor? When the State Governments shall have yielded to these measures, it will be time enough for Congress to declare that the rattling of the mail coaches shall no longer break the silence of this despotism. It is the duty of this Government to afford to *all,* to Jew or Gentile, Pagan or Christian, the protection and the advantages of our benignant institutions on *Sunday,* as well as every day of the week. Although this Government will not convert itself into an ecclesiastical tribunal, it will practice upon the maxim laid down by the founder of Christianity that it is lawful to do *good* on the Sabbath day. If the Almighty has set apart the first day of the week as time which man is bound to keep holy and devote exclusively to his worship, would it not be more congenial to the prospects of Christians to appeal exclusively to the Great Lawgiver of the Universe to aid them in making men better — in correcting their practices by purifying their hearts? Government will protect them in their efforts. When they shall have so instructed the public mind and awakened the consciences of individuals as to make them believe that it is a violation of God's law to carry the mail, open post offices, or receive letters on Sunday, the evil of which they complain will cease of itself, without any exertion of the strong arm of civil power. When man undertakes to be God's avenger he becomes a demon. Driven by the frenzy of a religious zeal he loses every gentle feeling, forgets the most sacred precepts of his creed, and becomes ferocious and unrelenting.

Our fathers did not wait to be oppressed when the mother country asserted and exercised an unconstitutional power over them. To have acquiesced in the tax of three pence upon a pound of tea would have led the way to the most cruel exactions; they took a bold stand against the principle, and liberty and independence was the result. The petitioners have not requested Congress to suppress Sunday mails upon the ground of political expediency but because they violate the sanctity of the first day of the week.

This being the fact, and the petitioners having indignantly disclaimed even the wish to unite politics and religion, may not the committee reasonably cherish the hope that they will feel reconciled to its decision in the case; especially as it is also a fact that the counter memorials, equally respectable, oppose the interference of Congress upon the ground that it would be legislating upon a religious subject and therefore unconstitutional.

6

On Keeping Religion out of Politics

THE PRINCIPLE OF the separation of church and state in its narrow meaning, that no church establishment was to be supported, was accepted in the first amendment to the Constitution of the United States. The extension of this principle, that no religious test should be required for the exercise of any of the rights or fulfillment of any of the duties of citizenship, was explicitly set forth in the body of the Constitution, and was accepted by particular states in cases such as those in North Carolina and Maryland which have been discussed in an earlier section of this book. The further general principle, that the government should not support teachers of any particular religious denomination, had been worked out by James Madison and others as a corollary of the breaking down of church establishments. There was, however, after fifty years of national existence, no clearly formulated policy concerning the extent to which the influence of religious groups, singly or in coalition, should be permitted to work on, in, and through governmental agencies.

In the nature of the case, this had to be so. Influence is a most tenuous and vague concept. Many of those who were elected to Congress or appointed to executive or judicial offices were earnest and devout members of various religious groups. Their religious backgrounds insensibly colored and modified their thinking on political matters. Others in federal office were members of anti-religious groups or were themselves confirmed in opposition to religion without being members of any organized opposition. Their rejection of religion colored their political decisions. Influence of this sort is unavoidable and even desirable. The more numerous and varied the factors entering into the making of democratic

119

decisions, the more likelihood there is that these decisions will be satisfactory to a variegated population. Furthermore, any attempt to place specific limits to as unspecific a matter as influence of this sort would have been foredoomed to failure. Something so evanescent and intangible cannot be pinned down by a legal formula.

Difficulties arose, however, when religious groups themselves made the attempt to formalize their influence, to transform their power into that of a pressure group. This overt activity, even when it was completely well intentioned and in no sense a violation of religious freedom or a breach in the wall of separation, called forth strong protest from opponents of all religious expansion. In fact, some of the polemical literature of the first thirty years of the nineteenth century, with religion as its subject, is reminiscent of the controversial literature of slavery of the following thirty years. In 1817, for example, a charitable society of which the Rev. Lyman Beecher was chairman appealed publicly for funds to educate a number of indigent young men for the ministry and thus "to assist in providing for our country a sufficient number of competent religious instructors." This was certainly a worthy and a legitimate object, and one which in no sense involved designs against religious liberty. Yet even this appeal for funds was the occasion for an almost hysterical accusation that Mr. Beecher and his colleagues had "designs . . . to unite church and state." True, in this case, the oppugner of the charitable group, a New Englander who masqueraded under the pseudonym of Ammah Philom, based his opposition on his views as a member of one of the anti-intellectual sects. The gravamen of his complaint is that the charitable society proposed to educate these indigent young men by sending them to "Yale or Andover colleges." "With all due deference to the learned clergy in New England," said Ammah Philom, "I believe a man may acquire a suitable knowledge of the scripture, by a prayerfull study of them, with the critical notes, to qualify him to preach, without going to college, where some have learned the abstract nonsense that there is no heat in fire, or cold in ice." Whatever his reasons for attacking this venture of the Connecticut Congregationalists, Philom was able to base his attack on a pretended intention to break down the wall of separation.

Feelings on religious organization must have been extremely sensitive to produce an attack of this sort during the very decade when national denominational organization was getting started, and when such interdenominational groups as the American Board of Foreign Missions, the American Bible Society, and the American Sunday School Union were formed.

If there was this much touchiness about a triviality, it is easy to imagine the consternation caused by Ezra Stiles Ely's 1827 sermon on "The Duty of Christian Freemen to Elect Christian Rulers." Ely's bold and untimely suggestion was that the "Christians" of the United States should form an intersectarian pressure group to prevent the election to governmental office of all "opponents of Christianity." Ely limited the group he considered as Christians to "five classes of true Christians": Presbyterians, Baptists, Methodists, Congregationalists, and — somewhat hesitantly — Protestant Episcopalians; these were to be supplemented by two other groups, the Lutheran and Dutch Reformed churches. Such a group, he maintained, could by sheer weight of numbers dominate elections, and vote for no candidate "who is not professedly friendly to Christianity, and a believer in divine Revelation," or who is an "open violater" of the sanctity of the Sabbath. A broad group of this sort, which Ely called "a Christian party in politics," might demand that "our civil rulers . . . act a religious part in all the relations which they sustain." One important effect of the program proposed, Ely believed, was that "it would at the very least create the necessity for [politicians'] appearing religious." If they are truly religious, so much the better; if not, "it is a matter of thankfulness if they are constrained to SEEM such persons." Ely defended his proposal by the specious argument that, since "infidels" were being chosen for the presidency, it was clear that infidels were exercising their political rights by voting for other infidels, and therefore Christians had the political right to vote as Christians. "Are Christians," he asked, "the only men in the community who may not be guided by their judgment, conscience, and choice in electing their rulers?" And he declared: "We are a Christian nation: we have a right to demand that all our rulers in their [official] conduct shall conform to Christian morality." Thus Ely was guilty of a flagrant attempt to defeat the purposes of religious freedom by advocating political action to gain religious ends, and by suggesting a religious criterion for political fitness.

Needless to say, the opposition to Ely's proposal was immediate and forthright. Ely's term, "a Christian party in politics," provided a peg on which other attempts at religious interference in the political life of the country could be hung. Much of the opposition is to be found in the free-thought press; Frances Wright and Robert Dale Owen, co-editors of *The Free Enquirer,* were voluble critics of Ely and Elyism. Miss Wright, especially, presented a vividly ironic picture of America dominated by the "Christian party":

> Washington carried by storm; a Baptist senate; a Methodist House of Representatives; an Episcopalian cabinet and a Presbyterian president! And to perfect the odor of sanctity of this New-Jerusalem upon earth, you must imagine a Supreme Court, compounded of Bishops, Presbyters, Elders, Deacons, and high-seat Fathers of double-refined orthodoxy, propounding the soundest theology of all the sound churches, and trying every case, domestic and foreign, national, international, and individual, by the church catechism, the thirty-nine articles, the Westminster confession of faith, the apostle's creed and the revelations of the apocalypse!

Opposition of this extreme sort was evidently as fanatical as what it opposed.

More sober and temperate, but no less firm against encroachments on religious liberty, was the opinion of the celebrated jurist, Joseph Story, a Unitarian layman and a conservative constitutional interpreter. In an address commemorating the anniversary of the first settlement of Salem, Massachusetts, which he delivered in 1828, Story seized the opportunity to name as "the fundamental error of our ancestors" their failure to allow to others the freedom of conscience for the sake of which they had left their native England. He maintained that religious and civil liberty were mutually interdependent. "If there is any right sacred beyond all others, because it imports everlasting consequences, it is the right to worship God according to the dictates of our own consciences," he declared, accusing any violator of this right of dishonoring "the profession of Christianity." Although Story presented this view in a framework of historical reference to the first settlers, he clearly meant his words to have application to his own times. Undoubtedly aware of Ely's suggestion, he asked the rhetorical question:

Is there any one, who would now for a moment justify the exclusion of every person from political rights and privileges who is not a Congregationalist of the straitest sect in doctrine and discipline? Is there any one, who would exclude the Episcopalian, the Baptist, the Methodist, the Quaker, or the Universalist . . .? If such there be, whatever badge they may wear, they are enemies to us and our institutions. They would sap the foundations of our civil as well as religious liberties.

Story's very omission of the Presbyterians from his catalogue of sects is as near as he comes to a direct indication that the program against which he is protesting is that of a Presbyterian group.

Intense and specific opposition to Ely's plan was voiced by many leaders of the Universalists. The members of this denomination were peculiarly aware of the problems of liberty. At this period they were going through an inner crisis which involved the question of how far a member might be permitted to differ from the opinion of the group. This internal controversy had sharpened their sensitivity to external limitations on liberty. When Ely had limited the term "true Christian" to several orthodox Calvinist and Lutheran groups, the same pen stroke had converted such excluded Christians as the Universalists into violent opposition. Leaders like David Pickering in Providence, and William Morse of Nantucket, spoke out firmly against Ely's "unhallowed attempt to effect a coalition of Church and State." Ely, they declared, was attempting to rivet the chains of mental slavery upon his fellow men. Morse asked: "What would liberty be, or the right of suffrage, but a name to such as belonged not to the union, if five of the most popular religious sects in this country should unite, and succeed in getting the reins of government into their own hands?" In summarizing the course of religious despotism in answer to this question, he erected storm warnings for "friends of liberty in this country." One of the Universalist attacks on Ely, that by Zelotes Fuller of Philadelphia, restates in more positive fashion the creed of the friends of liberty. It is a fine statement of fundamental American beliefs on religious freedom. Both for its own merits and as representative of the outstanding labors of American Universalists on behalf of freedom of religion, Zelotes Fuller's "The Tree of Liberty" is included here.

Zelotes Fuller

1830

THE TREE OF LIBERTY

AN ADDRESS IN CELEBRATION OF THE BIRTH OF WASHINGTON

To the Reader

In compliance with the earnest solicitations of a number of friends, the author of the following pages has consented to their publication.

If there ever was a time, when our civil and religious liberties, were in danger — if there ever was a time, when the political sons of the illustrious Washington, should be inspired with fresh zeal, in behalf of the cause of freedom — if ever a time, when the united exertions of the friends of equal rights were called for, to suppress clerical intolerance, and to defeat priestly *finess,* that time is the present.

The only apology we have to make to a certain "Christian party in politics," is, that we mean just what we say.

If the following address, should, in any degree, subserve the cause of civil, or religious freedom, the author will feel himself richly compensated for his labour. It is sent out with the best intentions; and respectfully submitted to the candid attention of the reading public. *Magna est veritas et prevalebit.* Great is truth, and mighty above all things — it shall ultimately prevail. She is the glory, beauty, wisdom and majesty of all ages. Blessed, thrice blessed by the God of truth.

TREE OF LIBERTY

Sons and daughters of Columbia! Deep on the tablet of your memory be registered the 22d of February 1732; for on that day was born the political father and saviour of our country — the illustrious Washington. Blest be the day, and let it ever be greeted with the rejoicings of happy millions, for in him were given to us, the genius of liberty, and the mild and popular government under which we now exist.

In the honored and renowned Hero of Mount Vernon, were to be found, all that deep penetration and sagacity, that moderation and prudence, yea, every quality requisite to constitute the truly great man. And in him were concentrated every virtue, necessary to constitute the man of genuine goodness. His public career was one of deep and lasting interest, to the people of America.

His achievements were indeed alone worthy of himself, and will be perpetuated to the latest posterity of time, as so many standing monuments of his excellent wisdom, and superior moral worth. His virtue and patriotism is the admiration of the world, and his memory one, which a grateful nation delights to honor. His invaluable services to his country, are above all praise. His whole life was devoted to the cause of freedom, civil and religious. Whilst the ambition of other heroes, aspired to regal authority, *his* aimed solely at the freedom and independence, the peace and happiness, of his beloved country. Well then might he be the admiration of the world — well may he be loved and esteemed by all the truly wise and good. His memory is justly embalmed in the cherished recollection of every true-hearted American, and while freedom has a consecrated spot upon the earth, or virtue a place in the human heart, the name of Washington shall be revered and his memory blest!

We shall not occupy the present opportunity, in giving you a history of the life of Washington, as with this you are all doubtless familiar — nor shall we, as is frequently the case on occasions like the present, dwell on the particular scenes of the Revolution, but shall content ourselves to lead your minds, principally, to the consideration of one grand point — the glorious liberty, civil and religious, which the immortal Washington and his noble compeers, gave us in peace to enjoy and in wisdom to improve — *that* liberty, declared by patriots in whose hearts the love of freedom beat high — whose illustrious spirits scorned to be slaves, and which was sealed and confirmed by the blood of gallant heroes!

Wisely and justly has it been asserted, that *all mankind are born free and with equal rights:* that the rights of conscience, of private judgment, and the freedom of opinion and of speech, are natural and unalienable — that they are, by the principles inherent in their very natures, born *free* and *equal,* by a certain code which existed before all civil governments — that these blessings, are, as a *legacy,* guaranteed by Almighty God, to every individual.

These invaluable privileges and blessings, Washington and his distinguished associates, restored to the people of America, after nearly eight years of bloody and unequal warfare; and secured the free exercise and enjoyment of the same, by the noble constitution, under which it is our country's boast, glory and happiness, still to exist.

This was an event which electrified every American bosom, and sent a powerful impulse of the love of liberty among the different nations of the world; and by it, was set an example, worthy of good men, and of the imitation of every nation under Heaven. By it monarchs were made to gather paleness on their tottering thrones, and holy inquisitors to contemplate the future, with direful apprehensions. It was, we trust, the dawning of an epoch, in the ultimatum of which, the lawless thrones of all tyrants shall crumble to dust, and those iron sceptres, which for ages have been wielded over the consciences and persons of degraded millions, shall fall harmless from the palsied hand of tyranny, to be grasped no more forever — and when civil and religious liberty shall unite to bless, to make thrice happy, the whole world of mankind!

Something more than half a century, gone by, a numerous widespread and happy nation was given to the world. Great has been our prosperity. Under the mild, liberal and wise government of our choice, we have flourished as a nation, beyond all others. Witness our fruitful fields — our flocks and herds upon a thousand hills — our commerce floating in every breeze of heaven — our homes and store houses filled with plenty — our colleges and seminaries of learning, and our temples and altars of religion. We have covered the seas with our ships; yea, we have rivalled Britain in her commerce, in mechanical ingenuity, and in every species of internal improvement. We are protected by just and equal laws, are blest with ample means of support for ourselves and families, the means of charity for our poor and aged, and the means of instruction for our children. Many learned institutions have grown up among us, that are in their nature powerful, but rigorous — free, but not licentious — and equal, without removing those distinctions, necessary to the order and subordination of society.

By the generous system of laws we have adopted, all religions are tolerated and protected. We enjoy the exalted privilege of worshipping Almighty God agreeably to the dictates of our own consciences, and there is no one to molest or to make us afraid. We can sit down under our own vine and fig tree, and enjoy the life that was made for man. Surely this is a boon worthy the holy religion of Jesus, yea, worthy an infinitely merciful God — worthy of Him, who has created all men free and the lawful proprietors of equal rights.

Ours is the only government under heaven, where liberty can, in truth, be said to dwell — and the numberless advantages of such a government, for moral, religious and intellectual improvement, may be learnt from the prosperous state of our country since the time she assumed her just and proper station among the nations of the earth. Contrast the situation of America, with those nations where tyranny reigns in all its cruelty, degrading millions of wretched subjects almost to a level with the overladen brute, which cringes beneath the cruel lash, of his more brutish and unfeeling master; and the superiority of our government over all others, will, *must* be apparent.

Here in our beautiful America, are enjoyed all the sweets of freedom and equality, of individual rights, and halcyon peace. Here just and liberal sentiments, civil and religious, are tolerated, and flourish in rich luxuriance and perennial beauty. Not so with other nations. Look to Switzerland and Poland, to Holland and Venice, to Russia, and instead of freedom and equality, civil and religious liberty, with all their attendant blessings, you will behold the ravages of tyranny and the dessolations of oppression — instead of liberty and its happy fruits, will be seen degrading vassalage, with all its concommitant evils and bitter consequences. You may indeed look to the empires of Europe, Asia, or Africa, and turn from them with disgust, to our own beloved and highly favoured America — the asylum of the persecuted and oppressed, the land of peace and plenty, yea, the paradise of the world.

What more could wisdom ask or desire for us, in a national

capacity, than what we now enjoy? What addition or alteration could be made, as it respects either our civil or religious liberties, that would be of any material advantage? No government, we humbly conceive, could possibly be more favourable to a general diffusion of knowledge, of correct and virtuous principles — more favourable to the cultivation and enriching of the human mind with all that is useful and good, with all that refines and embellishes the mind — more favourable to the promotion of moral and religious improvement, than the government under which we exist.

Wisely did the framers of the constitution of our government, after defining with unexampled accuracy the rights of the citizens, and limiting the authority of Congress, expressly prohibit the latter from interfering with the religious opinions of the people. There has been no change as yet in this particular, and we most sincerely pray, that there never may be. Every species of creeds, and varieties of faith, receive equal toleration and protection. The freedom of inquiry and the right of private judgment, the freedom of the press and of public speech, are still our rich inheritance — they are privileges which the laws of our common country, guarantee to every citizen. This is as it should be. These privileges are just and unalienable, they originate in perfect equity, they are the birthright of every individual, and should not be infringed by any one; nor will they be, willingly or designedly, by any *real* friend to the peace and happiness of human kind.

No government under heaven, affords such encouragement, as that of America, to genius and enterprise, or promises such rich rewards to talent and industry. Here, if a man rise to eminence, he rises by merit, and not by birth, nor yet by mammon. This is as it ought to be — this is perfect justice. By the liberal government of our country, ample provision is made, for the encouragement of the honest and ingenious artist, and due support is given to every laudable undertaking. Here, talent is not frowned into silence or trampled in the dust, for the want of gold to support its dignity, nor for the want of noble parentage; but commands the respectful attentions, of all the truly wise and candid, however obscure the corner from whence it emanates, and receives that encouragement and support from a generous government, to which it is justly and lawfully entitled.

Here, every man labours for himself, and not to pamper the pride of royalty, not to support kingly pomp, luxury and dissipation! Here, no ghostly priest stalks forth, and by virtue of her prerogative, seizes upon a tenth, of the hard earnings of the industrious poor, leaving them in a state of want and wretchedness; but they may apply their little all, to the conveniences of themselves and families. He who toils and labours, in the field or in the shop, or in whatever employment he may engage, has the high satisfaction to reflect, that it is wholly for the comfort and happiness of himself or family, if he so please, and that he is not bound by law, to contribute to the support of an artful, tyrannical and corrupted priesthood.

No country could possibly possess greater advantages and facilities, for continuing free and independent, than what is possessed by America. We are as a nation, enlightened, well informed, too much so, we think, ever to be duped or imposed upon. Nor are we wanting in zeal, neither do we believe that our courage will be called in question. We possess a vast extent of fruitful country, which yields a rich and beautiful variety, not only for the convenience, but also for the luxury of its inhabitants. Such is the state of our country, such the state of our agricultural and manufacturing departments, that it is not necessary, in order to obtain all the needed blessings, and most of the luxuries of life, that we should leave our own native shores. Such is the flourishing state of our country, that there is no real necessity, whatever may be the policy, of our going abroad for a single article, that is absolutely requisite for comfort or happiness; we have all that we really need at home. From Maine to Mexico, and from the Atlantic to the Western wilderness, is exhibited one continued scene of peace and plenty.

Our means of defence, are in every respect ample, we have, therefore, nothing to fear from foreign invasion. So long as we are true to ourselves, we have nothing to fear from any quarter whatever.

Our schools, colleges and universities, are not surpassed by any in the known world, so that there is no necessity of our going abroad in order to receive a complete education in any branch of erudition, or in order to be fitted to practice any of the learned professions, known to the present age.

Though young, yet we are a numerous, wealthy, popular and powerful nation. Our flag is everywhere respected. In our country, is found all that is grand, rich and beautiful — and in the constitution of our government, all that is truly wise, just and righteous. Our means of peace, safety, plenty and happiness, are abundant. We have enough and to spare. Our resources in every respect are, as it were, without limit. Nothing is wanting but industry, and faithfulness to ourselves, to secure every rational enjoyment, and to perpetuate the glory and happiness of our nation. If we do our duty, all will, *must* be well. We fear not, that the rights and privileges, guaranteed to us, by our most excellent constitution, will be infringed by those abroad, but they may be by a certain class at home, if no precaution be taken to prevent it.

Brethren and friends of America! Something more than half a century ago, Washington and his distinguished companions, nobly asserted, and more nobly defended, the rights and privileges we have been considering. The names of these men, and their unwearied exertions in the cause of freedom, are worthy of our highest admiration, and deserve to pass down the current of time to other generations, that they may live for ever in the grateful recollections of all the most virtuous of the human race. May we and our children rise up and call them blest — rise up and rally round the institutions they have given us, and prove ourselves worthy to be called their sons. May we preserve these rights and privileges, and hand them unimpaired, down to the generation that shall come after us, as a priceless inheritance, yea, the richest earthly boon to man.

If that was a righteous cause in which the fathers of our liberty bled, and who can doubt it, then does not justice demand, that we who now live and enjoy the glorious fruits of their toil and patriotic exertions, should be ready and willing to support and defend with our property, and if need there should be, with our lives, the rich inheritance they have left us!

If such be the feelings of our fellow countrymen, if such be the full purpose of their souls, if such their steadfast resolution; — if the principles and feelings, which led the heroes of '76, to declare themselves independent of the British crown, continue to cheer and warm the hearts of each succeeding generation of the happy sons of America, which may God send, then will it be safe to predict that, long shall she remain in the sanctuary of liberty, and the dwelling place of millions of happy freemen. Then will it be safe to say of America that —

The *union* of her states in rapture shall run,
Till nature shall freeze at the death of the sun!

Fifty-three years have we been in possession of national independence and political freedom. Our fathers willed themselves free and independent, and behold, liberty followed the sun in his path! *To continue free, we have but to will it!* And will you not do it, O people of America — ye who know the sweets of liberty? To support the liberties of your country, as did your fathers, so have ye pledged your lives, your fortunes, and your sacred honor. And are ye not ready to make good the pledge? Ye who are the friends of American freedom, and of humankind, have but one answer to give, and that answer is yea! Ye will duly honor the cause, that is committed to your keeping. Ye will never prove false to the liberties of your country — nor violate the pledge of your fathers — the pledge of yourselves as Americans.

Remember that the civil and religious liberty which ye enjoy, and which ye hold to be the birth-right of every man, was purchased with toil, and blood, and suffering. Dear was the price which it cost — precious the lives that were sacrificed. Never, O never suffer yourselves to be robbed of such an invaluable heritage, nor quietly submit to any infringement of the rights and privileges which it confers.

I have said, we fear not that the civil and religious rights and privileges, which our excellent constitution guarantees, will be infringed by those abroad, but they may be by a certain class at home, if no precaution be taken to prevent it. Yea, we deem it a truth, too evident to admit of doubt, and too generally conceded to require proof on the present occasion, that it is the intention of a certain religious sect in our country, to bring about, if possible, a union of church and state. To effect this purpose, a deep and artful scheme has been laid, and which may ultimately be consummated,

unless it is speedily and vigorously opposed. Yea, the declaration
has gone forth, that in ten years, or certainly in twenty, the political power of our country, will be in the hands of those who shall
have been educated to believe in, and probably *pledged* to support,
a certain creed. Merciful God! forbid the fulfilment of the proph-
ecy! Forbid it all ye, who have at heart, the prosperity and
happiness of our nation!

People of this free and happy land! we ask, will you give your
consent to the political dominancy of any one religious sect, and the
establishment of their religious creed by law? Will you in any way
encourage certain popular religious measures, got up by a certain
popular religious sect, in our humble opinion, for a very *unpopular*
object, but which in the view of many, is very popular to approve?
Be assured, whatever may be the *ostensive* objects of these measures, if they should be generally adopted, they will tend to infuse
the spirit of religious intolerance and persecution into the political
institutions of our country, and in the end, completely to annihilate
the political and religious liberty of the people. Are you willing
that a connection should be formed between politics and religion,
or that the equal rights of conscience, should in any degree be
mutilated? Are ye prepared to bow your necks to an intolerant
and persecuting system of religion; for instance, like that of England? Are ye prepared to submit to such an unrighteous system
of tithes, taxations and exactions, for the support of a *national
religion,* as the great mass of her people are compelled to submit
to? Are ye prepared to debase yourselves, like so many beasts of
burden, before a dissipated nobility and an intolerant corrupted
priesthood? It cannot be. I feel certain, that I am addressing those
of my countrymen, who are too enlightened and intelligent, too
patriotic and independent in their principles, whose feelings are
too lofty and whose souls are too noble, who love liberty too well
and prize it too highly, ever to submit to such degradation and
wretchedness. No! sooner may we perish — sooner let yonder
fields be strewed with our bones — sooner shall the tented battle
ground, be stained with our blood, as with the blood of our fathers!
for what is life without liberty to him, whose bosom glows with
the patriotic fire of '76, and who scorns to be a slave? Ye who
imbibe the principles and feelings of Washington and his associates,

in the days that tried men's souls; ye who are genuine republicans at heart, cannot we think, long debate, which of the two choose, slavery or death.

Be it your care, then, to repel every encroachment upon your sacred rights and privileges — to see that the equal rights of conscience — the freedom of religious opinion — the provisions and the spirit of the constitutions of the political government of our country, are never trampled in the dust, by bigotry, fanaticism, or superstition. Let not the base spirit, of civil and religious intolerance, that bane of our free institutions and misfortune of our country, ever receive from you the least encouragement. Forbid that clerical ambition should ever obtain a leading influence in the political councils of the nation. Keep down that spirit, where it ought to be kept, *in silence and darkness,* that would overthrow the liberty of our country, and establish on its ruins an ecclesiastical hierarchy. Crush the demon of tyranny in the very embryo of his existence. Certain it is, that you *now* have power to do this, and it is no less certain, that it is your imperious *duty* to do it.

Never I beseech of you, encourage a certain *"Christian party in politics,"* which under moral and religious pretences, is officiously and continually interfering with the religious opinions of others, and endeavouring to effect by law and other means, equally exceptionable, a systematic course of measures, evidently calculated, to lead to a union of Church and State. If a union of church and state should be effected, which may God avert, then will the doctrines of the prevailing sect, become the creed of the country, to be enforced by fines, imprisonment, and doubtless death! Then will superstition and bigotry frown into silence, everything which bears the appearance of liberality; the hand of genius will be palsied, and a check to all further improvements in our country, will be the inevitable consequence. If we now permit the glorious light of liberty to be extinguished, it may never more shine to cheer a benighted world with the splendour of its rays. Was it, may we ask, for a *few* years only, of freedom and independence, that our fathers raised the standard of rebellion? Was it for no more than this, they braved an empire's power, endured the toil, hardships and suffering, of an unequal and bloody warfare — that they closed their unarmed ports against the navies of Britain, and bid defiance to the authorities of ancient days and the threats of parliaments and thrones? It is for you to say, O people of America. The destinies of your country, are in your own hands. They are committed to your own keeping. It is for you to say, which ye will have, liberty or slavery, knowledge or ignorance, happiness or misery. I have said, *to continue free you have but to will it.*

If we do not choose the wiser and the better part — if by our negligence or want of zeal, we suffer the liberties of our country to be subverted — if we permit a corrupted priesthood to gain ascendency in the civil government, then shall the like direful fate of other countries, where this has been, and is still the case, be the fate of ours. The abuses which have been practised, the hellish cruelties which have been perpetrated, and the immense amount of suffering which has been inflicted, under governments where the clergy have borne rule, cannot easily be described. Youth and beauty, age and virtue, genius and rank, were equally unable to relax the iron grasp of clerical tyranny. Even now there are regions where the infuriated demon of persecution unfurles her bloodstained banner, and demands that unnumbered victims should bleed at the foot of her unrighteous throne! The past history of the Christian Church, should be a solemn warning to us, never to permit an alliance to be formed, between the priesthood and the civil magistracy — between *Church and State powers.*

To perpetuate our excellent government, and to defend it from the attacks of its enemies, is a duty we owe to ourselves, to our children, and to succeeding generations. It is what we owe to those, who fleeing from persecution, from slavery and wretchedness, in the land of their nativity, have here sought refuge, as the only country under heaven, where freedom and equality, peace and plenty, can be said to dwell — as the only genuine Republic, on the face of the whole earth. To perpetuate our excellent government, is a duty we owe to the whole world. It was long since predicted, that the fate of other Republics, ere this, would have been the fate of ours. "Oh, people of America! weighty is your responsibility! The destinies of mankind hang upon *your* breath. The fate of all the nations of the earth is entrusted to *your* keeping. On you devolves the task of vindicating our human nature, from the slanders heaped on it by superstitious ignorance, and the libels imagined by designing ambition. With you rests the duty, for with you is the power, to disprove the blasphemies of temporal tyrants, and spiritual craftsmen. On you the whole family of human kind turns the eye of expectation. From the Hellespont to the icy sea — from the Don to the Atlantic, suffering Europe hopes in your liberty, and waits for the influence of the virtue she dreams must be yours. On the shores of the ravaged Tagus, the ruined Tiber, the barbarous Tanais and Danube, the palace crowned Thames and Luxurious Seine, where wealth displays its splendour, and poverty its wretchedness — there, in each varied realm and distant region, does the oft defeated patriot, and oft disappointed believer in the latent excellence and final enfranchisement of trampled humanity, breathe his sighs, and wing his hopes to the far off land, which annually celebrates, not only its own, but the world's festival, and renews, in the name of human kind, the declaration of human independence.

Say, will you disappoint these high expectations? Will ye prove false to the cause ye have espoused? Will ye belie the sacred pledge ye have made?" It *cannot* be, that ye will.

"Proud, happy, thrice happy America! the home of the oppressed — the asylum of the emigrant — where the citizens of every clime, and the child of every creed, roams free and untrammelled as the wild winds of heaven — baptized at the font of liberty in fire and blood — cold must be the heart that thrills not at the mention of thy name! Search creation around my countrymen, and where do you find a land that presents such a glorious scene for contemplation! Look at our institutions — our seminaries — our agricultural and commercial interests — and above all, and more than all, look at the gigantic strides we are making in all that ennobles mankind! When the old world with its pride, pomp, and circumstance, shall be covered with the mantle of oblivion — when thrones shall have crumbled, and dynasties shall have been forgotten — then will our happy America, we trust, stand amid regal ruin, and national desolation, towering sublime like the last mountain in the deluge; majestic, immutable, and magnificent, in the midst of blight, ruin, and decay — the last remnant of earth's beauty — the last resting place of liberty and the light of heaven!"

7

Resistance to Imposed Religious Forms

WHEN THE FIRST constitution of the state of New York was drawn up in 1777, it explicitly rejected the colonial church establishment and provided for freedom of worship "without discrimination or preference." Both this early constitution and its revision in 1821 declared that ministers of the gospel or priests of any denomination were ineligible for any "civil or military office or place within this state." These provisions were intended to guarantee that the religion of the individual was to be protected against state interference, and that the government of the state was to be guarded against clerical domination.

For several years after 1777 these provisions were strictly adhered to. So, for example, sessions of the legislature did not open with prayer, because the appointment of legislative chaplains would have involved the use of civil funds for religious purposes. After a few years, however, the literal proscription was violated; without any formal change in the law, both houses of the legislature appointed chaplains by independent resolution. In the year 1829, when Revised Statutes were issued, the payment of chaplains for the legislature was provided for by law, and thus, in the minds of many, the constitutional prohibition was abrogated. As soon as this new law became widely known, the legislature received petitions, memorials, and remonstrances against the employment of legislative chaplains from groups of citizens all over the state. We do not have the text of these petitions; from the bare record in the legislative journal it is impossible to tell whether the objection was to *having* legislative chaplains, that is, to the violation of the constitution by the appointment of members of the clergy to posts

136

in the government; or to *paying* legislative chaplains, that is, giving support and maintenance to ministers, and thus supporting religious denominations. It is clear that there was some objection and that it was widespread.

So many petitions were received by the Assembly in 1832 that a special, or — as the phrase then went — "select," committee was appointed to bring in a report after considering the issues raised by the petitioners. The committee was composed of Assemblymen David Moulton, of Oneida County, John C. Kemble, of Rensselaer County, and Mordecai Myers, of New York City and County. On April 16, 1832, Messrs. Moulton and Myers brought in a report for the select committee; for some reason which is not disclosed in the record, Mr. Kemble did not sign the report. No action was taken on the report itself when it was presented to the Assembly, and the appended resolutions were tabled. The Moulton-Myers report is a fine statement of both philosophical and practical arguments against legislative chaplaincies and, in fact, against prayers in public assemblies.

The Moulton-Myers report begins by denying the value of an examination of the history of legislative prayer outside of the United States: it asserts that the only things certainly known from history are that no nation subject to "a union of political and ecclesiastical powers" was ever free nor its people able to "escape being depraved and miserable"; that there had never been a political despotism sustained without clerical support; and that no religion could remain undefiled when perverted to political purposes. Such results must be expected "from the combined operation of church and state machinery." This will generally be the case when political power is placed in the hands of those who consider themselves "to be elected ministers of a power above the people, and to possess authority 'beyond the civil law'!" Such men tend to regard their own "will and opinions" as the "will and word" of God. Further, since the promotion of their own particular denomination is their *"interest* and business calling," they have always tended to subordinate their duty to the community to their duty to their own creed, "and have always exercised their political power to sustain their own particular church and faith, to the detriment and exclusion of all others." Reasons such as these, "attested by historic evidence," lie behind the American rejection of any union of church and state.

The writers then review the provisions of the constitution of New York State and the practice, "never authorized by any provision of the constitution," of inviting chaplains to pray before the sessions of both houses of the legislature. They refer to the Revised Statutes of 1829 in which provision was made for the payment of chaplains for this service, and "priests thus recognized as *if* they were legitimate and necessary appurtenances to the legislative department of the State." This history is cited as "another illustration of the truth, that the least participation of clerical with civil authority, is dangerous to the liberties of the people." The writers maintain that through the breach thus made "the existence and continuance of several other laws on our statute books, which actually trench on religious liberty" are to be accounted for, and the contravention of the constitutional provisions explained.

Following the general preface, Moulton and Myers proceed to the establishment of their special point that the legislature has no legitimate authority to conduct or to appoint legislative chaplains, or to appropriate public funds for any religious service. The legislature is clearly vested with civil power alone; the only character which has been claimed for prayer is that of a religious duty. A civil legislature has no authority to perform an act of religious devotion officially, or to require others to do so, or to attend its performance: "The people have not delegated power to the Legislature to perform religious worship of any kind; and if prayers are acts of ecclesiastical character and of religious duty, legislative prayers are acts of supererogation."

Furthermore, the select committee contends, prayer often interferes with the proper business of the legislature. This is the result of the fact that, for various reasons, only a few of the legislators can at any one time join sincerely in the service. In the legislative assembly there are "persons of various religious sects and adverse religious opinions, and who are elected without reference to their religious creeds." This creates difficulty and disharmony and interferes with the business of the legislature because "mankind are generally averse to associate in religious devotion with any but those whose feelings and faith accord with their own"; while they may occasionally be induced to listen respectfully to a "sincere supplicant," yet, as legislators, compelled to listen frequently, they become "annoyed by the repeated annunciation of sentiments out of harmony with their own." They find their courtesy "greatly over taxed," their feelings "disobliged," their convictions "counteracted"; in the end they "usually absent themselves from the legislative chambers until after the ecclesiastical business of the house shall have been concluded."

Now, if the legislature is not empowered to conduct religious exercises or to "attempt, by official vote, to constrain the minority, against their religious opinions," Moulton and Myers maintain, "it is a self-evident and incontrovertible principle" that they have no right to empower others to do so. It is an assumed power, "dependent alone on the legislative will," and therefore can be used as precedent for any further extension of power "under religious and moral pretences." This is, it seems to me, the crux of the argument in this report and the heart of the case against legislative chaplaincies. A similar argument is used to suggest that, if the power to appoint legislative chaplains be assumed, the power to create other ecclesiastical officers could follow.

The legislature cannot appoint members of the clergy to civil office; this is expressly interdicted by the state constitution. No more can the legislature, whose authority is exclusively civil, appoint members of the clergy to ecclesiastical office. They may not, therefore, provide from the public treasury for the pay of those whom they have no right to appoint, "or for services which they have no better authority officially to require" — better, that is, than the assumed power of the legislature itself. If chaplains are used, they ought in justice to be paid, "not from the public purse, nor from the pockets of individuals who neither require nor approve *public* prayers, nor any *hired* religious devotion," but by those who require and use their services. It would not be contended that the legislature has the right to levy a direct tax on the people to pay for such services; how, then, has it the right to take money which has been raised for legitimate objects and thus misapply it?

This discussion ends the specific argument relating to legislative chaplaincies. Moulton and Myers take the opportunity to place on the record their comment on the contention "that the United States are a nation of christians; that christianity is the law of the land, and that all are infidels who disbelieve this doctrine or oppose it." They admit that a majority of the people are "professing christians," but maintain that there is some doubt "which particular *creed,* of the seventy different christian sects, is to be respected as the law of the land, and by which the other *sixty-nine* would be held as illegal." However, despite the numerical predominance of Christians, Moulton and Myers deny that "christianity as such is the law of the land." It is the constitution, they argue, which is "supreme." By the constitution all religions — "the *mosque,* the *synagogue,* the *christian church,* and all other churches" — are declared to stand on an equal footing. Therefore, say they, it is explicit in the supreme law of the land that "no religious creed, as such, can be recognized as the law of the State" and that, therefore, the whole question of appointment and payment of legislative chaplains is an unauthorized extension of the constitution. Whatever statutes allow legislative chaplaincies are unconstitutional and should be repealed.

One further detail remains to be noted. During the next session, on January 7, 1833, Assemblyman Dudley Burwell, of Herkimer County, introduced a bill repealing that section of the Revised Statutes which provided for the payment of legislative chaplains. The bill was passed by an overwhelming majority (110 to 9) on January 8, and presented to the Senate for concurrence. The Senate received the bill on January 9, referred it to the judiciary committee, who discharged it on January 17, and sent it to the committee of the whole. Here it was not brought up for action until March 25, when it was passed by a vote of eighteen to eleven. Thus a typical legislative compromise was effected: the principle of legislative chaplaincies was not determined, but an important area of contention, the statutory provision for payment of chaplains, was eliminated.

David Moulton and Mordecai Myers

1832

REPORT

OF THE SELECT COMMITTEE OF THE NEW YORK STATE
ASSEMBLY ON THE SEVERAL MEMORIALS AGAINST
APPOINTING CHAPLAINS TO THE LEGISLATURE

Mr. Moulton, from the select committee to whom were referred
twenty-six memorials from the inhabitants of various towns and
counties in this State, against appointing chaplains to the Legislature, and against the law by which money is drawn from the public
treasury to pay for religious services,
Respectfully Reports:
That they have taken the subject matter of the said memorials
into their serious consideration, and given to it that attentive
examination to which its great importance eminently entitles it.

Knowing that a great contrariety of opinions are entertained,
and that numerous and conflicting prejudices exist in the minds
of many honest and zealous religious sectarians on the subject
treated on in the said memorials; and being aware that the due
discharge of the duties assigned to the committee, requires them
to explore ground which, by some persons, is deemed *holy,* and
to disturb questions which, by many, have long been regarded as
fully and righteously settled; the committee have examined the
subjects referred to them with all that candor and circumspection
which they deem consistent with their duties to their constituents
— the due exercise of their own rights of conscience, and their
disposition to treat the opinions of their fellow men with all that
deference and respect to which, by the law of equal rights and the
provisions of the constitution of the civil government of the State,
they are entitled.

Your committee have not deemed it necessary or useful, on the
present occasion, to grope amidst the ignorance and superstition

of the darker ages, to discover the origin or utility of legislative prayers — nor to learn what nations *have,* or what have *not* practised them; nor to ascertain whether the custom was derived from human or divine authority. The "march of mind" must have progressed to a very limited extent and to very little useful purpose, if the civil and religious liberties of the people of this country were to be ascertained and measured by the opinions and customs of mankind in remote ages and in other nations, and under governments as dissimilar in their principles and character to those of our own country, as they were incompatible with the equal rights of man. Yet, amidst all the heterogeneous details of falsehood, fable and fact, which constitute the history of man, of nations and of governments, there are no truths more clearly illustrated by historic record and the concurrent testimony derived from the present state of the civilized world, than that no nation was ever free, or could be so, while subjected to a government constituted of a union of political and ecclesiastical powers; that no political despotism ever did or could long exist, unsustained by clerical influence; that no religion could be "pure and undefiled," when perverted to political purposes; and that no people could escape being depraved and miserable, when subjected to the double tyranny of spiritual and political power. Nor can a different result be rationally expected from the combined operation of church and state machinery; for it has generally happened, that when political authority has been given to men who believe themselves to be elected ministers of a power above the people, and to possess authority "beyond the civil law" — who are prone to regard their own will and opinions as the will and word of their master, and whose *interest* and business calling is to propagate their own religious creeds, they have ever been disposed to render their political influence subservient to their own views of religious duty, and have always exercised their political power to sustain their own particular *church* and *faith,* to the detriment and exclusion of all others. "In *some* instances," says the venerable and patriotic Madison, in his remonstrance to the Legislature of Virginia, against a bill establishing a provision for teachers of the christian religion, "they (ecclesiastical establishments) have been seen to erect a spiritual tyranny on the ruins of the civil authority: in *more* instances, they have been seen upholding the thrones of political tyranny; and in *no instance* have they been seen the guardians of the liberties of the people."

It was doubtless these truths, attested by historic evidence, and the observation of the American people, that induced them to hold as political axioms, that the union of church and state is incompatible with free government and destructive to the moral influence of all statutory religion; and that to vest with political power, those who claim to possess authority paramount to *that* derived from man, is dangerous or destructive to the civil and religious liberties of the people.

That the patriots of the American revolution, who adopted the State Constitution of 1777, recognized the aforementioned evils, and intended to guard against them, is proved by the unequivocal phraseology of those provisions of that instrument which were intended to sever the union of church and state powers, and to protect the civil and religious liberties of their country; the thirty-eighth article of which said constitution, is in the words following, viz: "And whereas we are required by the benevolent principles of rational liberty, not only to expel civil tyranny, but also to guard against that spiritual oppression and intolerance wherewith the bigotry and ambition of weak and wicked priests and princes have scourged mankind; this convention doth further, in the name of the good people of this State, ordain, determine and declare, that the free exercise and enjoyment of religious profession and worship, without discrimination or preference, shall forever hereafter be allowed within this State to all mankind: *Provided,* That the liberty of conscience hereby granted, shall not be so construed as to excuse acts of licentiousness, or justify practices inconsistent with the peace and safety of this State."

It was unquestionably with the same view that the convention when about to revive a portion of the laws of England and of the late province of New-York, all of which were effectually nullified by virtue of the declaration of independence, expressly excepted from such revival all laws by which church and state had been leagued together. Accordingly they declared, in the 35th article of the constitution, "That all such parts of the said common law, and all such of the statutes and acts aforesaid, or parts thereof, as may be construed to establish or maintain any particular denomination of christians or their ministers, or are repugnant to this constitution, be, and they are hereby abrogated and rejected." Thereby expressly confirming the logical and legal effect of the declaration of independence, to destroy all laws tending to an alliance of ecclesiastical and political powers, and also all laws by which ministers of religion could be maintained from the public treasury, or receive pay for their religious services, but from the private purse and voluntary contributions of those who chose to employ them.

It will be proper here to observe, that the 13th section of the 7th article of the new constitution, which, in concurrence with the above quoted article of the former constitution of this State, declares that "all such parts of the common law, and of the acts of the legislature of the colony of New-York, as together did form the law of the said colony on the nineteenth day of April one thousand seven hundred and seventy-five and the resolutions of the congress of the said colony, and of the *convention of the State of New-York,* in force on the twentieth day of April one thousand seven hundred and seventy-seven, which have not since expired, or been repealed or altered; and such acts of the legislature of this State as are now in force, shall be and continue to be the law of this State, subject to such alterations as the legislature shall make concerning the same: But all such parts of the said common law, and such of the said acts or parts thereof, as are repugnant to this constitution, are hereby abrogated." Thereby leaving *in statu quo,* where the declaration of independence and the constitution of 1777 had left them, *"abrogated and rejected,"* all those laws "which might be construed to establish or maintain any particular denomination of christians or their ministers," as well as all others tending to amalgamate ecclesiastical and political powers, or in any way to infringe the religious liberty of the people, or of any individual within this State.

In the same spirit and with the same view to religious liberty, it is declared in the first and the present constitution, that "no minister of the gospel or priest of any denomination whatsoever, shall, at any time hereafter, under any *pretence* or *description* whatever, be eligible to, or capable of holding any civil or military office or place within this state."

Yet, notwithstanding so much care had been taken to guard against ecclesiastical encroachments, we find, in a very few years after the adoption of the first constitution of this State, priests were ushered into the halls of political legislation, not only, (as we shall show), without legal authority, but in direct opposition to the spirit and express provisions of that instrument. This incipient step towards a union of religion and political legislation, is a measure but of recent date, and seems to have been introduced when the principles of our free republican government and the provisions of the constitution were not kept in view. Before the revolution, while New-York was a colony to a nation governed by a union of church and state powers, no provision was made by the provincial legislature for the support of chaplains, nor were any ever employed to officiate before that body. Such continued to be the case for a few years after the adoption of the constitution of 1777, no chaplain being appointed by either branch of the Legislature. The precise time when they first *received a legislative call* to mingle religion and politics together, is not fully ascertained. But [it] is well understood that the practice was never authorized by any provision of the constitution; and for many years was destitute of any statutory enactment to sanction it; nor was it ever based on higher authority than the naked *resolutions* of the two branches of the Legislature, each acting independently of the other, until the year 1829, when by the Revised Statutes, first part, page 161, section seventh, chapter seventh, title sixth, the *pay* of chaplains was first prescribed by law, and priests thus recognized as *if* they were legitimate and necessary appurtenances to the legislative department of the State.

The history of the incipient and successive measures, which resulted in the above mentioned statutory union of ecclesiastical and political concerns, is another illustration of the truth, that the least participation of clerical with civil authority, is dangerous to the liberties of the people; and proves the wisdom of the celebrated *Junius,* who strongly admonished his fellow-citizens, "never to suffer an invasion of their political constitution, however minute the instance might appear, to pass without a determined, persevering resistance. One precedent creates another. They soon accumulate and constitute law. What yesterday was fact, to day is doctrine. Examples are supposed to justify the most dangerous measures, and when they do not exactly suit, the defect is supplied by analogy. This is not the cause of faction, or of a party, or of an individual; but the common interest of every man in the community."

The adoption and continuance of the practice under consideration, after the nullification of all laws uniting church and state, "and after the adoption of a constitution of civil government repugnant to it, both in its spirit and provisions, is no sufficient reason for its further continuance; proof of its harmless influence on the religious liberties of the people. So intimate an association of official legislative duties, with religious forms and ceremonies, is a practical approximation to a union of church and state. The facility which it affords for the exercise of clerical influence in the legislative department of the government," militates against the equal rights of conscience, and also accounts for the existence and continuance of several other laws on our statute books, which actually trench on religious liberty, in contravention to those provisions of the constitution which were intended to repress the *evil spirit* of religious intolerance and persecution.

Your committee will now proceed to show that the Legislature possess no legitimate authority to associate religious prayers with legislative proceedings, nor to appoint legislative chaplains, nor to appropriate the public money to pay for any religious service: and because,

1st.   No such authority has been delegated to them; and,

2d.   Because the exercise of such powers is not only repugnant to the constitution, but expressly interdicted by it.

It will not be denied, and hence not necessary to prove that the Legislature is vested with civil powers *only;* and have not been clothed with spiritual jurisdiction. Nor will it be requisite to inquire into the utility of religious prayers, or the obligation to pray, as a religious duty. "Religion is a concern between a man's conscience and his God, with which no human tribunal has a right to meddle." If prayer be deemed an act of religious devotion, the Legislature have no authority officially to perform it, nor to require others to do so, or to attend its performance. The people have not delegated power to the Legislature to perform religious worship of any kind; and if prayers are acts of ecclesiastical character and of religious duty, legislative prayers are acts of supererogation; and legislative acts which transcend the powers delegated by the people to the Legislature, are an official exercise of "power beyond the law," and as unauthorized as they would be if expressly interdicted by those provisions of the constitution which are intended to prevent an alliance of political and ecclesiastical powers, and to preserve the unrestrained exercise and enjoyment of religious opinion.

But the absence of legal authority is not the only objection to which the practice under consideration is obnoxious. It often interferes with the legitimate business of the Legislature, and thus operates unpropitiously to the public interest. Some members of the Legislature, like many of their constituents, conscientiously disapprove of prayers altogether; others are averse to *legislative* prayers; others again do not hold to prayers in *public places;* and amidst the congregated assembly of persons of various religious sects and adverse religious opinions, and who are elected without reference to their religious creeds, there are but few who can at any one time join heartily in the *service.* And the effect produced in the minds of such as are induced by courtesy, or are constrained by a species of legal coercion to attend legislative *prayer meetings,* is anything but piety or "a praying spirit."

Mankind are generally averse to associate in religious devotion with any but those whose feelings and faith accord with their own; and although regard to the opinions of others may often induce some occasionally to listen with respectful attention to a sincere supplicant; yet being, as many of the members of the Legislature frequently are, annoyed by the repeated annunciation of sentiments out of harmony with their own; and finding at length their courtesy greatly overtaxed, their feeling constantly disobliged, and their convictions as often counteracted by attending prayers in which they have no *faith,* and with those with whom they cannot, consistently with their own *creeds,* have any religious communion or fellowship, they usually absent themselves from the legislative chambers until after the ecclesiastical business of the house shall have been concluded. Hence it is, that during prayer time there is seldom more than a lean quorum in attendance, and often less. It was doubtless owing to the extended operation of the same cause, that on one occasion during the present session the *Speaker* adjourned the House of Assembly for want of a quorum to transact legislative business, although a great majority of the members were in and about the Capitol, and appeared in the legislative chamber in a very few minutes after the adjournment.

Having shown that *getting up* legislative religious prayers are inconsistent with the authority delegated to the Legislature, unauthorized by the constitution, and hence an exercise of "powers beyond the law" it would seem superfluous to prove that the Legislature have no legitimate power to appoint legislative chaplains.

It is self-evident and incontrovertible principle, that no person nor body of men have a right to empower others to do *that* which no one, nor any number, have a right to do themselves. The Legislature having no right to convert the legislative chambers into "religious session rooms," nor to transform the legislative assemblies of the political delegates of the people into religious "prayer meetings;" nor any right to attempt, by official vote, to constrain the minority, against their religious opinions, to submit to such an incongruous intermixture of political and religious concerns: *consequently,* they have no right to appoint others to do so; and hence, *conclusively,* have no right to appoint ministers of religion, nor priests of any denomination, to say prayers, or to perform any other kind of religious service for the Legislature.

See to what extreme absurdities, and to what revolting results a concession of the power in question would lead.

The exercise of power by the Legislature, to employ priests to perform religious worship, not being authorized by the constitution or constitutional law, is altogether an *assumed* power. Originating in the bare *will* of the Legislature, it has no limit of time, place nor extent. Dependent alone on the legislative *will,* it is as uncertain and unstable as the fluctuating opinions of mankind, and as undefined and undefinable as the future opinions of different men at different times, who might in their turn assume authority to legislate on religious matters. Being subjected to legislative *will,* it can be altered at any time, moulded to any shape, directed to any object, used for any purpose, and carried, under religious and moral pretences, to any extent to which the Legislature, according to their good will and pleasure, may from time to time think proper to dictate.

If the right of the Legislature to appoint chaplains to *pray* were to be admitted, the right to employ them to *preach* and *sing psalms* could not be denied. *All* are religious *services,* and are deemed by many to be religious *duties.* By the like assumed authority by which the Legislature employ chaplains to *pray* at *one* time, they could employ them to do the like, or any other religious *service,* at any *other time;* on *Sunday* as well as on any *other day;* and at *one place* as well as *another.* If *in* the halls of legislation, why not *out* of them? If in the form of prayer, why *not* in any other manner? What then could prevent their assuming authority to direct and regulate religious worship throughout the State? The *precedent* for such a measure is before them; and can be followed as legally, and with as much propriety as that which attaches to the example set by the State *Executive,* who, under his official proclamation, with the air of legality, the apparent *forms* of law, and the language of recommendation, prescribes the performance of religious worship on *fast* and *thanksgiving* days throughout the State. And if the Legislature had a right to appoint any person to an *ecclesiastical office,* or any minister of religion to any *civil* office in the Legislature, they could follow their own precedent, and *create* ecclesiastical offices, and appoint persons to fill them, out of the Legislature; and with as good authority as *that* by which they have actually appointed priests to civil offices, both *in* and *out* of the legislative department of the government.

It is no sufficient apology for the official employment of *priests* by the Legislature, that the *clergy* of all sects in the city of Albany, *"without discrimination or preference,"* are appointed to the office of legislative chaplains. The words *"without discrimination or preference,"* are used in the provision of the constitution, which interdicts legislative interference with the religious concerns of their constituents, and guarantees the freedom of religious opinion, "without discrimination or preference to all mankind within this State," and affords no justification for the appointment of priests to civil or ecclesiastical office, "without discrimination or preference." Having no constitutional authority to appoint *any,* they can have no right to appoint *all* or any portion of the clergy to any office; nor in fact are chaplains appointed "without discrimination or preference."

It is true, that on the face of the *resolutions* by which the clergy in Albany are called to officiate in the Legislature, no discrimination *appears* to be made among the various sects. But can any person who knows the *true meaning* of those resolutions believe, that were there a *Shaker* society in Albany, they would be considered as included in those resolutions, or their *ministering elder* be permitted to perform any of his religious duties in the Legislature? Can it be imagined that the Legislature meant, under any circumstances, to give *a call* to *Shaker* chaplains, and to join in the devotions of that humble sect, whose *faith* and *trust* in God is such, they have no fear that he will do them any wrong, and therefore never *pray* to have him do as *he* or *they* think *right;* but with hearts inspired with gratitude and joy, they hymn his praise in music's moving strains, and perform with measured step, as *pious David* did, a solemn "dance before the Lord."

But the proof that a discrimination is made, and intended to be made, by which *all* the clergy in Albany have not been permitted to officiate even in *prayer,* at the instance of the Legislature, does not rest alone on hypothetical data. The committee are credibly informed and think, as the circumstance was noticed in the public prints, it may still be in the recollection of some of the members of this House, that some three or four years since, a respectable, regular, orthodox clergyman, who has the pastoral charge of a *coloured* flock in this city, knowing that the *resolutions* by which chaplains were appointed to make legislative prayers made no discrimination which excluded him from participating with his professional brethren in offering praise and supplication to an almighty and just God who is "no respecter of persons," nor the colour of "the outward man," he claimed his equal right to *pray* and to be paid. The dilemma thus produced was the subject of negotiation, which resulted in a compromise, by which the *sable* pastor was paid from the public purse, *not* for saying prayers for the Legislature, as other chaplains did, but for *not* saying them; and thus obtained "the penny without the pater noster." Whether it is true, as is said, that a similar arrangement is yearly made, your committee have not been able fully to ascertain, but believe the fact is so.

Your committee will close this part of the subject under discussion, with an item of testimony before noticed, and which is so clear and unequivocal, that he "who runs may read and understand" that the power to appoint chaplains to the legislature is expressly interdicted by the constitution; the enacting clause of the fourth section of the seventh article of which, is in the words following: "no minister of the gospel, or priest of any denomination whatsoever, shall at any time hereafter, under any *pretence* or *description* whatever, be eligible to or capable of holding any civil or military office or place within the State."

The office of chaplain to the Legislature, is a *civil* or an *ecclesiastical* office. Prayer is not a civil, but *religious* duty. To appoint priests or others to do *religious service,* is to appoint them to ecclesiastical office. Were the office of chaplain a civil office, the appointment of a priest to perform the duties connected with it, would be, as has been already proved, a palpable violation of the above recited provision of the constitution: and there being no ecclesiastical authority vested in the Legislature, they are as totally destitute of legitimate power to create an ecclesiastical office, or to appoint priests to perform any religious duty or service whatever, as if the official employment of chaplains for such purpose, by the Legislature were in *express terms* prohibited by the constitution.

After showing that the Legislature possess no legitimate power to associate religious devotion with legislative business proceedings, nor to appoint others to do so; it would seem to be superfluous to prove that it follows, as a necessary consequence, that they have no better warrant to take money from the public treasury to pay officers who they have no right to appoint; or for *services* which they have no better authority officially to require. Yet your committee trust it will not be deemed obtrusive if they offer a few observations on the subject of the *pay* of chaplains with the money of the people.

It is well said, in several of the memorials on this subject, that "the laborer is worthy of his hire;" and that when priests or other persons are *hired* to do religious duty, or to render any other *service,* they ought, in justice, to be paid, if they require it; but justice also requires that they should be paid by those at whose instance and for whose benefit their services may be rendered, and not from the public purse, nor from the pockets of individuals who neither require nor approve *public* prayers, nor any *hired* religious devotion. No person of mature understanding who is acquainted with the principles of our government and the provisions of the constitution will contend that the Legislature have a right to enact a law, expressly for the purpose of levying a direct tax on the people to pay the wages of priests appointed to say *prayers,* or to perform any other kind of *religious service* for the Legislature. Equally certain is it, that they have no better right to take money which has been paid by the people for legitimate objects, and apply it to purposes for which the Legislature have no constitutional right to impose a tax.

Again: your committee will repeat, if the Legislature have a right to grant the public money to such officers, for *religious services* performed for the Legislature *within* the doors of the halls of legislation; they have equally as good (assumed) authority to grant like pay for like services performed *out* of the pale of the legislative chambers. And as the *will* and *pleasure* of the Legislature are the only basis of all the measures and proceedings, against which your committee are reasoning, the same authority, with the same propriety, might with equal justice grant *per diem* pay for religious services performed under legislative auspices *anywhere* in the State; and by the exercise of power which would be as righteously assumed in *all* cases as in the appointment of a single chaplain, might honor *all* the clergy in the State with the *office;* and by recognizing the principle assumed in the case of the *coloured pastor,* and following that *precedent,* might appropriate the public taxes to the payment of *all* priests, whom they might choose to honor with the office of legislative chaplains, and so put them *all,* "without discrimination or preference," under per diem pay at the public expense, whether they actually officiated in the Legislature or not. Thus one united legislative and ecclesiastical encroachment would be followed by another, until their influence in the political councils of the State would, if suffered to prevail, endanger or destroy the civil and religious liberties of the people.

Your committee would be willing here to close their remarks, were they not aware that there is an *evil spirit* abroad, seeking to infuse its baleful influence among the people, to obtain a dominant power in the civil government, through which to manage all the political concerns of the nation, and thus to establish ecclesiastical dominion on the ruins of our free republican institutions, and the civil and religious liberties of our country.

To stifle thought, to suppress the exercise of human reason, and to prevent the use of argument, the name of God and of religion have often been profanely used to excite hostility and denunciation against *all* who oppose clerical domination, or any measures tending to a union of church and state, or who dare evince moral courage sufficient to exercise the rights of conscience, and maintain the freedom of opinion and the right of free discussion.

In opposition to the view which your committee have taken of the subject of the present report, it may again, as with like intent it often has been said, *"that the United States are a nation of christians; that christianity is the law of the land, and that all are infidels who disbelieve this doctrine or oppose it."*

Were it true that christianity, as such, is the law of the land, because a majority of the people are professing christians, it would be indispensable that every citizen should know *what christianity is;* because *all* ought to know the law, who are required to obey it. It would become essential then to ascertain which particular *creed,* of the seventy different christian sects, is to be respected as the law of the land, and by which the other *sixty-nine* would be held as illegal. If a majority can arbitrarily violate the provisions of the constitution by which the rights of the minority were intended to be secured, on the same principle then, *Methodism,* which is as much entitled to the name of christianity as the *creed* of any other sect, and the professors of which possess as much intelligence, integrity, and sincere religious *faith* as any other, and are far more *numerous* than any other christian sect in this country, would be justly deemed "the law of the land;" and the creed and worship of the minor christian sects would be adjudged illegal. And when we consider that *all may be wrong,* and *only one can be right,* it might become highly important, in order to know what kind of christianity is "the law of the land," to ascertain whether the religious *faith* of St. Paul or St. Peter, Martin Luther or John Calvin, would be considered as *the law of the* State; and which two or three of these would be denounced as illegal. Equally requisite would it be, in order to know "the law of the land," to understand whether *modern* or *primitive* christianity is such.

To settle all these questions or any of them would require the united effort of church and state. A religious inquisition would thence be indispensable; and all the horrid scenes of the darker ages, when ecclesiastical power reigned triumphant, would be again reacted. Our "happy land" would be as other nations have been, the bloody arena of religious strife, and church and state contention. The advocates of the miscalled christian *law,* would discuss its merits and its claims "sword in hand;" and *fire* and *faggot,* the *rack* and the *wheel,* would be used to prove the *truth,* enforce *conviction,* and to make converts to the *faith* sustained by the prevailing influence of such irresistible means of "adding to the church such as would be saved" from the power and tender mercies of the *holy office,* and the purifying flames of a religious *auto da fe!*

But to many honest and sincere professors of christianity, it ought to be a source of felicitation, that "the kingdom of Christ is not of this world;" and that the precepts and doctrines of *Jesus* are *not* "the law of the land:" for were they so, "prayers in *public places"* would be by law interdicted and suppressed; and men would be obliged, *"when they pray, to go into their closets and shut the doors and pray in secret."* And those who profess to be sent by God, to "go throughout all the earth and teach the gospel to every creature, without money and without price," would not be allowed by *law* to take *pay* for preaching or for *prayers:* nor would the people be *taxed* to pay *hire* for the performance of any religious *duty.* And were the precepts and doctrines of *Jesus* and his apostles, to be regarded as *"the law* of the land," none would be obliged, as by *statute law* they *now are against their religious faith,* to observe a religious Sabbath day, nor to respect "one day more holy than another." And all those, who, instigated by an *evil spirit* of intolerance and persecution, denounce, backbite and traduce those who *believe* in the truth and justice of the precepts and doctrines just alluded to, would be regarded as *hypocrites* and *infidels* to primitive christianity, and violaters of *"the law* of the land."

But it is not true that christianity as such is the law of the land. The constitution is the *supreme* law of the land; by virtue of which, the *mosque,* the *synagogue,* the *christian church,* and all other churches and religions are placed on equal grounds. It makes no discrimination between them, nor allows any preference to be given by law to any or either of them. It prohibits none — protects all, but permits no religious creed to be enforced as the law of the land. Hence the law of the land is, that no religious creed, as such, can be recognized as the law of the State; that "all mankind," and therefore every individual "within this State," have an equal and unalienable right to *believe* according to the dictates of their understanding," and no person, nor "human tribunal," has a right to use the name of *God* or *religion* to make men afraid to avow their honest and conscientious opinions, or in any way to coerce them to act the *hypocrite,* with a view to escape the wrath, or to propitiate the *evil spirit* of religious intolerance and persecution, which is denounced in the christian books and interdicted by the constitution of this State: both of which place clergymen precisely in that situation, which was recognized and approved by their great and acknowledged master. Neither he nor his apostles entered the halls of legislation, except when forced there by his persecutors; nor did he or his disciples ever claim or aspire to participate in the business of civil government, nor assume to be "judges or dividers in Israel." On the contrary, they shunned the political world as a source of contamination, tending to abstract the mind from the study and pursuit of eternal truth, and to pollute it with views and interests incompatible with their clerical vocation. They therefore neither sought nor received political aid, nor the pecuniary emoluments attached to services unknown to them, but which, in the revolution of time and events, have been sought and obtained by their successors.

The result of all the foregoing facts and arguments is, that your committee have arrived to the most satisfactory conclusion, that the association of ecclesiastical duties with political legislative proceedings, is unauthorized by any power delegated by the people — is incompatible with the character of a free government, predicated on the principle of equal rights — uncongenial with the spirit and provisions of the constitution of this State, and that the practice ought therefore to be abolished. That to appoint priests to the office of legislative chaplains, is to appoint them to ecclesiastical or civil office. The former is unauthorized, and the latter expressly interdicted by the constitution, and ought not in future to be repeated. That to take the people's money to pay for religious prayers or any religious service, transcends the legitimate power of the Legislature no less than would a statute law, if enacted expressly to levy a tax upon the people for such purposes.

Your committee therefore are of opinion that so much of the statute laws of this State as prescribe and allow chaplains to be paid out of the public funds, for the performance of religious services or duties are unconstitutional and ought to be expunged from the statute books of this State. For which purpose the chairman of your committee some time since brought in a bill.

And your committee further report, that in several of the memorials referred to their consideration, there are other laws which are represented to infringe the civil and religious liberties of your constituents; the alleged unconstitutionality of which is sustained by such facts and arguments as leave no doubt on the minds of the committee that the exceptions of the memorialists to the several subjects of complaint, are well taken. But your committee not having time to draw up a detailed report on all the matters contained in the said memorials; and not being willing that the memorialists should be misled to believe that their petitions have been neglected, their complaints disregarded or treated with any disrespect, and thus their grievances remain unredressed, your committee have deemed it proper to recommend the adoption of the following resolutions.

DAVID MOULTON, *Ch.*
M. MYERS.

Resolved, That all legislation on religion, other than pursuant to the constitution, to secure to "all mankind within this State without discrimination or preference" the free and unmolested enjoyment of the rights of opinion and free discussion, is unjust, unauthorized and unconstitutional.

Resolved, That all existing laws by which any person within this State is coerced against his conscientious opinions to conform to the religious creeds or doctrines of others, are unjust, unconstitutional, nugatory, and ought to be repealed.

Resolved, That to obstruct the public streets or highways with iron chains or other impediments to the free use thereof on Sunday or any other day, is an exercise of power without right, and ought to be interdicted under proper and effectual penalties.

8

On Keeping Religion out of Public Schools

EDUCATION HAS ALWAYS been taken seriously in the United States. Especially since independence was achieved and a government established on the basis of widespread participation of the citizenry in the processes of government, it has been clear that only an educated electorate could be a satisfactory electorate. When, during the Jacksonian era (not, it should be said, primarily under Jacksonian auspices), there came about a great development of the public schools, this growth was, in part, at least, the result of the broadened franchise. As the electorate was increased, it became necessary to extend education to the new citizens of the lower classes and to their children. As the problems on which citizen-electors must decide have grown graver and more complex, and as the analytic and historical tools necessary for making decisions have become more varied, larger and larger doses of schooling have been insisted upon. Today in the United States there is universal elementary schooling, and, in many sections of the country, universal secondary schooling.

The very universality of educational opportunity in America has brought in its train an important problem. Because all children, whatever their ethnic or religious background, are compelled to attend school, and because the public schools are supported by taxes paid by all citizens, everything that is included in the course of study must be equally acceptable to all the parents. An exception, of course, could be maintained where there was a clear public interest. In general, however, the schools have had to steer clear of themes whose desirability might be questioned by any group.

157

Two areas have been particularly affected by this implicit ban: sex education and religious education.

Of these, religious education has become a central issue of discussion in our own day. In the earliest periods of American educational history, when, perhaps, there was more consistency in the backgrounds of the children attending any school or school system, there was less difficulty in deciding what was to be taught of religion; but, as immigration brought large groups of adherents of different religious views to America, the problem became acute. Without attempting to present a definitive solution here, it might be well to indicate some of the facets of the argument.

Americans believe that the conscience of each individual shall be his only guide in the choice of religious belief. Therefore no religious belief which is specific to any sect can be taught in American public schools. But there is a minority of those who have chosen unbelief; their right to unbelief is implied in the guarantee of freedom of conscience. Any religious teaching is unacceptable to them because it is in opposition to their nonreligion. Thus it is maintained there is nothing of religion which can be taught in public schools.

On the other hand, citizenship is more than the right and duty of making politico-economic decisions; it necessarily involves the making of moral decisions. Traditionally and in practice the source and sanction of most of our moral ideas is to be found in religion. If the school is established for the purpose of moral training, it must give some form of religious education or lose one of morality's fundamental sanctions. Now, it can be shown that there is a wide area of agreement in morality paralleling the wide area of disagreement in religion. One would think that the schools might teach the agreed moral principles, and steer clear of religious disagreements. In practice, this is what has been done. But this does not satisfy many earnest people, because they do not feel that these moral principles can or should be taught apart from their religious sanctions. The attempt to do so, which they call "secularization," is in their view doomed to failure.

Furthermore, as the amount of time spent in schools has increased, the amount of time left over for other types of educational experience, including the religious, has decreased. Religion, once (we are told) a dominant and central aspect of the lives of men, has been driven toward the periphery. Births, marriages, and deaths are still religiously signalized; but, beyond these vital statistics, religion is of little importance in the lives of a large part of the American people. To offset this decrescence of religion, in the interests of morality, we must find a way within the letter of religious freedom to bring religion back into the schools. This, in brief sketch, is our problem.

The same problem which is faced today was faced in an earlier time by Horace Mann, who, as secretary of the Massachusetts Board of Education, was the key figure in education in that state for twelve years. As occupant of this central position, he was subjected to constant pressure to permit the reintroduction of sectarian religious teaching into the public schools. Mann was a deeply religious person, convinced that no community can be moral unless it is religious, and that no community can be religious unless it has facilities for religious education. He did not question the desirability of religious education — far from it. He questioned, rather, what method was to be used in giving religious education: "In the measures we adopt to give a religious education to others, shall we ourselves abide by the dictates of religion? or . . . shall we seek to educate the community religiously through the use of the most irreligious means?" To these questions and the issues which gave rise to them, Mann addressed himself in his twelfth annual report as secretary of the Massachusetts Board of Education, his valedictory to the people of the state he had served so long and so well.

His defense begins with a division into two groups of all schemes devised by government to secure the continuance and growth of religion. The first of these is the support of a church establishment, thus making "the regulation and control of the religious belief of the people to be one of the functions of government, like the command of the army or the navy." This is the system which has been applied, for the most part, over all the Christian world. The alternative, of the belief in which the United States seemed to Mann to furnish "almost a solitary example among the nations of the earth," holds that "religious belief is a matter of individual and parental concern." Under this system, beyond providing an atmosphere within which religious belief can be developed, the government has no authority to determine the form or content of the religious views of the individual.

The chief difficulty which follows the more usual method is that, when the government assumes the regulation of religion, the government must define both what religion is and what religion is not, upholding what is included and suppressing what is omitted. To enforce such a definition, the government would have to impose penalties for independent thinking and nonconformity. Ultimately the government would have to become inquisitorial in its attempt "to secure faith by force." Among the myriad creeds professed throughout the world, each appearing to its adherents to have the force of eternal and immutable truth, each demanding the whole-hearted devotion of its followers, the government would have to select and impose one. In making this decision and in tracking down dissenters, government would be under the necessity of placing itself in the hands of ecclesiastical hierarchs. Yet "each man is bound to follow his own best light and guidance" in matters of faith, and this obligation is "an express negation of any other man's rights, and of any government's right, of forcible interference."

Reasoning, thus, from the ultimate duty of the individual to follow his own conscience in matters of religious belief, Horace Mann could not but reject the view that government should concern itself with the fixing of religious truth. On the other hand, as himself a faithful believer, he could not accept "those dreadful reactions" to established religion, "which have abjured all religion, spurned its obligations, and voted the Deity into nonexistence." Intermediate between these two extremes, he accepts the traditional American principle "that government should do all that it can to facilitate the acquisition of religious truth, but shall leave the decision of the question, what religious truth is, to the arbitrament, without human appeal, of each man's reason and conscience." Although this is the established American way, it is not yet securely established. Religious impositions have become so universal and commonplace all over the world that they are taken for granted; "men have become tolerant of intolerance." As an example of this acceptance, Mann points to the fact that sectarian teaching in the public schools of Massachusetts was not made unlawful until 1827; and, more than ten years later, on his first official supervisory visit to the schools of the state, he found many schools still giving "doctrinal" instruction. He found sectarian textbooks in use. He found "printed directions, given by committee-men to teachers, enjoining upon them the use of a catechism in school, which is wholly devoted to an exposition of the doctrine of one of the denominations amongst us."

Both as the servant of the people of the state and as a firm adherent of the view that sectarian instruction would destroy the public schools, Horace Mann exerted his authority to have these sectarian types of instruction eliminated. His activity in this regard brought down upon his head the attacks of those who accused him of "hostility to religion." The decision of the Board of Educational Commissioners not to make public reply denying these allegations was responsible, in Mann's opinion, for the lack of co-operation with which he met in some instances. The Massachusetts schools, he maintained, were more genuinely serving the interests of religion than were those that would compel the teaching of sectarian dogmas. In a pungent and well-considered analogy, Mann compared political education with religious education:

The elements of a political education are not bestowed upon any school child for the purpose of making him vote with this or that political party when he becomes of age, but for the purpose of enabling him to choose for himself with which party he will vote. So the religious education which a child receives at school is not imparted to him for the purpose of making him join this or that denomination when he arrives at years of discretion, but for the purpose of enabling him to judge for himself, according to the dictates of his own reason and conscience, what his religious obligations are, and whither they lead.

To introduce religion into the schools on such a basis, he advocates the study of the Bible, apparently without comment, for he insists that the Bible must be permitted "to speak for itself."

Up to this point, it has been possible for us to agree with all that Mann has said. Here, however, out of the simplicity of his times, he has unwittingly introduced an additional area of controversy. For now we should have to ask, "Whose Bible?" When Mann wrote, the King James version was the standard English translation of the Bible. Today there are several, many of which have official sanction and acceptance in different denominations. To read one's Bible in one translation or another has become a new criterion of orthodoxy. We must, then, go a step beyond Horace Mann, and, with deep regrets, exclude the Bible from the public schools in order to achieve the absence of sectarian pressure which was his goal as it is ours.

With this exception duly noted, it remains only to say that, a century ago, Horace Mann gave definitive statement to the position American educators have taken on keeping religion out of public schools.

Horace Mann
1848

RELIGIOUS EDUCATION
FROM THE TWELFTH ANNUAL REPORT FOR 1848
OF THE SECRETARY
OF THE BOARD OF EDUCATION OF MASSACHUSETTS

It will be said that this grand result in practical morals is a con-
summation of blessedness that can never be attained without
religion, and that no community will ever be religious without a
religious education. Both these propositions I regard as eternal
and immutable truths. Devoid of religious principles and religious
affections, the race can never fall so low but that it may sink still
lower; animated and sanctified by them, it can never rise so high
but that it may ascend still higher. And is it not at least as pre-
sumptuous to expect that mankind will attain to the knowledge of
truth, without being instructed in truth, and without that general
expansion and development of faculty which will enable them to
recognize and comprehend truth in any other department of human
interest as in the department of religion? No creature of God of
whom we have any knowledge has such a range of moral oscilla-
tion as a human being. He may despise privileges, and turn a
deaf ear to warnings and instructions such as evil spirits may never
have known, and therefore be more guilty than they; or, ascending
through temptation and conflict along the radiant pathway of duty,
he may reach the sublimest heights of happiness, and may there
experience the joys of a contrast such as ever-perfect beings can
never feel. And can it be that our nature in this respect is taken out
of the law that governs it in every other respect, — the law,
namely, that the teachings which supply it with new views, and the
training that leads it to act in conformity with those views, are
ineffective and nugatory?

Indeed, the whole frame and constitution of the human soul show, that, if a man be not a religious being, he is among the most deformed and monstrous of all possible existences. His propensities and passions need the fear of God as a restraint from evil; and his sentiments and affections need the love of God as a condition and preliminary to every thing worthy of the name of happiness. Without a capability or susceptibility, therefore, of knowing and reverencing his Maker and Preserver, his whole nature is a contradiction and a solecism: it is a moral absurdity, as strictly so as a triangle with but two sides, or a circle without a circumference, is a mathematical absurdity. The man, indeed, of whatever denomination or kindred or tongue he may be, who believes that the human race, or any nation, or any individual in it, can attain to happiness, or avoid misery, without religious principle and religious affections, must be ignorant of the capacities of the human soul, and of the highest attributes in the nature of man. We know, from the very structure and functions of our physical organization, that all the delights of the appetites and of the grosser instincts are evanescent and perishing. All bodily pleasures over-indulged become pains. Abstemiousness is the stern condition of prolonged enjoyment, — a condition that balks desire at the very moment when it is most craving. Did the fields teem, and the forests bend, and the streams flow, with the most exquisite delicacies, how small the proportion of our time in which we could luxuriate in their sweets without satiety and disgust! Unchastened by temperance, the richest earthly banquets stimulate, only to end in loathing. Perpetual self-restraint on the one side, or intolerable pains on the other, is the law of all our animal desires; and it may well be questioned which are the sharper sufferings, the fiercest pangs of hunger and of thirst, or the agonizing diseases that form the fearful retinue of epicurism and bacchanalian indulgence. Were the pleasures of sense the only pleasures we could enjoy, immortality might well be scoffed at as worthless, and annihilation welcomed; for if another Eden were created around us, filled with all that could gratify the appetite or regale the sense, and were the whole range and command of its embowering shades and clustering fruits bestowed upon us, still, with our present natures, we should feel intellectual longings which not all the objects of sight and of sense could appease; and luxuries would sate the palate, and beauties pall upon the eye, in the absence of objects to quicken and stimulate the sterner energies of the mind.

The delights of the intellect are of a far nobler order than those of the senses; but even these have no power to fill up the capacities of an immortal mind. The strongest intellect tires. It cannot sustain an ever-upward wing. Even in minds of Olympian vastness and vigor, there must be seasons for relaxation and repose,— intervals when the wearied faculties, mounted upon the topmast of all their achievements, must stop in their ascending career to review the distance they traversed, and to replenish their energies for an onward flight. And although, in the far-off cycles of eternity, the stature of the intellect should become lofty as an archangel's; although its powers of comprehension should become so vast, and its intuitions so penetrating, that it could learn the history of a planet in a day, and master at a single lesson all the sciences that belong to a system of stars,— still, I repeat, that, with our present nature, we should be conscious of faculties unoccupied, and restless, yea, tormented with a sense of privation and loss, like lungs in a vacuum gasping vainly for breath, or like the eye in darkness straining to catch some glimmering of light. Without sympathy, without spiritual companionship with other beings, without some Being, all-glorious in his perfections, whom the spirit could commune with and adore, it would be a mourner and a wanderer amid all the splendors of the universe. Through the lone realms of immensity would it fly, calling for love as a mother calls for her departed first-born; but its voice would return to it in echoes of mockery. Nay, though the intellect of man should become as effulgent as the stars amid which he might walk, yet sympathetic and devout affections alone can fertilize the desolations of the heart. Love is as necessary to the human heart as knowledge is to the mind; and infinite knowledge can never supply the place of infinite good. The universe, grand, glorious, and beautiful as it is, can be truly enjoyed only through the worship as well as the knowledge of the great Being that created it. Among people where there is no true knowledge of God, the errors, superstitions, and sufferings of a false religion always rush in to fill the vacuum.

There is not a faculty nor a susceptibility in the nature of man, from the lightning-like intuitions that make him akin to the cherubim, or the fire and fervor of affection that assimilate him to seraphic beings, down to the lowest appetites and desires by which he holds brotherhood with beast and reptile and worm,— there is not one of them all that will ever be governed by its proper law, or enjoy a full measure of the gratification it was adapted to feel, without a knowledge of the true God, without a sense of acting in harmony with his will, and without spontaneous effusions of gratitude for his goodness. Convictions and sentiments such as these can alone supply the vacuity in the soul of man, and fill with significance and loveliness what would otherwise be a blank and hollow universe.

How limited and meagre, too, would be the knowledge which should know all things else, but still be ignorant of the self-existent Author of all! What is the exquisite beauty of flowers, of foliage, or of plumage, if we know nothing of the great Limner who has painted them, and blended their colors with such marvellous skill? So the profundity of all science is shallowness if we know nothing of the eternal Mind that projected all sciences, and made their laws so exact and harmonious, that all the objects in an immensity can move onward throughout an eternity without deviation or error. Even the visible architecture of the heavens, majestic and refulgent as it is, dwindles and glooms into littleness and darkness in the presence of the great Builder, who "of old laid the foundation of the earth," and "meted out heaven with a span." Among all the objects of knowledge, the Author of knowledge is infinitely the greatest; and the microscopic animalcule, which, by a life of perseverance, has circumnavigated a drop of water, or the tiny insect which has toiled and climbed until it has at last reached the highest peak of a grain of sand, knows proportionately more of the height and depth and compass of planetary spaces than the philosopher who has circuited all other knowledge, but is still ignorant of God. In the acquisition of whatever art, or in the pursuit of whatever science, there is a painful sense of incompleteness and imperfection while we remain untaught in any great department known to belong to it. And so, in the development and culture of the human soul, we are conscious not merely of the want of symmetry, but of gross disfigurement and mutilation, when the noblest and most enduring part of an appropriate development and culture is wanting. In merely an artistical point of view, to be presented with the torso of Hercules, or with the truncated body of Minerva, when we were expecting to behold the fulness of their majestic proportions, would be less painful and shocking than a system of human culture from which religious culture should be omitted.

So, too, if the subject be viewed in relation to all the purer and loftier affections and susceptibilities of the human soul, the results are the same. If, in surveying the highest states of perfection which the character of man has ever yet reached upon earth, we select from among the whole circle of our personal or historical acquaintances those who are adorned with the purest quality and the greatest number of excellences as the objects of our most joyful admiration and love, why should not the soul be lifted into sublimer ecstasies, and into raptures proportionately more exalted and enduring, if it could be raised to the contemplation of Him whose "name alone is excellent"? If we delight in exhibitions of power, why should we pass heedlessly by the All-powerful? If human hearts are touched with deeds of mercy, there is One whose tender mercies are over all his works. If we reverence wisdom, there is such perfect wisdom on high, that that of angels becomes "folly" in its presence. If we love the sentiment of love, has not the apostle told us that God is love? There are many endearing objects upon earth from which the heart of man may be sundered; but he only is bereaved of all things who is bereaved of his Father in heaven.

I here place the argument in favor of a religious education for the young upon the most broad and general grounds, purposely leaving it to every individual to add for himself those auxiliary arguments which may result from his own peculiar views of religious truth. But such is the force of the conviction to which my own mind is brought by these general considerations, that I could not avoid regarding the man who should oppose the religious education of the young as an insane man; and, were it proposed to debate the question between us, I should desire to restore him to his reason before entering upon the discussion. If, suddenly summoned to eternity, I were able to give but one parting word of advice to my own children, or to the children of others; if I were sinking beneath the wave, and had time to utter but one articulate breath; or were wasting away upon the death-bed, and had strength to make but one exhortation more,— that dying legacy should be, "Remember thy Creator in the days of thy youth."

I can, then, confess myself second to no one in the depth and sincerity of my convictions and desires respecting the necessity and universality, both on abstract and on practical grounds, of a religious education for the young; and, if I had stronger words at command in which to embody these views, I would not fail to use them. But the question still remains, How shall so momentous an object be pursued? In the measures we adopt to give a religious education to others, shall we ourselves abide by the dictates of religion? or shall we do, as has almost universally been done ever since the unhallowed union between Church and State under Constantine,— shall we seek to educate the community religiously through the use of the most irreligious means?

On this subject I propose to speak with freedom and plainness, and more at length than I should feel required to do but for the peculiar circumstances in which I have been placed. It is matter of notoriety, that the views of the Board of Education,— and my own, perhaps, still more than those of the Board,— on the subject of religious instruction in our public schools, have been subjected to animadversion. Grave charges have been made against us, that our purpose was to exclude religion, and to exclude that, too, which is the common exponent of religion,— the Bible,— from the common schools of the State; or, at least, to derogate from its authority, and destroy its influence in them. Whatever prevalence a suspicion of the truth of these imputations may have heretofore had, I have reason to believe that further inquiry and examination have done much to disabuse the too credulous recipients of so groundless a charge. Still, amongst a people so commendably sensitive on the subject of religion as are the people of Massachusetts, any suspicion of irreligious tendencies will greatly prejudice any cause, and, so far as any cause may otherwise have the power of doing good, will greatly impair that power.

It is known, too, that our noble system of free schools for the whole people is strenuously opposed by a few persons in our own State, and by no inconsiderable numbers in some of the other states of this Union; and that a rival system of "parochial" or "sectarian schools" is now urged upon the public by a numerous, a powerful, and a well-organized body of men. It has pleased the advocates of this rival system, in various public addresses, in reports, and through periodicals devoted to their cause, to denounce our system as irreligious and anti-Christian. They do not trouble themselves to describe what our system is, but adopt a more summary way to forestall public opinion against it by using general epithets of reproach, and signals of alarm.

In this age of the world, it seems to me that no student of history, or observer of mankind, can be hostile to the precepts and the doctrines of the Christian religion, or opposed to any institutions which expound and exemplify them; and no man who thinks, as I cannot but think, respecting the enduring elements of character, whether public or private, can be willing to have his name mentioned while he is living, or remembered when he is dead, as opposed to religious instruction and Bible instruction for the young. In making this final Report, therefore, I desire to vindicate my conduct from the charges that have been made against it; and, so far as the Board has been implicated in these charges, to leave my testimony on record for their exculpation. Indeed, on this point, the Board and myself must be justified or condemned together; for I do not believe they would have enabled me, by their annual re-elections, to carry forward any plan for excluding either the Bible or religious instruction from the schools; and, had the Board required me to execute such a purpose, I certainly should have give them the earliest opportunity to appoint my successor. I desire, also, to vindicate the system with which I have been so long and so intimately connected, not only from the aspersion, but from the suspicion, of being an irreligious or anti-Christian or an un-Christian system. I know full well, that it is unlike the systems which prevail in Great Britain, and in many of the Continental nations of Europe, where the Established Church controls the education of the young in order to keep itself established. But this is presumptive evidence in its favor, rather than against it.

All the schemes ever devised by governments to secure the prevalence and permanence of religion among the people, however variant in form they may have been, are substantially resolvable into two systems. One of these systems holds the regulation and control of the religious belief of the people to be one of the functions of government, like the command of the army or the navy, or the establishment of courts, or the collection of revenues. According to the other system, religious belief is a matter of individual and parental concern; and, while the government furnishes all practicable facilities for the independent formation of that belief, it exercises no authority to prescribe, or coercion to enforce it. The former is the system, which, with very few exceptions, has prevailed throughout Christendom for fifteen hundred years. Our own government is almost a solitary example among the nations of the earth, where freedom of opinion, and the inviolability of conscience, have been even theoretically recognized by the law.

The argument in behalf of a government-established religion, at the time when it was first used, was not without its plausibility; but the principle, once admitted, drew after it a train of the most appalling consequences. If religion is absolutely essential to the stability of the State as well as to the present and future happiness of the subject, why, it was naturally asked, should not the government enforce it? And, if government is to enforce religion, it follows, as a necessary consequence, that it must define it; for how can it enforce a duty, which, being undefined, is uncertain? And again: if government begins to define religion, it must define what it is not, as well as what it is; and, while it upholds whatever is included in the definition, it must suppress and abolish whatever is excluded from it. The definition, too, must keep pace with speculation, and must take cognizance of all outward forms and observances; for if speculation is allowed to run riot, and ceremonies and observances to spring up unrestrained, religion will soon elude control, emerge into new forms, and exercise, if it does not arrogate, a substantial independence. Both in regard to matters of form and of substance, all recusancy must be subdued, either by the deprivation of civil rights, or by positive inflictions; for the laws of man, not possessing, like the laws of God, a self-executing power, must be accompanied by some effective sanction, or they will not be obeyed. If a light penalty proves inadequate, a heavier one must follow,— the loss of civil privileges by disfranchisement, or of religious hopes by excommunication. If the non-conformist feels himself, by the aid of a higher power, to be secure against threats of future perdition, the civil magistrate has terrible resources at command in this life,— imprisonment, scourging, the rack, the fagot, death. Should it ever be said that these are excessive punishments for exercising freedom of thought, and for allowing the heart to pour forth those sentiments of adoration to God with which it believes God himself has inspired it, the answer is always ready, that nothing is so terrible as the heresy that draws after it the endless wrath of the Omnipotent; and, therefore, that Smithfield fires, and inquisitorial tortures, and *auto-da-fés,* and St. Bartholomews, are cheap offerings at the shrine of truth: nay, compared with the awful and endless consequences of a false faith, they are of less moment than the slightest puncture of a nerve. And assuming the truth of the theory, and the right of the government to secure faith by force, it surely would be better, infinitely better, that every hilltop should be lighted with the fires of Smithfield, and every day in the calendar should be a St. Bartholomew's, than that errors so fatal should go unabolished.

In the council-hall of the Inquisition at Avignon, there still is, or lately was, to be seen, a picture of the Good Samaritan painted upon the wall. The deed of mercy commemorated by this picture was supposed to be the appropriate emblem of the inquisitor's work. The humanity of pouring oil and wine into the wounds of the bleeding wayfarer who had fallen among thieves; the kindness of dismounting from his own beast, and setting the half-dead victim of violence upon it; and the generosity of purchasing comfort and restoration for him at an inn,— were held to be copied and imitated, upon an ampler and a nobler scale, by the arrest of the heretic, by the excruciating tortures that at last wrenched soul and body asunder. The priests who sentenced, and the familiars that turned the wheel or lighted the fagot, or, with red-hot pincers, tore the living flesh from the quivering limbs, were but imitators of the Good Samaritan, binding up moral wounds, and seeking to take a lost traveller to a place of recovery and eternal repose. So when the news of the Massacre of St. Bartholomew's,— on which occasion thirty thousand men, women, and children were butchered at the stroke of a signal-bell — reached Rome, the pope and his cardinals ordained a thanksgiving, that all true believers might rejoice together at so glorious an event, and that God might be honored for the pious hearts that designed, and the benevolent hands that executed, so Christian a deed. And, admitting their premises, surely they were right. Could communities, or even individuals, be rescued from endless perdition at the price of a massacre or an *auto-da-fé,* the men who would wield the sword, or kindle the flame, would be only nobler Samaritans; and the picture upon the Inquisition walls at Avignon would be but an inadequate emblem of their soul-saving beneficence.

But, in all the persecutions and oppressions ever committed in the name of religion, one point has been unwarrantably assumed; namely, *that the faith of their authors was certainly and infallibly the true faith.* With the fewest exceptions, the advocates of all the myriad conflicting creeds that have ever been promulgated have held substantially the same language: *"Our* faith we know to be true. For its truth, we have the evidence of our reason and our conscience; we have the Word of God in our hands, and we have the Spirit of God in our hearts, testifying to its truth."* The answer to this claim is almost too obvious to be mentioned. The advocates of hundreds and thousands of hostile creeds have placed themselves upon the same ground. Each has claimed the same proof from reason and conscience, the same external revelation from God, and the same inward light of his Spirit. But if truth be *one,* and hence necessarily harmonious; if God be its author; and if the voice of God be not more dissonant than the tongues of Babel, — then, at least, all but one of the different forms of faith ever promulgated by human authority, so far as these forms conflict with each other, cannot have emanated from the Fountain of all truth. These faiths must have been more or less erroneous. The believers in them must have been more or less mistaken. Who, on an impartial survey of the whole, and a recollection of the confidence with which each one has been claimed to be infallibly true, shall dare to affirm that anyone of them all is a perfect

---

* Or, as I once heard the same sentiment expressed in the pulpit, from the lips of an eminent divine, "I am right; and I know I am right; and I know I know it."

transcript of the perfect law as it exists in the Divine Mind, *and that that one is his?*

But here arises a practical distinction, which the world has lost sight of. It is this: after seeking all possible light from within, from without, and from above, each man's belief is his own standard of truth; *but it is not the standard for any other man.* The believer is bound to live by his belief under all circumstances, in the face of all perils, and at the cost of any sacrifice. But his standard of truth is the standard for himself alone; *never for his neighbor.* That neighbor must have his own standard, which to him must be supreme. And the fact that each man is bound to follow his own best light and guidance is an express negation of any other man's right, and of any government's right, of forcible interference. Here is the dividing-line. On one side lie personal freedom and the recognition of freedom in others; on the other side are intolerance, oppression, and all the wrongs and woes of persecution for conscience' sake. The hierarchs of the world have generally reversed this rule of duty. They have been more rigid in demanding that others should live according to their faith than in living in accordance with it themselves.

Did the history of mankind show that there has been the most of virtue and piety in those nations where religion has been most rigorously enforced by law, the advocates of ecclesiastical domination would have a powerful argument in favor of their measures of coercion; but the united and universal voice of history, observation, and experience, gives the argument to the other side. Nor is this surprising. Weak and fallible as human reason is, it was too much to expect that any mere man, even though aided by the light of a written revelation, would ever fathom the whole counsels of the Omnipotent and the Eternal. But the limitations and short-sightedness of men's reason did not constitute the only obstacle to their discovery of truth. All the passions and perversities of human nature conspired to prevent so glorious an achievement. The easily-acquired but awful power possessed by those who were acknowledged to be the chosen expounders of the divine will tempted men to set up a false claim to be the depositaries of God's purposes towards men, and the selected medium of his communication with them; and to this temptation erring mortals were fain to yield. Those who were supposed able to determine the destiny of the soul in the next world came easily to control opinion, conduct, and fortune in this. Hence they established themselves as a third power,— a power between the creature and the Creator,— not to facilitate the direct communion between man and his Maker, but to supersede it. They claimed to carry on the intercourse between heaven and earth as merchants carry on commerce between distant nations, where the parties to the interchange never meet each other. The consequence soon was, that this celestial commerce degenerated into the basest and most mercenary traffic. The favors of heaven were bought and sold like goods in the marketplace. Robbery purchased pardon and impunity by bribing the judge with a portion of the wealth it had plundered. The assassin bought permission to murder, and the incendiary to burn. A price-current of crime was established, in which sins were so graduated as to meet the pecuniary ability of both rich and poor offenders. Licenses to violate the laws of God and man became luxuries, for which customers paid according to their several ability. Gold was the representative of all virtues as well as of all values. Under such a system, men lost their conscience, and women their virtue; for the right to commit all enormities was purchasable by money, and pardonable by grace,— save only the guilt of heresy; and the worst of all heresies consisted in men's worshipping the God of their fathers according to the dictates of their consciences.

Those religious exercises which consist in a communion of the soul with its Father in heaven have been beautifully compared to telegraphic communications between distant friends; where, silent as thought, and swift as the lightning, each makes known to the other his joys and his desires, his affection and his fidelity, while the busy world around may know nought of their sacred communings. But, as soon as hierarchies obtained control over men, they changed the channel of these communications between heaven and earth. An ecclesiastical bureau was established; and it was decreed that all the telegraphic wires should centre in that, so that all the communications between man and his Maker should be subject to the inspection of its chiefs, and carried on through their agency alone. Thus, whether the soul had gratitude or repentance to offer to its God, or light or forgiveness to receive from on high, the whole intercourse, in both directions, must go through the government office, and there be subject to take such form, to be added to or subtracted from, as the ministers or managers in possession of power might deem to be expedient. Considering the nature of man, one may well suppose that many of the most precious of the messages were never forwarded; that others were perverted, or forged ones put in their place; and that, in some instances at least, the reception of fees was the main inducement to keep the machinery in operation.

Among the infinite errors and enormities resulting from systems of religion devised by man, and enforced by the terrors of human government, have been those dreadful re-actions which have abjured all religion, spurned its obligations, and voted the Deity into non-existence. This extreme is, if possible, more fatal than that by which it was produced. Between these extremes, philanthropic and godly men have sought to find a medium, which should avoid both the evils of ecclesiastical tyranny and the greater evils of atheism. And this medium has at length been supposed to be found. It is promulgated in the great principle, that government should do all that it can to facilitate the acquisition of religious truth, but shall leave the decision of the question, what religious truth is, to the arbitrament, without human appeal, of each man's reason and conscience; in other words, that government shall never, by the infliction of pains and penalties, or by the privation of rights or immunities, call such decision either into prejudgment or into review. The formula in which the constitution of Massachusetts expresses it is in these words: "All religious sects and denominations demeaning themselves peaceably and as good citizens shall be equally under the protection of law; and no subordination of one sect or denomination to another shall ever be established by law."

The great truth recognized and expressed in these few words of our constitution is one which it has cost centuries of struggle and of suffering, and the shedding of rivers of blood, to obtain; and he who would relinquish or forfeit it, virtually impetrates upon his fellow-men other centuries of suffering and the shedding of other rivers of blood. Nor are we as yet entirely removed from all danger of relapse. The universal interference of government in matters of religion, for so many centuries, has hardened the public mind to its usurpations. Men have become tolerant of intolerance; and, among many nations of Christendom, the common idea of religious freedom is satisfied by an exemption from fine and imprisonment for religious belief. They have not yet reached the conception of equal privileges and franchises for all. Doubtless the time will come when any interference, either by positive infliction or by legal disability, with another man's conscience in religious concernments, so long as he molests no one by the exercise of his faith, will be regarded as the crowning and supereminent act of guilt which one human being can perpetrate against another. But this time is far from having yet arrived, and nations otherwise equally enlightened are at very different distances from this moral goal. The oppressed, on succeeding to power, are prone to become oppressors in their turn, and to forget, as victors, the lessons, which, as victims, they had learned.

The Colonial, Provincial, and State history of Massachusetts shows by what slow degrees the rigor of our own laws was relaxed, as the day-star of religious freedom slowly arose after the long, black midnight of the past. It was not, indeed, until a very recent period, that all vestige of legal penalty or coercion was obliterated from our statute-book, and all sects and denominations were placed upon a footing of absolute equality in the eye of the law. Until the ninth day of April, 1821, no person in Massachusetts was eligible to the office of governor, lieutenant-governor, or councillor, or to that of senator, or representative in the General Court, unless he would make oath to a belief in the particular form of religion adopted and sanctioned by the State. And until the eleventh day of November, 1833, every citizen was taxable, by the constitution and laws of the State, for the support of the *Protestant* religion, whether he were a Protestant, a Catholic, or a believer in any other faith. Nor was it until the tenth day of March, 1827 (St. 1826, ch. 143, 7), that it was made unlawful to use the common schools of the State as the means of proselyting children to a belief in the doctrines of particular sects, whether their parents believed in those doctrines or not.

All know the energetic tendency of men's minds to continue in a course to which long habit has accustomed them. The same law is as true in regard to institutions administered by bodies of men as in regard to individual minds. The doctrine of momentum, or head-way, belongs to metaphysics as much as to mechanics. A statute may be enacted, and may even be executed by the courts, long before it is ratified and enforced by public opinion. Within the last few years, how many examples of this truth has the cause of temperance furnished! And such was the case in regard to the law of 1827, prohibiting sectarian instruction in our public schools. It was not easy for committees at once to withdraw or to exclude the books, nor for teachers to renounce the habits, by which this kind of instruction had been given. Hence, more than ten years subsequent to the passage of that law, at the time when I made my first educational and official circuits over the State, I found books in the schools as strictly and exclusively *doctrinal* as any on the shelves of a theological library. I heard teachers giving oral instruction as strictly and purely *doctrinal* as any ever heard from the pulpit or from the professor's chair. And more than this: I have now in my possession printed directions, given by committee-men to teachers, enjoining upon them the use of a catechism in school, which is wholly devoted to an exposition of the doctrines of one of the denominations amongst us. These directions bear date a dozen years subsequent to the prohibitory laws above referred to. I purposely forbear to intimate what doctrine or what denomination was "*favored*," in the language of the law, by these means, because I desire to have this statement as impersonal as it can be.

In the first place, then, I believed these proceedings not only to be wholly unwarranted by law, but to be in plain contravention of law. And, in the next place, the legislature had made it the express duty of the Secretary, "diligently to apply himself to the object of collecting information of the condition of the public schools (throughout the State), of the fulfilment of the duties of their office by all members of the school-committees of all the towns, and the circumstances of the several school-districts in regard to all the subjects of teachers, pupils, books, apparatus, and methods of education," and so forth. I believed then, as now, that religious instruction in our schools, to the extent which the constitution and laws of the State allowed and prescribed, was indispensable to their highest welfare, and essential to the vitality of moral education. Then as now, also, I believed that sectarian books and sectarian instruction, if their encroachments were not resisted, would prove the overthrow of the schools. While, on the one hand, therefore, I deplored, in language as earnest and solemn as I was capable of commanding, the insufficiency of moral and religious instruction given in the schools; on the other hand, instead of detailing what I believed to be infractions of the law in regard to sectarian instruction, I endeavored to set forth what was supposed to be the true meaning and intent of the law. Such a general statement of legal limitations and prohibitions, instead of a specific arraignment of teachers or of committees for disregarding them, I judged to be the milder and more eligible course. Less I could not do, and discharge the duty which the law had expressly enjoined upon me. More I deemed it unadvisable to do, lest transgressors should take offence at what they might deem to be an unnecessary personal exposure. And, further, I had confidence, that when the law itself, and the reasons of equity and public policy on which it was founded should be better understood, all violations of it would cease. Every word of my early Reports having any reference to this subject was read in the presence of the Board, on which sat able lawyers and distinguished clergymen of different denominations; and no word of exception was ever taken to the views there presented, either on the ground that they were contrary to law, or had any sinister or objectionable tendency.

No person, then, in the whole community, could have been more surprised or grieved than myself at finding my views in regard to the extent and the limitation of religious instruction in our public schools attributed to a hostility to religion itself, or a hostility to the Scriptures, which are the "lively oracles" of the Christian's faith. As the Board was implicated with me in these charges (they never having dissented from my views, and continuing to re-elect me annually to the office of Secretary), it is well known to its earlier members that I urged the propriety of their meeting these charges with a public and explicit denial of their truth. In so grave a matter, I did not think that a refutation of the calumny would derogate from their dignity, but only evince the sensitiveness of their moral feelings, and the firmness of their moral principles. Such was the course pursued by the Board of Commissioners of

Education in Ireland, composed of some of the most pious and elevated dignitaries in both communions, and at whose head was that most able and venerable prelate, Archbishop Whately. When their conduct was assailed, and their motives impugned, because they refused to turn the national schools into engines for proselyting from one sect to another, they met the charges from year to year in their Annual Reports, and finally discomfited and put to shame their bigoted assailants.

To my suggestion in regard to vindicatory measures, the reply was, that, as the charges were groundless, they probably would be temporary; and that a formal reply to the accusations might bestow an undeserved importance upon the accusers. Were it not that the opinion of the Board, at that time, did not coincide with my own, I should still think that an early, temperate, but decided refutation, by the Board itself, of the charges against them, and against the system administered by them or under their auspices, would have been greatly preventive of evil, and fruitful of good. The pre-occupancy of the public mind with error on so important a subject is an unspeakable calamity; and errors that derive their support from religious views are among the most invincible. But different counsels prevailed; and for several years, in certain quarters, suspicions continued rife. I was made to see, and deeply to feel, their disastrous and alienating influence as I travelled about the State; sometimes withdrawing the hand of needed assistance, and sometimes, when conduct extorted approval, impeaching the motives that prompted it. For no cause, not dearer to me than life itself, could I ever have persevered, amid the trials and anxieties, and against the obstacles, that beset my path. But I felt that there is a profound gratification in standing by a good cause in the hour of its adversity. I believed there must be a deeper pleasure in following truth to the scaffold than in shouting in the retinue where error triumphs. I felt, too, a religious confidence that truth would ultimately prevail; and that it was my duty to labor in the spirit of a genuine disciple, who toils on with equal diligence and alacrity, whether his cause is to be crowned with success in his own lifetime, or only at the end of a thousand years. And, as the complement of all other motives, I felt that a true education would be among the most efficient of means to prevent the re-appearance, in another generation, of such an aggressive and unscrupulous opposition as the Board and myself were suffering under in this.

After years of endurance, after suffering under misconstructions of conduct, and the imputation of motives whose edge is sharper than a knife, it was at my suggestion, and by making use of materials which I had laboriously collected, that the Board made its Eighth Annual Report,— a document said to be the ablest argument in favor of the use of the Bible in schools anywhere to be found. This Report had my full concurrence. Since its appearance, I have always referred to it as explanatory of the views of the Board, and as setting forth the law of a wise commonwealth and the policy of a Christian people. Officially and unofficially, publicly and privately, in theory and in practice, my course has always been in conformity with its doctrines. And I avail myself of this, the last opportunity which I may ever have, to say, in regard to all affirmations or intimations that I have ever attempted to exclude religious instruction from school, or to exclude the Bible from school, or to impair the force of that volume, that they are now, and always have been, without substance or semblance of truth.

But it may still be said, and it is said, that however sincere, or however religiously disposed, the advocates of our school-system may be, still the character of the system is not to be determined by the number nor by the sincerity of its defenders, but by its own inherent attributes; and that, if judged by these attributes, it is, in fact and in truth, an irreligious, an un-Christian, and an anti-Christian system. Having devoted the best part of my life to the promotion of this system, and believing it to be the only system which ought to prevail, or can permanently prevail, in any free country, I am not content to see it suffer, unrelieved, beneath the weight of imputations so grievous; nor is it right that any hostile system should be built up by so gross a misrepresentation of ours. That our public schools are not theological seminaries, is admitted. That they are debarred by law from inculcating the peculiar and distinctive doctrines of any one religious denomination amongst us, is claimed; and that they are also prohibited from ever teaching that what they do teach is the whole of religion, or all that is essential to religion or to salvation, is equally certain. But our sys-

tem earnestly inculcates all Christian morals; it founds its morals
on the basis of religion; it welcomes the religion of the Bible; and,
in receiving the Bible, it allows it to do what it is allowed to do in
no other system,— *to speak for itself*. But here it stops, not because it claims to have compassed all truth, but because it disclaims
to act as an umpire between hostile religious opinions.

The very terms "public school" and "common school" bear
upon their face that they are schools which the children of the
entire community may attend. Every man not on the pauper-list
is taxed for their support; but he is not taxed to support them as
special religious institutions; if he were, it would satisfy at once the
largest definition of a religious establishment. But he is taxed to
support them as a *preventive* means against dishonesty, against
fraud, and against violence, on the same principle that he is taxed
to support criminal courts as a *punitive* means against the same
offences. He is taxed to support schools, on the same principle
that he is taxed to support paupers,— because a child without
education is poorer and more wretched than a man without bread.
He is taxed to support schools, on the same principle that he would
be taxed to defend the nation against foreign invasion, or against
rapine committed by a foreign foe,— because the general prevalence of ignorance, superstition, and vice, will breed Goth and
Vandal at home more fatal to the public well-being than any Goth
or Vandal from abroad. And, finally, he is taxed to support schools,
because they are the most effective means of developing and training those powers and faculties in a child, by which, when he
becomes a man, he may understand what his highest interests and
his highest duties are, and may be in fact, and not in name only, a
free agent. The elements of a political education are not bestowed
upon any school child for the purpose of making him vote with
this or that political party when he becomes of age, but for the
purpose of enabling him to choose for himself with which party
he will vote. So the religious education which a child receives at
school is not imparted to him for the purpose of making him join
this or that denomination when he arrives at years of discretion,
but for the purpose of enabling him to judge for himself, according
to the dictates of his own reason and conscience, what his religious
obligations are, and whither they lead. But if a man is taxed to

support a school where religious doctrines are inculcated which he believes to be false, and which he believes that God condemns, then he is excluded from the school by the divine law, at the same time that he is compelled to support it by the human law. This is a double wrong. It is politically wrong, because, if such a man educates his children at all, he must educate them elsewhere, and thus pay two taxes, while some of his neighbors pay less than their due proportion of one; and it is religiously wrong, because he is constrained by human power to promote what he believes the divine power forbids. The principle involved in such a course is pregnant with all tyrannical consequences. It is broad enough to sustain any claim of ecclesiastical domination ever made in the darkest ages of the world. Every religious persecution since the time of Constantine may find its warrant in it, and can be legitimately defended upon it. If a man's estate may be taken from him to pay for teaching a creed which he believes to be false, his children can be taken from him to be taught the same creed. And, in regard to the extent of the penalties which may be invoked to compel conformity, there is no stopping-place between taking a penny and inflicting perdition. It is only necessary to call a man's reason and conscience and religious faith by the name of recusancy or contumacy or heresy, and so to inscribe them on the statute-book, and then the non-conformist or dissenter may be subdued by steel or cord or fire; by anathema and excommunication in this life, and the terrors of endless perdition in the next. Surely that system cannot be an irreligious, an anti-Christian, or an un-Christian one, whose first and cardinal principle it is to recognize and protect the highest and dearest of all human interests and of all human rights.

Again: it seems almost too clear for exposition, that our system, *in one of its most essential features,* is not only not an irreligious one, but that it is more strictly religious than any other which has ever yet been adopted. Every intelligent man understands what is meant by the term "jurisdiction." It is the rightful authority which one person, or one body of men, exercises over another person or persons. Every intelligent man understands that there are some things which are within the jurisdiction of government, and other things which are not within it. As Americans, we understand that there is a line dividing the jurisdiction of the State governments from the jurisdiction of the Federal government, and that it is a violation of the constitutions of both for either to invade the legitimate sphere of action which belongs to the other. We all understand, that neither any State in this Union, nor the Union itself, has any right of interference between the British sovereign and a British subject, or between the French government and a citizen of France. Let this doctrine be applied to the relations between the creature and the Creator, just as political rights embrace the relations between subject and sovereign, or between a free citizen and the government of his choice, and just as parental rights embrace the relation between parent and child. Rights, therefore, which are strictly religious, lie out of and beyond the jurisdiction of civil governments. They belong exclusively to the jurisdiction of the divine government. If, then, the State of Massachusetts has no right of forcible interference between an Englishman or a Frenchman, and the English or French government, still less, far less, has it any right of forcible interference between the soul of man and the King and Lord to whom that soul owes undivided and supreme allegiance. Civil society may exist, or it may cease to exist. Civil government may continue for centuries in the hands of the same dynasty, or it may change hands, by revolution, with every new moon. The man outcast and outlawed to-day, and to whom, therefore, we own no obedience, may be rightfully installed in office to-morrow, and may then require submission to his legitimate authority. The civil governor may resign or be deposed; the framework of the government may be changed, or its laws altered; so that the duty of allegiance to a temporal sovereign may have a succession of new objects, or a succession of new definitions. But the relation of man to his Maker never changes. Its object and its obligations are immutable. The jurisdiction which God exercises over the religious obligations which his rational and accountable offspring owe to him excludes human jurisdiction. And hence it is that religious rights are inalienable rights. Hence, also, it is, that it is an infinitely greater offence to invade the special and exclusive jurisdiction which the Creator claims over the consciences and hearts of men than it would be to invade the jurisdiction which any foreign nation rightfully possesses over its own subjects or citizens. The latter would be only an offence against international law; the former is treason against the majesty of Heaven. The one violates secular and temporal rights only; the other violates sacred and eternal ones. When the British government passed its various statutes of *praemunire,* as they were called, — statutes to prevent the Roman pontiff from interfering between the British sovereign and the British subject,— it was itself constantly enacting and enforcing laws which interfered between the Sovereign of the universe and his subjects upon earth, far more directly and aggressively than any edict of the Roman see ever interfered with any allegiance due from a British subject to the self-styled defender of the faith.

It was in consequence of laws that invaded the direct and exclusive jurisdiction which our Father in heaven exercises over his children upon earth, that the Pilgrims fled from their native land to that which is the land of our nativity. They sought a residence so remote and so inaccessible, in the hope that the prerogatives of the Divine Magistrate might no longer be set at nought by the usurpations of the civil power. Was it not an irreligious and an impious act on the part of the British government to pursue our ancestors with such cruel penalties and privations as to drive them into banishment? Was it not a religious and a pious act in the Pilgrim Fathers to seek a place of refuge where the arm of earthly power could neither restrain them from worshipping God in the manner which they believed to be most acceptable to him, nor command their worship in a manner believed to be unacceptable? And if it was irreligious in the British government to violate freedom of conscience in the case of our forefathers two centuries ago, then it is more flagrantly irreligious to repeat the oppression in this more enlightened age of the world. If it was a religious act in our forefathers to escape from ecclesiastical tyranny, then it must be in the strictest conformity to religion for us to abstain from all religious oppression over others, and to oppose it whenever it is threatened. And this abstinence from religious oppression, this acknowledgement of the rights of others, this explicit recognition and avowal of the supreme and exclusive jurisdiction of Heaven, and this denial of the right of any earthly power to encroach upon that jurisdiction, is precisely what the Massachusetts

school-system purports to do in theory and what it does actually
in practice. Hence I infer that our system is not an irreligious
one, but is in the strictest accordance with religion and its obligations.

It is still easier to prove that the Massachusetts school-system
is not anti-Christian nor un-Christian. The Bible is the acknowledged expositor of Christianity. In strictness, Christianity has no
other authoritative expounder. This Bible is in our common schools
by common consent. Twelve years ago, it was not in all the
schools. Contrary to the genius of our government, if not contrary
to the express letter of the law, it had been used for sectarian
purposes,— to prove one sect to be right, and others to be wrong.
Hence it had been excluded from the schools of some towns by an
express vote. But since the law, and the reasons on which it is
founded, have been more fully explained and better understood,
and since sectarian instruction has, to a great extent, ceased to be
given, the Bible has been restored. I am not aware of the existence
of a single town in the State in whose schools it is not now introduced, either by a direct vote of the school-committee, or by such
general desire and acquiescence as supersede the necessity of a
vote. In all my intercourse for twelve years, whether personal or
by letter, with all the school-officers in the State, and with tens of
thousands of individuals in it, I have never heard an objection
made to the use of the Bible in school, except in one or two instances; and, in those cases, the objection was put upon the ground
that daily familiarity with the Book in school would tend to impair
a reverence for it.

If the Bible, then, is the exponent of Christianity; if the Bible
contains the communications, precepts, and doctrines which make
up the religious system called and known as Christianity; if the
Bible makes known these truths, which, according to the faith of
Christians, are able to make men wise unto salvation; and if this
Bible is in the schools,— how can it be said that Christianity is
excluded from the schools? or how can it be said that the school-
system which adopts and uses the Bible is an anti-Christian or an
un-Christian system? If that which is the acknowledged exponent
and basis of Christianity is in the schools, by what tergiversation
in language, or paralogism in logic, can Christianity be said to be

shut out from the schools? If the Old Testament were in the schools, could a Jew complain that Judaism was excluded from them? If the Koran were read regularly and reverently in the schools, could a Mahometan say that Mahometanism was excluded? Or, if the Mormon Bible were in the schools, could it be said that Mormonism was excluded from them?

Is it not, indeed, too plain to require the formality of a syllogism, that if any man's creed is to be found in the Bible, and the Bible is in the schools, then that man's creed is in the schools? This seems even plainer than the proposition, that two and two make four; that is, we can conceive of a creature so low down in the scale of intelligence, that he could not see what sum would be produced by adding two and two together, who still could not fail to see, that, if a certain system called Christianity were contained in and inseparable from a certain book called the Bible, then, wherever the Bible might go, there the system of Christianity must be. If a vase of purest alabaster, filled with myrrh and frankincense and precious ointments, were in the school, would not their perfumes be there also? And would the beautiful vase, and the sweet aroma of spice and unguent, be any more truly there, if some concocter of odors, such as Nature never made, should insist upon saturating the air with the products of his own distillations, which, though pleasant to *his* idiosyncrasy, would be nauseous to everybody else? But if a man is conscious or suspicious that his creed is not in the Bible, but resolves that it shall be in the schools at any rate, then it is easy to see that he has a motive either to exclude the Bible from school, or to introduce some other book, or some oral interpreter in company with it, to misconstrue and override it. If the Bible is in the schools, we can see a reason why a Jew, who disbelieves in the mission of our Saviour, or a Mahometan, who believes in that of the Prophet, should desire, by oral instruction or catechism or otherwise, to foist in his own views, and thereby smother all conflicting views; but even they would not dare to say that the schools where the Bible was found were either anti-Christian or un-Christian. So far from this, if they were candid, they would acknowledge that the system of Christianity was in the schools, and that they wished to neutralize and discard it by hostile means.

And further: our law explicitly and solemnly enjoins it upon all teachers, without any exception, "to exert their best endeavors to impress on the minds of children and youth committed to their care and instruction the principles of piety, justice, and a sacred regard to truth, love to their country, humanity, and universal benevolence, sobriety, industry, and frugality, chastity, moderation, and temperance, and those other virtues which are the ornament of human society, and the basis upon which a republican constitution is founded." Are not these virtues and graces part and parcel of Christianity? In other words, can there be Christianity without them? While these virtues and these duties towards God and man are inculcated in our schools, any one who says that the schools are anti-Christian or un-Christian expressly affirms that his own system of Christianity does not embrace any one of this radiant catalogue; that it rejects them all; that it embraces their opposites.

And further still: our system makes it the express duty of all the "resident ministers of the gospel" to bring all the children within the moral and Christian inculcations above enumerated; so that he who avers that our system is an anti-Christian or an un-Christian one avers that it is both anti-Christian and un-Christian for a "minister OF THE GOSPEL" to promote, or labor to diffuse, the moral attributes and excellences which the statute so earnestly enjoins.

So far, the argument has been of an affirmative character. Its scope and purpose show, or at least tend to show, *by direct proof,* that the school-system of Massachusetts is not an anti-Christian nor an un-Christian system. But there is still another mode of proof. The truth of a proposition may be established by showing the falsity or absurdity of all conflicting propositions. So far as this method can be applied to moral questions, its aid may safely be invoked here.

What are the other courses which the State of Massachusetts might adopt or sanction in relation to the education of its youth? They are these four:—

1. It might establish schools, but expressly exclude all religious instruction from them, making them merely schools for secular instruction.

2. It might adopt a course directly the reverse of this. It might define and prescribe a system of religion for the schools, and ap-

point the teachers and officers, whose duty it should be to carry out that system.

3. It might establish schools by law, and empower each religious sect, whenever and wherever it could get a majority, to determine what religious faith should be taught in them. And,

4. It might expressly disclaim and refuse all interference with the education of the young, and abandon the whole work to the hazards of private enterprise, or to parental will, ability, or caprice.

1. A system of schools from which all religious instruction should be excluded might properly be called un-Christian, or rather non-Christian, in the same sense in which it could be called non-Jewish or non-Mahometan; that is, as having no connection with either. I do not suppose a man can be found in Massachusetts who would declare such a system to be his first choice.

2. Were the State to establish schools, and prescribe a system of religion to be taught in them, and appoint the teachers and officers to superintend it, could there be any better definition or exemplification of an ecclesiastical establishment? Such a system would create at once the most formidable and terrible hierarchy ever established upon earth. It would plunge society back into the dark ages at one precipitation. The people would be compelled to worship the image which the government, like another Nebuchadnezzar, might set up; and, for any refusal, the fiery furnace, seven times heated, would be their fate. And worse than this. The sacerdotal tyranny of the dark ages, and of more ancient as well as of more modern times, addressed its commands to *men*. Against *men* it fulminated its anathemas. On *men* its lightnings fell. But *men* had free agency. They could sometimes escape. They could always resist. They were capable of thought. They had powers of endurance. They could be upheld by a sense of duty here, and by visions of transcending rewards and glories hereafter. They could proclaim truth in the gaspings of death,— on the scaffold, in the fire, in the interludes of the rack,— and leave it as a legacy and a testimony to others. But children have no such resources to ward off tyranny, or to endure its terrors. They are incapable of the same comprehensive survey of truth, of the same invincible resolve, of being inspired with an all-sustaining courage and endurance from the realities of another life. They would die under

imprisonment. Affrighted at the sight of the stake, or of any of the dread machinery of torture, they would surrender their souls to be distorted into any deformity, or mutilated into any hideousness. Before the process of starvation had gone on for a day, they would swallow any belief, from Atheism to Thuggery.

For any human government, then, to attempt to coerce and predetermine the religious opinions of children by law, and contrary to the will of their parents, is unspeakably more criminal than the usurpation of such control over the opinions of men. The latter is treason against truth; but the former is sacrilege. As the worst of all crimes against chastity are those which debauch the infant victim before she knows what chastity is, so the worst of all crimes against religious truth are those which forcibly close up the avenue and bar the doors that lead to the forum of reason and conscience. The spirit of ecclesiastical domination in modern times, finding that the principles of men are too strong for it, is attempting the seduction of children. Fearing the opinions that may be developed by mature reflection, it anticipates and forestalls those opinions, and seeks to imprint upon the ignorance and receptiveness of childhood the convictions which it could never fasten upon the minds of men in their maturity. As an instance of this, the "Factories Bill," so called, which, in the year 1843, was submitted by Sir James Graham to the British Parliament, may be cited. Among other things, this bill provided that schools should be established in manufacturing districts, under the auspices of the nation, and partly at its expense. These schools were to be placed under the immediate superintendence and visitation of officers appointed by the government. No teacher was to be eligible, unless approved by a bishop or archbishop. Any parent who hired out his child to work in a factory for half a day, unless he should go to this sectarian or government school the other half of the day, was to be fined; and, for non-payment of the fine, imprisonment was the legal consequence. So any overseer or factory proprietor, who should employ a child for half a day who did not attend school the other half, was also subject to a fine; and, of course, to imprisonment, if the fine were not paid. It did not at all alter the principle, that in a few excepted cases, owing to the peculiar nature of the work, the children were allowed to prosecute it for a whole day, or for two or three days in succession; because, just so long as they were permitted to work, just so long were they required to go to the school after the work. Nor, in the great majority of cases, was it any mitigation of the plan, that, if the parents would provide a separate school for their children at their own expense, they might send to it; because not one in ten of the operatives had either time or knowledge to found such a school, or pecuniary ability to pay its expenses if it were founded. The direct object and effect, therefore, of the proposed law, were to compel children to attend the government school, and to be taught the government religion, under the penalty of starvation or the poor-house. Children were debarred from a morsel of bread, unless they took it saturated with the government theology.

Now, to the moral sentiments of every lover of truth, of every lover of freedom for the human soul, is there not a meanness, is there not an infamy, in such a law, compared with which the bloody statutes of Elizabeth and Mary were magnanimous and honorable? To bring the awful forces of government to bear upon and to crush such lofty and indomitable souls as those of Latimer and Cranmer, of Ridley and Rogers, one would suppose to be diabolical enough to satisfy the worst spirits in the worst regions of the universe; but for a government to doom its children to starvation unless they will say its catechism, and to imprison the parent, and compel him to hear the wailings of his own famishing offspring,— compel him to see them perish, physically by starvation, or morally by ignorance, unless he will consent that they shall be taught such religious doctrines as he believes will be a peril and a destruction to their immortal souls,— is it not the essence of all tyrannies, of all crimes, and of all baseness, concreted into one?

Such a system as this stands in the strongest possible contrast to the Massachusetts system. Will those who call our system un-Christian and anti-Christian adopt and practise this system as Christian and religious?

3. As a third method, the government might establish schools by law, and empower each religious sect, whenever and wherever it could get a majority, to determine what religious faith should be taught in them.

Under such a system, each sect would demand that its own faith should be inculcated in all the schools, and this on the clear and simple ground that such faith is the only true one. Each differing faith believed in by all the other sects, must, of course, be excluded from the schools; and this on the equally clear and simple ground that there can be but one true faith: and which that is has already been determined, and is no longer an open question. Under such a system, it will not suffice to have the Bible in the schools to speak for itself. Each sect will rise up, and virtually say, "Although the Bible from Genesis to Revelation is in the schools, yet its true meaning and doctrines are not there: Christianity is not there, unless our commentary, our creed, or our catechism, is there also. A revelation from God is not sufficient. Our commentary or our teacher must go with it to reveal what the revelation means. Our book or our teacher must be superadded to the Bible, as an appendix or an erratum is subjoined at the end of a volume to supply oversights and deficiencies, and to rectify the errors of the text. It is not sufficient that the Holy Ghost has spoken by the mouth of David; it is not sufficient that God has spoken by the mouth of all his holy prophets which have been since the world began; it is not sufficient that you have the words of one who spoke as never man spake: all this leaves you in fatal ignorance and error, unless you have our 'addenda' and 'corrigenda,' — our things to be supplied, and things to be corrected. Nay, we affirm, that, without our interpretation and explanation of the faith which was once delivered unto the saints, all that the Holy Ghost and God and Christ have promulgated, and taught to men, still leaves your system an un-Christian and an anti-Christian system. To accept a revelation directly from Jehovah is not enough. His revelation must pass through our hands; his infinite Mind must be measured and squared by our minds: we have sat in council over his law, his promises, and his threatenings, and have decided, definitively, unappealably, and forever, upon the only true interpretation of them all. Your schools may be like the noble Bereans, searching the Scriptures daily; but, unless the result of those searchings have our countersign and indorsement, those schools are un-Christian and anti-Christian."

Now, it is almost too obvious to be mentioned, that such a claim as the above reduces society at once to this dilemma: if one religious sect is authorized to advance it for itself, then all other sects are equally authorized to do the same thing for themselves. The right being equal among all the sects, and each sect being equally certain and equally determined, what shall be done? Will not each sect, acting under religious impulses,— which are the strongest impulses that ever animate the breast of man,— will not each sect do its utmost to establish its supremacy in all the schools? Will not the heats and animosities engendered in families and among neighbors burst forth with a devouring fire in the primary or district school-meetings? and, when the inflammable materials of all the district meetings are gathered together in the town-meeting, what can quell or quench the flames till the zealots themselves are consumed in the conflagration they have kindled? Why would not all those machinations and oppressions be resorted to, in order to obtain the ascendency, if religious proselytism should be legalized in the schools, which would be resorted to, as I have endeavored, in a preceding part of this Report, to explain, if political proselytism were permitted in the schools? Suppose, at last, that different sects should obtain predominance in different schools,— just as is done by different religions in the different nations in Europe; so that, in one school, one system of doctrines should be taught to the children under the sanctions of law as eternal truth; and, in the neighboring schools, other and opposite systems should also be taught as eternal truth. Under such circumstances, perhaps it is not too much to suppose, that although some of the weaker sects might be crushed out of existence at once, yet that all the leading denominations, with their divisions and subdivisions, would have their representative schools. Into these, their respective catechisms or articles of faith would be introduced. And though the Bible itself might accompany them, yet, if we may judge from the history of all the religious struggles by which the world has been afflicted, the Bible would become the incident, and the catechism or articles the principal. And if these various catechisms or articles do declare, as is averred by each party, what the Bible means, and what the Christian religion is, then what a piebald, heterogeneous, and self-contradictory system does Christianity become! Suppose these schools to be brought nearer together, within hearing distance of each other, how discordant are the sounds they utter! Bring them under the same roof, remove partition, or other architectural barrier, so that they may occupy the same apartment, so that the classes may sit side by side; and does the spectacle which they now exhibit illustrate the one indivisible, all-glorious system of Christianity? or is it the return of Babel? Would such a system as this be called Christian by those who denounce our system as anti-Christian?

Is there not, on the contrary, an unspeakable value in the fact, that, under the Massachusetts system, the Bible is allowed to speak for itself? Under a system opposite to ours, this right of speaking for itself would never be vouchsafed to it. And how narrow is the distance between those who would never allow the Bible to be read by the people at all, and those who will allow it to be read only in the presence of a government interpreter! If government and teachers really believe the Bible to be the word of God,— as strictly and literally given by his inspiration as the tables of the law which Moses brought down from the mount were written by his finger,— then they cannot deny that, when the Bible is read, God speaks, just as literally and truly as an orator or a poet speaks when his oration or his poem is rehearsed. With this belief, it is no figure of speech to say, when the lids of the Bible are opened in school that its oracles may be uttered, that the lips of Jehovah are opened that he may commune with all his children, of whatever faith, who may be there assembled. Is that a time and an occasion for a worm of the dust, a creature of yesterday, to rush in and close the book, and silence the Eternal One, that he may substitute some form of faith of his own,— some form, either received from tradition, or reasoned out or guessed out by his fallible faculties,— and impose it upon the children as the plainer and better word of God? Or when the allotted hour for religious instruction comes, or the desire arises in the teacher's mind that the children of the school should hold communion with their heavenly Father, suppose that Father, instead of the medium of the Bible, should send an angel from his throne to make known to them his commands and his benedictions by living lips and in celestial words. Would that be a time for the chiefs of twenty different sects to rush in with their twenty different catechisms, and thrust the heavenly messenger aside, and struggle to see which could out-vociferate the rest in proclaiming what the visitant from on high was about to declare?

I hold it, then, to be one of the excellences, one of the moral beauties, of the Massachusetts system, that there is one place in the land where the children of all the different denominations are brought together for instruction, where the Bible is allowed to speak for itself; one place where the children can kneel at a common altar, and feel that they have a common Father, and where the services of religion tend to create brothers, and not Ishmaelites. If this be so, then it does violence to truth to call our system anti-Christian or un-Christian.

Thus far, under this head, I have supposed that the different sects, in their contests for supremacy, would keep the peace. But every page in the history of polemic struggles shows such a supposition to be delusive. In the contests for victory, success would lead to haughtiness, and defeat to revenge. Affinities and repulsions would gather men into bodies: these bodies would become battalions, and would set themselves in hostile array against each other. Weakness of argument would re-enforce itself by strength of arm; and the hostile parties would appeal from the tribunal of reason to the arbitrament of war. But after cities had been burned, and men slaughtered by thousands, and every diabolical passion in the human breast satiated, and the combatants were forced, from mere exhaustion, to rest upon their arms, it would be found, on a re-examination of the converted grounds, that not a rule of interpretation had been altered, not the tense of a single verb in any disputed text had been changed, not a Hebrew point nor a Greek article had been added or taken away, but that every subject of dispute remained as unsettled and uncertain as before. Is any system, which, by the law of the human passions, leads to such results, either Christian or religious?

4. One other system, if it may be so called, is supposable; and this exhausts the number of those which stand in direct conflict with ours. It is this: Government might expressly disclaim and refuse all interference with the education of the young, abandoning the whole work to the hazards of private enterprise, or to parental will, ability, or caprice.

The first effect of this course would be the abandonment of a

large portion of the children of every community to hopeless and
inevitable ignorance. Even with all the aids, incitements, and
bounties now bestowed upon education by the most enlightened
States in this Union, there exists a perilous and a growing body
of ignorance, animated by the soul of vice. Were government systems to be abolished, and all government aids to be withdrawn,
the number of American children, who, in the next generation,
would be doomed to all the wants and woes that can come in the
train of ignorance and error, would be counted by millions. This
abandoned portion of the community would be left, without any
of the restraints of education, to work out the infinite possibilities
of human depravity. In the more favored parts of the country, the
rich might educate their own children; although it is well known,
even now, that, throughout extensive regions of the South and
West, the best education which wealth can procure is meagre and
stinted, and alloyed with much error. The "parochial" or "sectarian" system might effect something in populous places; but what
could it do in rural districts, where so vast a proportion of all the
inhabitants of this country reside? In speaking of the difficulties
of establishing schools at the West, Miss Beecher gives an account
of a single village which she found there, consisting of only four
hundred inhabitants, where there were *fourteen* different denominations. "Of the most numerous portions of these," she says, "each
was jealous lest another should start a church first, and draw in
the rest. The result was, neither church nor Sunday school of any
kind was in existence." Of another place she says, "I found two
of the most influential citizens arrayed against each other, and
supported by contending partisans, so that whatever school one
portion patronized the other would oppose. The result was, no
school could be raised large enough to support any teacher." And
again: "In another large town, I was informed by one of the clergymen that no less than twenty different teachers opened schools and
gave them up in about six months."

In a population of four hundred, there would be about one
hundred children who *ought* to attend school; although this proportion, on an average of the whole country, is nearly threefold
the number of actual attendants. One hundred children would
furnish the materials for a good school, but, divided between four-

teen different schools, would give only seven children and one-seventh of a child to each school. How impossible to sustain schools on such a basis! The more numerous sects, it is true, would have a larger proportion; but just so much less would be the proportion of the smaller sects, and doubtless there would be some who would be fully represented by the above-mentioned fraction of one-seventh of a child. But let us see how insane and suicidal would be such a course of policy even with us. Leaving out all the *cities,* there are three hundred and five *towns,* in Massachusetts: and these comprise most of the rural and sparsely-populated portion of the State. These three hundred and five towns have an average of eleven schools (wanting a very small fraction) for each. Two hundred and twenty-six of these three hundred and five towns have a population, according to the last census, of less than twenty-two hundred each. If there are twenty-two hundred inhabitants and eleven schools in a town, each school represents an average of two hundred inhabitants. Including every child who was found in *all* our public schools last year, for any part either of the summer or winter terms, they would make a mean average for those terms of only forty-eight to a school. Now, suppose these forty-eight scholars to be divided, not between *"fourteen,"* but only between *four* different denominations, there would be but *twelve* to a school. Connect this result with the fact that Massachusetts has a population five times as dense as the average of the residue of the Union, and it will be seen, by intuition, that only in a few favored localities could the system of "sectarian" schools be maintained. This obstacle might be partially overcome by a union of two or more sects, between whom the repellency resulting from some punctilios in matters of form or ceremonial observance would not overcome the argument from availability; but this union, having been purchased by the sacrifice of a portion of what each holds to be absolute truth, why, when any one of the allies should become sufficiently powerful to stand alone, would it not dissolve the alliance, set up for itself, and abandon its confederates to their fate?

In making the above computation, which gives an average of forty-eight scholars to each school, it will be observed that *all* the schools in the State are included,— the numerously-attended schools of the cities as well as the small ones of the country. And although the number of districts in the two hundred and twenty-six towns whose population is less than twenty-two hundred each may be somewhat less than in the remaining seventy-nine towns, yet the fact unquestionably is, that an allowance of forty-eight scholars to a school is much too large an average for the schools in these two hundred and twenty-six, of the three hundred and five towns in the State. Of course, twelve scholars to a school would be much too large an average, if the schools were divided only between four different sects. Nor has any mention been made of the large numbers who connect themselves with no religious sect, and who, therefore, if united at all, would be united on the principle of opposition to sect. Surely the very statement of the case supersedes argument in regard to the possibility of maintaining schools for any considerable portion of the children of the country on such a basis.

The calamities necessarily resulting from so partial and limited a system as the one now under consideration would inflict retributive loss and weakness upon all classes in the community; but upon the children of the poor, the ignorant, and the unfortunate, would the blow fall with terrible severity. And what class of children ought we most assiduously to care for? Christ came to save that which would otherwise be lost. All good men, and all governments, so far as they imitate the example of Christ, strive to succor the distressed, and to reclaim the guilty; in an *intellectual* and in a *moral* sense, to feed the hungry, to clothe the naked, to visit the sick and the imprisoned; amid the priceless wealth of character, to find the lost piece of silver; and, amid the wanderings from the fold of truth, to recover the lambs. Before Heaven, it is now, today, the first duty of every government in Christendom to bring forward those unfortunate classes of the people, who, in the march of civilization, have been left in the rear. Though the van of society should stand still for a century, the rear ought to be brought up. The exterminating decree of Herod was parental and beneficent compared with the cruel sway of those rulers who dig the pit-falls of temptation along the pathway of children, and suffer them to fall, unwarned and unassisted, into the abysses of ruin. What, then, shall be said of that opposition to our system, which, should it prevail, would doom to remediless ignorance and vice a great majority of all the children in this land? Is such a system, as contradistinguished from our free system, Christian and religious?

It is a very surprising fact, but one which is authenticated by a report, made in the month of July last, by a committee of the Boston primary-schools, that, of the *ten thousand one hundred and sixty-two* children belonging to said schools, *five thousand one hundred and fifty-four* were of foreign parentage. Let sectarianism be introduced into the Boston schools, or rather let it be understood that the schools are to be carried on for the avowed purpose of building up any one of the New-England denominations, and what a vast proportion of these *five thousand one hundred and fifty-four* children would be immediately withdrawn from the schools! Their parents would as soon permit them to go to a lazar-house as to such schools; and this, too, from the sincerest of motives. The same thing would prove relatively true in regard to no inconsiderable number of the less populous cities, and of the most populous towns, in the State. Now, what would be the condition of such children at the end of twenty years? and what the condition of the communities which had thus cruelly closed the school-house doors upon them? Would not these communities be morally responsible for all the degradation, the miseries, the vices, and the crimes consequent upon such expulsion from the school? And would such a result be one of the fruits of a Christian and a religious system?

But there would be another inseparable accompaniment of such a system. In Massachusetts, the average compensation paid to male teachers is very much larger than that which is paid in any other State in the Union. It is nearly double what is given in most of the States; and yet, even with us, the great body of ambitious and aspiring young men pass by the profession of teaching, and betake themselves to some other employment, known to be more lucrative, and falsely supposed to be more honorable. How degrading, then, must be the effect upon the general character and competency of teachers as a profession, when, on the abolition of the public schools, and the substitution of private and sectarian schools in their stead, the wages of teachers, for the poorer classes, shall be reduced to a pittance, and the collection of even this pittance shall be precarious! What will be the social rank and standing

of teachers, when their customary income encourages no previous
preparation for their work, doles out only a niggardly subsistence
even while they are engaged in the service, and leaves no surplus
for the probable wants of sickness, or the certain ones of age?
And among whom shall the teacher seek his associates, when he
is shunned by the learned for his want of culture, and ridiculed
for his poverty by the devotees of wealth? Even in England, where
the population is so dense that hardly a spot can be selected as a
centre, which will not embrace, within a circumference of convenient distance, a sufficient number of children for a school,—
even there, the voluntary and sectarian system leaves at least two-
thirds of the agricultural and manufacturing classes in a state of the
most deplorable ignorance; supplying them with teachers, so far
as it supplies them with teachers at all, who fulfil the double office
of perpetuating errors in school, and degrading the character of
the profession out of it.

There is another fact of fearful significance, which no one who
has any regard for the common interests of society can be pardoned
for forgetting. It is known to all, that, in many parts of the Union,
the population is so sparse, and can command so little of ready
means for paying salaries, that no *resident* clergyman of any denomination is to be found throughout wide districts of country;
and many of those who do devote themselves to the spiritual welfare of their fellow-men are most scantily provided for. If un-
married, they can barely live; if they have a family, there is, often-
times, a real scantiness of the comforts and necessities of life.
They have neither books to peruse; nor leisure to read, even if
they had books. They may be a pious, but they cannot be a learned
clergy. At least in one respect, they are compelled to imitate
St. Paul; for as he wrought at his own "craft" for a subsistence,
so must they. And now, if existing means are too scanty to give a
respectable support even to the ministry, how disastrous must be
the effect of dividing these scanty means between the institution of
the gospel and the institution of the school! Will not the vineyard
of the Lord be overgrown with weeds, will not its hedges be
broken down, and the wild beasts of the forests make their lair
therein, if the servants who are set to tend and to dress it are so
few in number, and so miserably provided for? Is not this another

criterion by which to determine whether our present system is not as Christian and as religious as that which would supplant it?

I know of but one argument, having the semblance of plausibility, that can be urged against this feature of our system. It may be said, that if questions of doctrinal religion are left to be decided by men for themselves, or by parents for their children, numerous and grievous errors will be mingled with the instruction. Doubtless the fact is so. If truth be one, and if many contradictory dogmas are taught as truth, then it is mathematically certain that all the alleged truths but one is a falsity. But, though the statement is correct, the inference which is drawn from it in favor of a government standard of faith is not legitimate; for all the religious errors which are believed in by the free mind of man, or which are taught by free parents to their children, are tolerable and covetable, compared with those which the patronage and the seductions of government can suborn men to adopt, and which the terrors of government can compel them to perpetuate. The errors of free minds are so numerous and so various, that they prevent any monster-error from acquiring the ascendency, and therefore truth has a chance to struggle forward amid the strifes of the combatants; but if the monster-error can usurp the throne of the civil power, fortify itself by prescription, defend its infallibility with all the forces of the State, sanctify its enormities under sacred means, and plead the express command of God for all its atrocities,— against such an antagonist, Truth must struggle for centuries, bleed at every pore, be wounded in every vital part, and can triumph at last, only after thousands and tens of thousands of her holiest disciples shall have fallen in the conflict.

If, then, a government would recognize and protect the rights of religious freedom, it must abstain from subjugating the capacities of its children to any legal standard of religious faith with as great fidelity as it abstains from controlling the opinions of men. It must meet the unquestionable fact, that the old spirit of religious domination is adopting new measures to accomplish its work,— measures which, if successful, will be as fatal to the liberties of mankind as those which were practised in bygone days of violence and terror. These new measures are aimed at children instead of men. They propose to supersede the necessity of subduing free thought *in the mind of the adult,* by forestalling the development of any capacity of free thought *in the mind of the child.* They expect to find it easier to subdue the free agency of children by binding them in fetters of bigotry than to subdue the free agency of men by binding them in fetters of iron. For this purpose, some are attempting to deprive children of their right to labor, and, of course, of their daily bread, unless they will attend a government school, and receive its sectarian instruction. Some are attempting to withhold all means even of secular education from the poor, and thus punish them with ignorance, unless, with the secular knowledge which they desire, they will accept theological knowledge which they condemn. Others still are striving to break down all free public-school systems where they exist, and to prevent their establishment where they do not exist, in the hope, that, on the downfall of these, their system will succeed. The sovereign antidote against these machinations is free schools for all, and the right of every parent to determine the religious education of his children.

9

On Keeping God out of the Constitution

BY THE MIDDLE of the nineteenth century, it was quite clear that
the wall of separation built by the Founding Fathers was lasting
well. As we have seen, the application of the principle of freedom
of religion had to be clarified; its corollaries had to be explored
and made specific. Attempts to circumvent the separation had
to be exposed and defeated. Despite the necessity for such defenses, it is fair to say that the Jeffersonian mechanism of the separation of church and state, expressing the more general principle of
freedom of religion, was achieving its purposes. American politics
was, for the most part, free from religious intervention; American
religious bodies were completely free from political direction, and,
for the most part, free from political ambitions; each inhabitant of
the United States was secure in his freedom to choose the religion
which satisfied him, without political disadvantage and with a
minimum of economic and social discrimination. There had been
developed, against the will of a minority of extremists on either
side, a distinctively American attitude towards religion which
might be summarized in some such terms as these: It is generally
desirable that each person should make choice of some religious
group, and affiliate with it. There should, however, be no public
pressure on anyone to force such affiliation. Furthermore, while
religious organization is a good and a necessary thing if each individual is to have free choice, any organization, religious or not,
must be watched; any organization contains the threat of becoming,
in its expansion, a self-perpetuating, oligarchic danger to free individuals. Churches are especially likely to develop into a menace
because of the necessarily oligarchic character of their ministry.

Any ministry contains the germs of a priesthood, and must be prevented from developing into a priestly class. In a word, the middle-of-the-road American attitude was proreligious, but anticlerical and antiecclesiastical.

It was obvious, then, to proponents of greater churchly influence in the United States in the middle of the nineteenth century that they were not going to achieve the uniformity or the power they desired under the conditions of what William Leggett, in one of his editorials, had so tellingly described as "free trade in religion." Ecclesiasticism had gone as far as it could under the Constitution; the only road that seemed to be open to advocates of more religion in government was that of amending the Constitution. When this was first suggested, a more important issue, that of slavery, occupied the immediate foreground. There were only a few voices to suggest the importance of "putting God into the Constitution" by amending that document. Then came the "irrepressible conflict" of fratricidal war between the states to provide the occasion for further organized attempts to introduce the so-called "Christian amendment."

In the early days of the Civil War, the fortunes of the United States were at a low ebb. Lacking in military strength, weak in diplomatic position, divided in council and in leadership, confused, disoriented, and defeated, the Northern states were backed into a corner at the close of the year 1862. The despairing citizenry, especially in the more evangelical and fundamentalist sections of the Middle West, returned from their heart-searching with the message, reminiscent of the Old Testament prophets, that the ill success of the Unionist cause was a manifestation of God's dissatisfaction with the secular Constitution of the United States. So desperate were conditions that even this idea was taken seriously; on the third day of February, 1863, eleven Christian denominations, through their representatives assembled at Xenia, Ohio, demanded that the United States of America should place their allegiance to God on record in the Constitution. In 1864, this action was followed by the formation of the National Reform Association, largely under Presbyterian and Episcopalian domination, to agitate and to lobby for the passage of some form of Christian amendment.

There were various forms proposed for the amendment. One, which was widely advocated, appeared in the first issue of *The Christian Statesman,* a journal started in 1867 as the organ of the National Reform Association. It required the amendment of the Preamble to the Constitution to read as follows: "We, the people of the United States, acknowledging Almighty God as the source of all authority and power in civil government, the Lord Jesus Christ as the Ruler among the nations, and His Will, revealed in the Holy Scriptures, as of supreme authority, in order to constitute a Christian government, form a more perfect union, establish justice, . . ." Men of learning and influence were at the forefront of this movement. Justice William Strong of the Supreme Court of the United States was, for a time, its president. Among its vice-presidents were four men who had been governors of their states: John W. Geary and James Pollock of Pennsylvania, James M. Harvey of Kansas, and John W. Stewart of Vermont. President Julius Seelye of Amherst College was one of the educational leaders who played an important part in the National Reform Association; others were Thomas Bicknell, Commissioner of Public Schools of Rhode Island, and Professors Tayler Lewis of Union College, George Junkin of Lafayette, and J. H. McIlvaine of Princeton. This was a considerable movement, not one to be trifled with. Its popular support, as expressed in mass meetings and signatories to petitions, was large. Its activities persisted, though with diminished intensity, into the twentieth century.

Needless to say, there was steady and relentless opposition to the objectives and activities of the National Reform Association. So many and diverse were the leaders of this opposition that it is almost without point to single out a few for special mention. All the liberal religious groups were represented, frequently by members of the clergy. Charles Sumner of Massachusetts led the opposition in the Senate. One of his acts was to present, in 1874, a petition against the "Christian amendment," bearing nearly thirty-five thousand signatures gathered chiefly in the East and the Middle West. This petition was started in 1872 by the distinguished liberal religionist, Francis Ellingwood Abbot, and pushed by him in his weekly paper, *The Index.* As presented in the Senate, this petition measured 953 feet! It is clear what lengths the people of the

United States were willing to go to defeat any such attempt to infringe upon their hard-bought freedom. The *Daily Globe* of Boston, on January 8, 1874, remarked editorially on the physical
length of the petition which, it was said, went far "in demonstrating
the absurdity of the proposed constitutional plan of salvation."
The *Globe* also pointed out that "the most truly religious men in
the country are opposed to the amendment."

Recognizing that in some cases at least the best defense is to
attack, Abbot and other leaders of the liberal opposition proclaimed
that the very existence of such a movement as that sponsored by
the National Reform Association indicated that, despite the wall of
separation, there was still too much religious influence in the
American government. On January 4, 1873, Abbot's leading article in *The Index,* entitled "Burn Your Ships," was a demand for
positive action on the part of religious liberals to eradicate the last
vestiges of "mediaevalism" from the American system. He listed
eight "glaring infringements of all liberty and justice" for the consideration of those who believed that America was "free enough."
To close these breaches in the wall of separation, Abbot had formulated in 1872, and reprinted elsewhere in the January 4, 1873,
issue of *The Index,* "Nine Demands of Liberalism" as a platform
for the organization of Liberal Leagues. By July, 1876, there
were about forty local organizations in various parts of the country
which had accepted the "Nine Demands" and had enrolled themselves as Liberal Leagues.

Abbot's next step, taken in 1874, was to fight fire with fire by
recommending that the first amendment to the Constitution of the
United States be made more specific and affirmative by the adoption of a "Religious Freedom Amendment." In revised form
(1876) incorporating the suggestions of others beside its origina-
tor, this proposed substitute for the first amendment read as follows:

Section 1. Neither Congress nor any State shall make any law
respecting an establishment of religion, or favoring any particular
form of religion, or prohibiting the free exercise thereof; or permitting
in any degree a union of Church and State, or granting any special
privilege, immunity, or advantage to' any sect or religious body or to
any number of sects or religious bodies; or taxing the people of any
State, either directly or indirectly, for the support of any sect or

religious body or of any number of sects or religious bodies; or abridging the freedom of speech or of the press, or of the right of the people peaceably to assemble and to petition the Government for a redress of grievances.

Section 2. No religious test shall ever be required as a condition of suffrage, or as a qualification to any office or public trust, in any State. No person shall ever in any State be deprived of any of his or her rights, privileges, or capacities, or disqualified for the performance of any public or private duty, or rendered incompetent to give evidence in any court of law or equity, in consequence of any opinions he or she may hold on the subject of religion. No person shall ever in any State be required by law to contribute directly or indirectly to the support of any religious society or body of which he or she is not a voluntary member.

Section 3. Neither the United States, nor any State, Territory, municipality, or any civil division of any State or Territory, shall levy any tax, or make any gift, grant or appropriation, for the support, or in aid of any church, religious sect, or denomination, or any school, seminary, or institution of learning, in which the faith or doctrines of any religious order or sect shall be taught or inculcated, or in which religious practices shall be observed; or for the support, or in aid, of any religious charity or purpose of any sect, order, or denomination whatsoever.

Section 4. Congress shall have power to enforce the various provisions of this Article by appropriate legislation.

July 4, 1876, the hundredth anniversary of the signing of the Declaration of Independence, was a day of inventory for the American people. It was, for most of the throngs who participated in activities all over the country, a day for the backward glance, usually somewhat smug, if the addresses of that centennial Fourth tell us true. For all, in some way, the day was one of dedication. For a small group who met together on that day in Concert Hall in Philadelphia, and who had been meeting for several days before that, it was a day of extraordinary dedication. This was the band of liberals who had come together to organize their scattered Liberal Leagues into a National Liberal League. This Centennial Congress of Liberals was no group of fire-eaters; they spent most of their time listening to very dull papers, all intellectually honest and carefully elaborated, but lacking the spirit and rhetorical abandon of earlier declarations in behalf of religious freedom. They argued over minute points in their resolutions, which were many.

The delegates took their stand with their president, Dr. Abbot, against the Christian amendment and for the Religious Freedom amendment.

Their moment of greatest liveliness came when, at the instigation of Benjamin F. Underwood, a tough old atheist, they passed a resolution approving of the prohibition of the passage of obscene matter through the mails. This does not seem unusual to our eyes; in 1876, the days of Anthony Comstock, it was unusual in what was omitted rather than in what was said. For the Comstock postal laws of 1873 and 1876 banned not only obscene, but also blasphemous, matter from passing through the mails, and Comstock himself, as postal inspector, was the judge of what constituted blasphemy and obscenity. As Stow Persons has pointed out in his excellent study of *Free Religion,* internal disagreement on the degree to which liberals would support Comstock's power was the rock upon which the National Liberal League foundered.

Underwood, in addition to introducing and sponsoring this most important resolution of the Centennial Congress of Liberals, also made the most telling speech of the Congress, at the evening session on Sunday, July 2, 1876. Entitled "The Practical Separation of Church and State," it is a strong plea for the liberation of morality from the shackles of theological sanctions. Thus it meets the argument of the proponents of the Christian amendment directly and at their central point. For it had been the contention of the National Reform Association and of its unorganized predecessors that government must be a religious institution because government depends upon morality, and morality is established and sanctioned by religion. This was the position which Underwood undertook to controvert. Parts of this speech, as well as the "Nine Demands of Liberalism," are printed here to show how the relatively well-organized extremists among the liberal religionists of the 1870's fought to keep God out of the Constitution.

Francis Ellingwood Abbot

1873

NINE DEMANDS OF LIBERALISM

1. We demand that churches and other ecclesiastical property shall be no longer exempt from taxation.

2. We demand that the employment of chaplains in Congress, in the legislatures, in the navy and militia, and in prisons, asylums, and all other institutions supported by the public money, shall be discontinued.

3. We demand that all public appropriations for educational and charitable institutions of a sectarian character shall cease.

4. We demand that all religious services now sustained by the government shall be abolished; and especially that the use of the Bible in the public schools, whether ostensibly as a textbook or avowedly as a book of religious worship, shall be prohibited.

5. We demand that the appointment, by the president of the United States or by the governors of the various states, of all the religious festivals and fasts shall wholly cease.

6. We demand that the judicial oath in the courts and in all other departments of the government shall be abolished, and that simple affirmation under the pains and penalties of perjury shall be established in its stead.

7. We demand that all laws directly or indirectly enforcing the observance of Sunday as the Sabbath shall be repealed.

8. We demand that all laws looking to the enforcement of "Christian" morality shall be abrogated and that all laws shall be conformed to the requirements of natural morality, equal rights and impartial liberty.

9. We demand that not only in the Constitution of the United States and of the several states, but also in the practical ad-

ministration of the same, no privileges or advantage shall be conceded to Christianity or any other special religion; that our entire political system shall be founded and administered on a purely secular basis; and whatever changes shall prove necessary to this end shall be consistently, unflinchingly, and promptly made.

Benjamin F. Underwood

1876

THE PRACTICAL SEPARATION OF
CHURCH AND STATE

To some it may seem superfluous, in this country, and at this day, to make a plea for the separation of Church and State. There are persons ready to declare that with us there is no connection between the two, that nobody *wants* them united, that everybody believes in and exercises religious liberty in this country, and that there is no use and no reason in agitating this subject, especially at a time when we should all join in viewing the results and celebrating the triumphs of our hundred years of national existence. Loud professions and boastful claims never fail to impress the crowd. The majority of men assume that what they have always heard must be true. Loudness of assertion is taken for argument, and extravagance of statement for evidence. The fact that millions of human beings were held in slavery under our flag a few years ago, never modified the claims of the ordinary Fourth of July orator, nor did it abate in the least the enthusiasm of the average audience, whenever reference was made to this country as the exclusive abode of the goddess of Liberty,— as the "land of the free and the home of the brave." *Now* the inconsistency is seen and acknowledged by those, even, who a few years ago were ready to cry "fanatic," "freedom shrieker," "traitor," whenever any one hinted at the inconsistency between profession and performance, pretension and practice, in this American Republic. The time will come, when it will be seen, not less clearly, that the popular notion that there is an utter disconnection between Church and State in America, and that all our laws are in harmony therewith, is a notion which is *at variance with the real facts*. Nor is there a universal recognition of the right of all persons to avow and advocate their religious beliefs. There is in this country a class by no means inconsiderable in numbers or insignificant in influence that show by their acts, and a certain party among them by the frank avowal of their purposes, that they are *opposed* to equal rights and impartial religious liberty. Nothing will satisfy them but the incorporation of their own religious dogmas into the National Constitution, so as to make them a part of the organic law. Then, while we should not be insensible to the great achievements of a century, while indeed, we should feel gratified with the numerous evidences of progress, and among them the undoubted increase in liberality of sentiment, yet patriotism does not require, nor will a reasonable prudence and forethought permit us, to ignore the existence of evils which have descended to us, or those which have sprung up and assumed prominence in our own time, and, if not checked, may be a source of mischief in the future.

Here, as in other countries, there is a large class in whose education the principles of morality have been subordinated to the dogmas of theology, and whose devotion to their religion, in consequence, is far stronger than their sense of justice, or their understanding of its requirements in their relations with their fellow men. They are willing, at any time, to support measures that they think will promote the interests of their faith, without regard to the personal or legal rights of those who cannot adopt their views. Many of them lack the breadth of thought and catholicity of spirit to understand that there is any wrong in censuring and punishing those who reject their creeds, which they not only firmly believe to be true, but regard as surpassing in importance all other truths. Hence they would conscientiously, to the extent of their ability, prevent all discussions and suppress all doubts tending to disparage them, and interdict any denial of their truth or divine origin. They would gladly have the government changed to correspond with their religious views, and so administered as to favor and enforce exclusively their religious beliefs.

There are others who are more intellectual, but quite as much under the influence of theological creeds, who are in favor of a union between Church and State, because they see that, from their standpoint, there is a logical necessity for it, to make the government harmonize with the teachings and demands of their religion.

Upon the acceptance of their views depend the eternal interests of mankind, as well as that less important concern — the welfare of the State. They, therefore, ask that their religion be sustained by the government and enforced, if necessary, by coercive measures, for reasons compared with which all other reasons seem petty and insignificant: namely, to save multitudes from eternal torture, and secure for them an inheritance of eternal glory. If Christ died for this, can they be true followers of him (they argue) if they allow any mere theories of religious liberty — which are nowhere sustained by the word of God — to prevent their using all means within their power for crushing every error and delusion that stands in the way of the religion of the Cross? Bigoted and fanatical the men who reason thus may be; but they are earnest and conscientious, consistent, possess the courage of their opinions, and are really the most dangerous class that we have to contend with in opposing the Christianization of this government.

We have also an army of political demagogues who are ever watching and waiting to spring to the support of any movement, however unjust, which promises them office or influence. The moment they discover a large and increasing public sentiment in favor of a measure, it has for them, a special attraction. They are not less zealous in opposing any *reform,* however beneficent, than the removal of any abuse, however great, if behind it there is not sufficient numerical strength and popular approval to make it for their personal interest to come out in favor of it. Their assumed piety and reverence are so great that it pains them to hear of any movement which threatens to disturb the institutions of the past, or the time-honored customs of their fathers, so long indeed as they are sustained by popular ignorance and prejudice; but just as soon as they see a growing sentiment in favor of the movement, their veneration and pious regard for the notions of their ancestors forsake them, and they are profuse with words of approval and admiration. These are men to be ranked among the enemies of all reforms in their inception, and their influence with the masses makes them formidable foes of progress. Morally, they are most despicable men. . . .

With such elements as these in the country, and with the lessons of the past before us, the relation of the State to the religious beliefs of the people cannot be a matter of small concern. Although I am of the opinion that there is a very large element in this country in favor of the complete secularization of the State, sufficient, if aroused to its importance, to give us, through legislative enactments, all needed guarantees of impartial religious liberty, yet, if there were but twelve individuals in sympathy with the movement, it would be none the less the duty of those twelve persons to work for its triumph. Indeed, to the truly wise mind the disposition to labor for it would be even greater — greater in proportion to its need of friends and the amount of work to be accomplished. . . .

The American Revolution found and left every State, Rhode Island only excepted, so related to the Church that there was a complete inter-dependence. This relation was continued by special provision in the new Constitutions which were adopted after the Declaration of Independence, in every State, with the exception of New York. Some of the States, among them Massachusetts, Pennsylvania, Delaware and Maryland, inserted a clause requiring a statement of religious belief as a condition of office. In 1780, Benjamin Franklin wrote to Richard Price:—

"I am fully of your opinion respecting religious tests; but though the people of Massachusetts have not in the new Constitution kept quite clear of them, yet, if we consider what that people were one hundred years ago, we must allow they have gone great lengths in liberality of sentiment on religious subjects; and we may hope for greater degrees of perfection when their Constitution, some years hence, shall be revised."

North and South Carolina and Georgia required all officers of the State to be of the Protestant faith. Since those days, the Constitutions of all the States have been revised, and the connection beween Church and State has been made more indirect and greatly lessened. Yet there are several States in which belief in the existence of a God is required as a condition of office, and in nearly all it is impossible for an atheist to testify in the courts, if he frankly avows his opinions. Only by compromising with his conscience, by equivocating, or by concealing his own views, can he avoid the humiliation of having his testimony excluded. What a premium on dishonesty and hypocricy is thus offered by the State! But we are not here so much concerned with the moral effects as with the great injustice of such a religious test, and its utter incongruity with the principles of equal rights and religious liberty. How can any man who is in favor of such a law look a freethinker in the face, and say that he is in favor of impartial liberty!

Then in every State we have official legislative prayers, which, being acts of devotion, involve a connection between Church and State, as must any official act of any department of the government which enforces, favors, or aids any religious doctrine or duty. The direction or performance by the State of religious worship is a combined clerical and political service. When our political representatives convert the legislative halls into rooms for religious worship, and transform the legislative bodies into prayer meetings, such association of political and religious acts is an actual union of Church and State.

So the custom of appointing days of fasting, thanksgiving, and prayer, by the State, through its chief magistrate, is another link connecting the two. It is an official declaration of the existence of a God, the duty of fasting, praying and giving thanks to God.

Nearly all the States have laws enforcing the observance of Sunday as the Sabbath, and not unfrequently individuals are arrested and fined for doing work or indulging in amusements on that day, when their acts in no way disturb others. If the State is independent of the Church, what right has it to require the observance of one day as a Sabbath more than another? And how can it punish any man for doing work at any time, when he does not thereby infringe on the rights of other members of society? The judicature of the country is disgraced, so long as our courts serve as tribunals for such sectarian purposes.

The use of the Bible and the performance of religious exercises in our public schools, sustained and enforced by State authority and public appropriations for religious institutions, are utterly inconsistent with that complete separation of Church and State which is so often declared to exist in this country.

The exemption of churches, church property and religious institutions from taxation, thereby forcing indirectly into their support persons who do not believe in their utility, is an outrage on the rights of all such persons, and a remnant of that religious despotism which once treated mankind as slaves, and robbed its victims, in the name of God, to build costly cathedrals, and enable ecclesiastics to live in luxury and ease.

Our National Constitution, thanks to the wisdom of our fathers, is a purely secular instrument. It declares that Congress shall make no laws respecting an establishment of religion, and that no religious test shall be required for any office or public trust. In the treaty with Tripoli, which was signed by George Washington, it was declared that the United States Government is not founded on the Christian religion. Undoubtedly the feeling of the framers of the Constitution on this subject were well expressed by Franklin, when, in a letter to a friend, he wrote:—

"When a religion is good, I conceive it will support itself, and when it cannot support itself, and God does not care to support it, so that its professors are obliged to call for the help of the civil power, it is a sign, I apprehend, of its being a bad one."

But notwithstanding the entirely secular character of the National Constitution, from the first there was in the administration of the general movement a yielding to ecclesiastical influence, backed up as it was by a strong religious sentiment. Days of fasting, thanksgiving and prayer were appointed by the early Presidents, as well as by the Governors of States. The first, by Washington, was at the close of his first administration, by the special request of Congress. Jefferson refused to follow the example of his predecessors, and thereby incurred the wrath of the clergy and all persons of Puritanical proclivities. "I know," he wrote, "it will give great offence to the clergy; but the advocate of religious freedom is to expect neither peace nor forgiveness from them." "I consider," he wrote, "the government of the United States as interdicted by the Constitution from intermeddling with religious institutions, their doctrine, discipline, or exercises." "Fasting and prayer are religious exercises; the enjoying them is an act of religious discipline. Every religious society has a right to determine for itself the time for these exercises, and the objects proper to them, according to its own peculiar tenets; and this right can never be safer than in their own hands, where the Constitution has deposited it. Civil powers alone have been given to the President of the United States, and he has no authority to direct the religious exercises of his constituents."

This view, so clearly the only correct and just one, has been generally disregarded, and the appointment by the President of the United States of days for religious exercises has become established as a custom. There are persons, now indifferent to its religious character, who justify it on the plea of *custom* alone. But the repetition of practices unauthorized by, and contrary to, the Constitution, is no reason for their further continuance. Custom, in legal parlance, signifies a usage from time immemorial *neither against law, nor individual nor public right*. It is no justification of any wrong that the aggressor has for a long time been accustomed to wrong-doing.

The presence of Chaplains in the halls of legislation, in the army and navy, and in other departments of the general government, is as unconstitutional as it is unjust. Congress, having been invested with no ecclesiastical authority, has no constitutional right to create an ecclesiastical office, or to induct any person into such office created by the Church. The appointment of Chaplains by the Government of the United States is an unauthorized act of political legislation, as little in keeping with the spirit of our Constitution as praying in public places — for instance in Congress — is in accordance with the teachings of the Nazarene reformer.

Not content, however, with these unjust discriminations in favor of believers in the Christian religion, some of them now demand that such changes be made in the Constitution and in the government as shall be necessary to make the main dogmas of this religion part of the organic law. The movement, having for its object the accomplishment of this change by Constitutional amendments and such legislature as may be necessary to enforce them, has during the past few years acquired considerable strength and influence. It numbers among its friends eminent clergymen, Presidents of Colleges, Governors of States, Members of Congress, and Judges of the Supreme Court. We cannot ignore it.

In all ages and countries, in proportion as the adherents of religion have come to agree in belief and be consolidated in organization, their disposition and power have increased to influence the government to enforce theological dogmas and impose disabilities on dissenters. Fortunately for us, the number of sects, and the competitive strife between them in this country, have been unfavorable to the encroachment of the Church on the State. Occupied chiefly with increasing their numbers and adding to their wealth, and more or less envious of one another, they have had but little disposition to unite their forces and organize for concerted and concentrated action. But, with the growth of Liberalism and the subordination of many of the doctrinal points which have heretofore distinguished them as separate bodies to those fundamental doctrines which they hold in common, one of the chief obstacles to their union has been removed, and the danger of their interference with the government is thereby greatly increased. The rapid growth of anti-Christian sentiments, with the more bigoted and intolerant of all sects, is the strongest reason for a union, when in the absence of danger to their faith their chief pleasure consists in cursing and anathematizing one another on account of differences so small that they are scarcely perceptible to the unregenerate mind. Evangelical alliances, presenting to us the spectacle of sects heretofore hostile assembled on terms of apparent friendship for a common purpose, even though they are an evidence of a growing liberality of the sects towards one another, are not without portentous significance, well calculated to arouse apprehensions in the minds of those who are acquainted with history and are lovers of religious liberty. A religious element that will maintain the rightfulness of forcing all tax-payers to pay taxes which religious societies only should pay, of excluding from the courts the testimony of citizens who differ from it on speculative subjects, of keeping in our schools a religious service that is objectionable to a large and respectable portion of the patrons of these schools, who are taxed equally with others for their support, *goes no farther, simply because it lacks the power*. If it could, it would force Jews, spiritualists, and free-thinkers of every phase of thought, to attend churches and help pay the salary of the clergy, and prevent all gatherings and prohibit all expressions of belief not in accordance with its own belief, as was done in New England by the Puritans and their pious and persecuting descendants. Whatever those who are petitioning Congress for an amendment to our Constitution that shall recognize "God as the source of all authority, Jesus Christ as the Ruler among Nations, and the Bible as the supreme authority" may disclaim now, it is plain that they purpose to make belief in Christianity a test of office and of citizenship, and thereby disfranchise all Jews, Infidels, Buddhists, Mohammedans, and others who cannot accept Christianity as a supernatural religion. The incorporation of their dogmas in the Constitution means the legislative and executive enforcement of them by governmental authority. To be consistent, the government will have to give directions in regard to the worship of God, and see that the citizens make their conduct conform to the revealed will of God, which is to be the authority from which no appeal can be made.

The sect that finds itself in the numerical majority will have the power to enforce by acts of Congress its own peculiar dogmas as the supreme law, because these will be declared authoritatively the revealed will of God. Free-thinkers and non-Christians of all classes have no rights the Church will be bound to respect. Says the Methodist *Home Journal:*

"We hold that, to be consistent with ourselves, Infidelity should not be tolerated in our country, much less encouraged by those who openly profess and teach its doctrines."

Only a few weeks ago in Baltimore, at the general conference of the Methodist church, was offered a resolution declaring that all the blessings of civil and religious liberty which we so abundantly enjoy are due to the enlightening influence of the Christian religion, and recommending "to the members of the Church throughout the country that they use every just and proper means to place in all the civil offices of our government only such men as are known to possess and maintain a true Christian character and principles." We have here the expression of the views and wishes of thousands of Orthodox Protestants, many of whom are less frank in the avowal of their ultimate designs. . . .

Independently of the lessons of history, teaching us the terrible consequences of a union of civil and ecclesiastical power, a complete separation of Church and State is demanded by the imprescriptible rights of the human mind. The right to life, liberty, and the pursuit of happiness involves the right to profess and advocate our views. Whether they be true or false affects not the sacredness of the right of the believer. He has a right to one God, or three, or three thousand, or none at all; to worship or not as he pleases, at any time and in any manner that he thinks proper, when he does not thereby interfere with the equal rights of others. No human power, no earthly tribunal can justly dictate to any individual what he shall believe in regard to religion, or how, or when, or where he shall worship. If his views are such that they require him to violate the rules of decency or the acknowledged principles of morality, let him be restrained — if necessary, punished, for such violation; but let no one suppose that by an appeal to extreme cases, even involving the right of society to deal with dangerous monomaniacs, or disturbers of the peace, any justification can be found for interference by the State. With men's religious beliefs, no individual, no number of individuals, with direct or delegated authority, have the right to use coercive measures to prevent any persons from promulgating any religion, or to induce him to subscribe to any creed, perform any worship, acknowledge any God, or support any religion on earth.

The Puritans have been eulogized for braving the dangers of the ocean and the privations of the wilderness, that they might worship God as conscience dictated. It is not strange that with the imperfect views of religious freedom then prevailing, they or their immediate descendants soon re-established in the new world a religious despotism more intolerant than that in the old world from which they had fled; but when we see men who lack language strong enough to denounce their persecutors, or to praise their sincerity and courage, earnestly advocating measures to-day to deprive of religious liberty such of their fellow citizens as cannot subscribe to their own views, we are most painfully impressed with the power of bigotry and superstition so to distort the mind as to make enemies of those who should be our friends, verifying the saying that "a man's foes shall be those of his own household."

There are millions in this country who cannot conscientiously support any kind of supernatural religion. Have they no rights the Church is bound to respect? We are told that the views of such are an offence to God. This is the teaching of theologians. But many things which have been pronounced by them an offence to God, have in succeeding generations, by the same class, been discovered to be right; so we cannot resist the conviction that these men who talk so confidently about the will and wishes of God, as an argument against equal rights and religious freedom, simply give expression to the will and wishes of their own minds. When they declare that God is displeased with the omission of his name from the national Constitution, and that it is his requirement that this government recognize Jesus Christ as "Ruler among nations," we accept these statements as evidence that those who utter them, however sincerely, see the spread of those liberal sentiments that are gradually undermining their spiritual authority, and that they feel the necessity of securing the aid of the civil power to guard against the innovations of scepticism and science.

Further, those who are in favor of uniting Church and State, after declaring (what is so evident that none dispute it) that morality is necessary to the State, coolly assure us that morality depends upon the Christian religion, and without its light and authority virtue has no fixed standard, no guarantee, no sanctions. Here we have the real difference reduced to its last terms between many of those who would Christianize and those who would secularize the government. Both parties hold to the importance of good morals. But one believes there can be no true morality except in connection with Christianity; while the other maintains that morality is natural and secular, and does not depend for its existence, or for the practice of its precepts, upon any religion whatever. Thus is involved in this contest the true nature and the real basis of morality, without an understanding of which there can hardly be an intelligent appreciation of the merits of the controversy.

To us nothing is more clear than that morality depends not upon any system of faith: it requires no miraculous evidence; it is independent of theological dogma; no supernatural halo can heighten its beauty; no ecclesiastical influence can strengthen its obligations; it is confined to no one country, limited to no one age, restricted to no one form of faith, the exclusive possession of no one class, sect, order, nation, or race of men; it requires no written decalogue; it needs no single individual authority; theology can not add to it, neither can it take from it. It has its indestructible basis in the nature of man, as a feeling, thinking, acting being, and in society as an aggregation of such beings, with the manifold relations and the acknowledged rights and duties that spring therefrom. Empires rise and perish; religions grow and decay;

special forms of civilization appear and give way to other types; but as, amid all the mutations of human existence, the nature of man remains essentially the same, and through all these changes the social condition everlastingly persists, morality can never be without a foundation as broad and deep and enduring as humanity itself. It changes not, but, as Cicero says, it is "the same at Rome and at Athens, to-day and to-morrow; alone, eternal, and invariable, it binds all nations and all times." Its highest *standard* is the enlightened reason of man. The better man understands his nature, and the more he is capable, by reason of intelligence and culture, of comprehending the object of society and his relations thereto, the better understanding will he have of the principles of morality.

Theologians could have no ideas of moral qualities, unless they had discovered them in humanity. They are observed in man, and as in him they are admired in contrast to the opposite qualities, they are ascribed to God; and then theologians, having invested God with human qualities and denied to him what they have borrowed from him with which to invest God before they could form any conception of him as a moral being, most ungratefully as well as inconsistently declare there can be no morality independently of their theological system and book revelation. Of course, it is nothing to ignore the fact that, before either the one or the other appeared, society existed and nations flourished essentially the same as they do to-day!

One would suppose, from the claims which are frequently made, that there was no morality before the Christian era; that men were entirely wanting in knowledge of what is right, and the disposition to do it; in short, that all men were thieves, robbers, and murderers, before they heard of Jesus Christ. I do not wonder that a system which through its representatives gives currency to such a falsehood as this wants the aid of civil power to enforce its teachings.

The morality of the advanced nations to-day is commonly called Christian morality, but only with the same disregard of truth which is implied in denying the existence of virtue and goodness before Christ and outside of Christendom. The morality of this age does not owe its existence to any religion, to any book, to any historic character, however much or little any one of these has influenced mankind. Our present conception of morality has grown through many centuries of human experience, and exists now only because by many mistakes and much suffering man has learned its adaptedness to his wants. It is the result of the combined influence of our natural character and education. To ascribe it to the dominant religion were as absurd as to attribute the enlightenment of the ancient Greeks to their mythology, or the enlightenment of the Saracens of Spain in the ninth and tenth centuries, when darkness enveloped Christian Europe, to the Koran. The fact is, with the advancement of the human mind, with the discoveries in science and progress in morality, believers in all systems of religion modify their views so as to adjust them to the new order of things, always claiming, in ancient and in modern times, in Egypt, India, Rome, Turkey, England, America, that they find authority for the new ideas or reforms in their sacred books or religious systems. Soon they claim these religions are entitled to the exclusive credit of having *produced* the beneficent change which they have been powerless to prevent. Thus, while the Bible teaches the subordination of woman in plain and unequivocal language, sanctions and authorizes human slavery, and condemns to unresisting submission to their condition the subjects of oppressive governments, today in this country the Orthodox believers deny the plain signification of the Bible on these points, and claim that it has been effective in the destruction of all kinds of political and social bondage; this, too, in spite of the fact, that its most zealous advocates, within the memory of men who are yet young, were quoting its texts to show the wickedness of the reforms which they now have the hardihood to claim as the outgrowths of that book! Those portions of a religious system or book revelation which are shown to be false, or which come to be repudiated by the enlightened moral sense of the age, are either absolutely ignored or twisted out of their obvious and natural meaning. By keeping in the background the teachings of the Bible which have been outgrown, by giving prominence to the precepts of morality which are attached to all systems of religion, by *stamping them all as Christian,* although they were known and practised before Christianity was ever heard of, theologians impress the masses with the conviction that the Bible and the Christian religion are the foundation of all virtue, and the only hope of the world. It then presents the theological dogmas — which have nothing whatever in common with morality (such as that Jesus Christ is Ruler among Nations) — which indeed have been the faith, the sincere, unquestioning faith of multitudes of the most cruel and vicious men of all ages since they have been taught, and demand their acceptance and incorporation in our Constitution from purely *moral considerations!* Making all allowance for the fact that transitional periods such as the present are always characterized by grave inconsistencies which imply no dishonesty, it is difficult to believe that, in these common representations regarding Christianity and morality, there is not a good deal of disingenuousness and selfish disregard of the rights of those who will not sustain them in the theological views they advocate.

This much on this point I have thought it right and proper to say, not for the purpose of discrediting theology or reflecting on its advocates, but to meet the assertion so commonly made, one which has great influence with the masses, that Christianity is entitled to recognition and support by the State on the ground that it is necessary to that morality without which the State cannot exist. This argument can impose only on the uninformed or such as are blinded by prejudice and bigotry to the most unquestionable facts and the most unanswerable logic. There is no argument worthy of the name that will justify the union of the Christian religion with the State. Every consideration of justice and equality forbids it. Every argument in favor of free Republican institutions is equally an argument in favor of a complete divorce of the State from the Church. History in warning tones tells us there can be no liberty without it. Justice demands it. Public safety requires it. He who opposes it is, whether he realizes it or not, an enemy of freedom. He who sees its justice and fails to use his influence in its favor is recreant to duty and unworthy the name of freeman. Those who today when we are about to celebrate the one hundredth anniversary of American Independence, are suffering from disabilities, however slight, on account of religious beliefs, and who are disposed tamely to submit to such an outrage on their rights as men and citizens, are in disposition *spaniels* — a disgrace to the very name of Freethinker, and utterly undeserving the inheritance which has come to them from the illustrious dead — from those, as Carlyle says, "whose heroic sufferings rise up melodiously together unto heaven, out of all times and out of all lands, as a sacred *Miserere;* their heroic actions also, as a boundless everlasting Psalm of triumph." Every sentiment of honor, every manly feeling, a righteous indignation at injustice, a determination to submit to no religious intolerance, love of peace and the welfare and prosperity of our country, with an ardent and unfaltering attachment to republican institutions — all combine to induce us to demand a separation of Church and State, total and complete, "now, henceforth, and forever." And we ought never to be content, ought never to relax our efforts until this is effected, and secured beyond peril by Constitutional Amendment. Whatever is of worth comes by exertion, and whatever is valuable needs watchful care. "Eternal vigilance is the price of liberty."

Thankful for all the blessings that have been secured to us by the struggles and sacrifices of our fathers, let us show our gratitude and pay the debt we owe them to those who shall come after us, by adding to what we have received in strengthening the foundations of freedom, so that no fury of religious fanaticism will ever be able to destroy them. Long live the Republic! May she continue to grow in greatness and grandeur till her light and glory shall fill the earth!

10

The Fight against "Released Time"

IN THE TWENTIETH CENTURY, thus far, the major battle in the perennial struggle to maintain religious liberty has been the battle of the schools. Once again, as in the days of Horace Mann, there is a desperate attempt being made by highly organized groups of orthodox adherents of various religions to use American schools to indoctrinate sectarian teachings. And again, as in every earlier instance when religious liberty was threatened, it has found stalwart defenders.

When Ezra Stiles Ely suggested that the "Christians" of the country should organize politically to prevent the election of anyone not of their number, he assured his listeners that he was not advocating a church establishment, but merely trying to prevent the dominance of the "infidels" in national affairs. Similarly, those who advocate the teaching of religion in our schools today assert that they do not strive to establish the pre-eminence of their own sect, but merely to "rescue" our public schools "from being an unwilling agent in consecrating secularism as the religion of America," as one of their number wrote several years ago. In thus attempting to prevent the "establishment" of secularism, they maintain that they are the true defenders of religious freedom. Let us examine their program.

Its first plank is "released time." This is an arrangement made by the schools to permit pupils whose parents so request to be dismissed during regular school hours for a set period of time in order to attend classes in religion, staffed by denominational teachers and usually conducted off the school premises. There is no

225

universal pattern for the administration of released-time programs in different parts of the country. In some instances, the public schools have no more to do with the program after its establishment. At the other extreme stand the school systems which permit the released-time programs to be conducted in the school buildings. In between is to be found every possible variation of method.

The second plank in the program of those who are resisting "secularization" of the American public schools involves the effort to restore the Bible and the Lord's Prayer to the curriculum. Once again the argument is used that Bible study and prayer constitute an indispensable basis for moral training, and that the return to such classroom activities will preclude the spread of delinquency and crime. State legislatures and local school boards are especially prone to accept this reintroduction. Members of these elective bodies can see no positive harm in Bible reading, and can endear themselves at little cost to an organized and vocal pressure group by approving of it. Needless to say, the opposition to Bible study includes Roman Catholics. In Illinois, some years ago, a ruling of the court enjoining Bible reading as a violation of religious freedom was gained as a result of an action instituted by Catholics.

On the other hand, Catholic groups are ardently in support of — and, in fact, are in the forefront of the advocates of — the third plank of the orthodox program. This is the supreme effort to gain at least partial public support for parochial schools. Some of the specific tactical moves in this campaign are extremely hard to oppose; it is, indeed, harsh to suggest that the Federal government's subsidy lunch program, designed to assure adequately nutritive lunches at a minimum cost to all the children, should be restricted to all the children who do not attend parochial schools. Yet, if hot lunches be provided, why not medical and dental services, textbooks, bus transportation to and from school, and ultimately — as some have advocated — public support of that part of the parochial-school program which is not specifically religious in content? It requires a very nice discrimination to avoid making even humanitarianism a warrant and precedent for broader destruction of the wall of separation. The United States Supreme Court has held, in two separate cases, that free textbooks might be furnished to parochial-school pupils as well as to those in public schools, and that the States might transport children to parochial schools at the public expense. In one Vermont town, the building of an adequate public high school was held up by pressure until the guarantee was given that its new and well-equipped gymnasium would be available for use by parochial-school students. A condition of Catholic support for Federal bills to aid education in our poorer and less able states has been that this aid should be made available to "non-public" schools, *without public direction of the ways in which this aid would be used.*

Enough has been said to demonstrate beyond cavil that today's invasion of education by the forces of organized and orthodox religion constitutes a major battlefront in the struggle to hold our Jeffersonian wall of separation. Increasingly this is coming to be realized by the less fanatical sects among orthodox religionists. In the past few years, many Episcopalian, Methodist, and other conservative Protestant groups have joined with such liberal religionists as the Unitarians, Reformed Jews, Ethical Culturists, and Humanists to resist further encroachment and to beat back the advance guard of infiltration. In the heated atmosphere of charges and countercharges, a member of the Humanist faith, Mrs. Vashti McCollum, brought suit in the courts of Illinois, charging that the released-time program as administered in Champaign was an infringement of her religious rights. In Champaign the program involved the use of public-school classrooms for religious education. Pressure of various sorts had been brought to bear upon Mrs. McCollum to enroll her son in the program. An essential feature of her complaint was that these pressures violated the constitutional guarantee of her freedom of conscience. The Supreme Court of the State of Illinois pronounced judgment for the Champaign Board of Education, defendant in the case, on the ground that there was no official pressure inflicted upon Mrs. McCollum or her son.

On appeal to the United States Supreme Court, the verdict of the Illinois court was reversed in a decision which gained nationwide attention. However, the Supreme Court declared the Champaign program a violation of constitutional rights on the ground that public buildings were used for religious education, and *not* on the ground of the pressures brought to bear on the complainant. Thus

the decision does not hold all released-time programs as infringements of religious rights, but only those in which public rooms are
used. Even this decision was not unanimous, Mr. Justice Reed
having dissented from the opinion of the remainder of his colleagues
on the ground that "when pupils compelled by law to go to school
for secular education are released from school so as to attend the
religious classes, churches are [not] unconstitutionally aided. Whatever may be the wisdom of the arrangement as to the use of the
school buildings made with The Champaign Council of Religious
Education it is clear to me that past practice shows such co-
operation between the schools and a non-ecclesiastical body is not
forbidden by the First Amendment. . . . The prohibition of
enactments respecting the establishment of religion do [sic] not
bar every friendly gesture between church and state. . . . Devotion to the great principle of religious liberty should not lead us
into a rigid interpretation of the constitutional guarantee that conflicts with accepted habits of our people."

Furthermore, although the remaining members of the Court
disagreed with Mr. Justice Reed, their grounds of disagreement
were so diverse that three at least partially inconsistent opinions
were required to set them forth: the Court's opinion, written by
Mr. Justice Black, who was joined by Justices Murphy, Douglas,
Rutledge, and Burton and by Chief Justice Vinson; a concurring
opinion by Mr. Justice Frankfurter, joined by Justices Rutledge,
Burton, and Jackson, two of whom had also subscribed to the
Court's opinion; and a second concurring opinion by Mr. Justice
Jackson, who joined in Mr. Justice Frankfurter's opinion, but not in
that of the Court. The result of this fragmentation of opinion, in
the words of Leo Pfeffer, an opponent of released-time programs,
is that "it can hardly be denied that there is at least superficial
validity to the claim that the Court's decision is not so clear and
unambiguous as to require complete abandonment of all systems
of religious instruction in any way connected with the public school"
(*The Standard,* Nov., 1948, pp. 4-5).

The question of released time is, therefore, despite the historic
decision of March 8, 1948, still a very live issue. Because this is
so, and because there is every indication that the released-time
program will continue to be the subject of debate and litigation

for many years to come, it is advisable that as many Americans as possible should familiarize themselves with the various aspects of the question. As a means toward becoming familiar with the history of the relations between religion and public education in the United States —-as well as with the background of the released-time question — the concurring opinion of Mr. Justice Frankfurter in the McCollum case is reprinted here. This opinion takes a middle ground between that of the Court and that of Justice Jackson, and does so to the accompaniment of a very competent historical survey. The deep scholarship and the broad humanity of Justice Frankfurter appear clearly in this opinion, establishing more securely his place as a great American of our age, and suggesting that the future may assign him a still higher place in the line of defenders of religious freedom in all ages.

Felix Frankfurter

1948

CONCURRING OPINION IN
THE VASHTI McCOLLUM CASE
(PEOPLE OF THE STATE OF ILLINOIS V. BOARD OF EDUCATION)

We dissented in Everson v. Board of Education, 330 U.S. 1, 67 S. Ct. 504, 512, because in our view the Constitutional principle requiring separation of Church and State compelled invalidation of the ordinance sustained by the majority. Illinois has here authorized the commingling of religious with secular instruction in the public schools. The Constitution of the United States forbids this.

The case, in the light of the Everson decision, demonstrates anew that the mere formulation of a relevant Constitutional principle is the beginning of the solution of a problem, not its answer. This is so because the meaning of a spacious conception like that of the separation of Church from State is unfolded as appeal is made to the principle from case to case. We are all agreed that the First and the Fourteenth Amendments have a secular reach far more penetrating in the conduct of Government than merely to forbid an "established church." But agreement, in the abstract, that the First Amendment was designed to erect a "wall of separation between Church and State," does not preclude a clash of views as to what the wall separates. Involved is not only the Constitutional principle but the implications of judicial review in its enforcement. Accommodation of legislative freedom and Constitutional limitations upon that freedom cannot be achieved by a mere phrase. We cannot illuminatingly apply the "wall-of-separation" metaphor until we have considered the relevant history of religious education in America, the place of the "released time" movement in that history, and its precise manifestation in the case before us.

To understand the particular program now before us as a conscientious attempt to accommodate the allowable functions of Government and the special concerns of the Church within the framework of our Constitution and with due regard to the kind of society for which it was designed, we must put this Champaign program of 1940 in its historic setting. Traditionally, organized education in the Western world was Church education. It could hardly be otherwise when the education of children was primarily study of the Word and the ways of God. Even in the Protestant countries, where there was a less close identification of Church and State, the basis of education was largely the Bible, and its chief purpose inculcation of piety. To the extent that the State intervened, it used its authority to further aims of the Church.

The emigrants who came to these shores brought this view of education with them. Colonial schools certainly started with a religious orientation. When the common problems of the early settlers of the Massachusetts Bay Colony revealed the need for common schools, the object was the defeat of "one chief project of that old deluder, Satan, to keep men from the knowledge of the Scriptures." The Laws and Liberties of Massachusetts, 1648 edition (Cambridge 1929) 47.[1]

The evolution of colonial education, largely in the service of religion, into the public school system of today is the story of changing conceptions regarding the American democratic society, of the functions of State-maintained education in such a society, and of the role therein of the free exercise of religion by the people. The modern public school derived from a philosophy of freedom reflected in the First Amendment. It is appropriate to recall that the Remonstrance of James Madison, an event basic in the history of religious liberty, was called forth by a proposal which involved support to religious education. See Mr. Justice Rutledge's opinion in the Everson case supra, 330 U.S. at pages 36, 37, 67 S. Ct. ; pages 521, 522. As the momentum for popular education increas' and in turn evoked strong claims for State support of religious ed cation, contests not unlike that which in Virginia had prodv Madison's Remonstrance appeared in various form in other Si New York and Massachusetts provide famous chapters in th

---

[1] References are to the notes at the end of the chapter.

tory that established dissociation of religious teaching from State-maintained schools. In New York, the rise of the common schools led, despite fierce sectarian opposition, to the barring of tax funds to church schools, and later to any school in which sectarian doctrine was taught.[2] In Massachusetts, largely through the efforts of Horace Mann, all sectarian teachings were barred from the common school to save it from being rent by denominational conflict.[3] The upshot of these controversies, often long and fierce, is fairly summarized by saying that long before the Fourteenth Amendment subjected the States to new limitations, the prohibition of furtherance by the State of religious instruction became the guiding principle, in law and feeling, of the American people. In sustaining Stephen Girard's will, this Court referred to the inevitable conflicts engendered by matters "connected with religious polity" and particularly "in a country composed of such a variety of religious sects as our country." Vidal et al. v. Girard's Executors, 2 How. 127, 198, 11 L. Ed. 205. That was more than one hundred years ago.

Separation in the field of education, then, was not imposed upon unwilling States by force or superior law. In this respect the Fourteenth Amendment merely reflected a principle then dominant in our national life. To the extent that the Constitution thus made it binding upon the States, the basis of the restriction is the whole experience of our people. Zealous watchfulness against fusion of secular and religious activities by Government itself, through any of its instruments but especially through its educational agencies, was the democratic response of the American community to the particular needs of a young and growing nation, unique in the composition of its people.[4] A totally different situation elsewhere, as illustrated for instance by the English provisions for religious education in State-maintained schools, only serves to illustrate that free societies are not cast in one mould. See the Education Act of 1944, 7 and 8 Geo. VI, c. 31. Different institutions evolve from different historic circumstances.

It is pertinent to remind that the establishment of this principle of separation in the field of education was not due to any decline in the religious beliefs of the people. Horace Mann was a devout Christian, and the deep religious feeling of James Madison is stamped upon the Remonstrance. The secular public school did

not imply indifference to the basic role of religion in the life of the people, nor rejection of religious education as a means of fostering it. The claims of religion were not minimized by refusing to make the public schools agencies for their assertion. The non-sectarian or secular public school was the means of reconciling freedom in general with religious freedom. The sharp confinement of the public schools to secular education was a recognition of the need of a democratic society to educate its children, insofar as the State undertook to do so, in an atmosphere free from pressures in a realm in which pressures are most resisted and where conflicts are most easily and most bitterly engendered. Designed to serve as perhaps the most powerful agency for promoting cohesion among a heterogeneous democratic people, the public school must keep scrupulously free from entanglement in the strife of sects. The preservation of the community from divisive conflicts, of Government from irreconcilable pressures by religious groups, of religion from censorship and coercion however subtly exercised, requires strict confinement of the State to instruction other than religious, leaving to the individual's church and home, indoctrination in the faith of his choice.

This development of the public school as a symbol of our secular unity was not a sudden achievement nor attained without violent conflict.[5] While in small communities of comparatively homogeneous religious beliefs, the need for absolute separation presented no urgencies, elsewhere the growth of the secular school encountered the resistance of feeling strongly engaged against it. But the inevitability of such attempts is the very reason for Constitutional provisions primarily concerned with the protection of minority groups. And such sects are shifting groups, varying from time to time, and place to place, thus representing in their totality the common interest of the nation.

Enough has been said to indicate that we are dealing not with a full-blown principle, nor one having the definiteness of a surveyor's metes and bounds. But by 1875 the separation of public education from Church entanglements, of the State from the teaching of religion, was firmly established in the consciousness of the nation. In that year President Grant made his famous remarks in the Convention of the Army of the Tennessee:

"Encourage free schools and resolve that not one dollar appropriated for their support shall be appropriated for the support of any sectarian schools. Resolve that neither the state nor the nation, nor both combined, shall support institutions of learning other than those sufficient to afford every child growing up in the land the opportunity of a good common school education, unmixed with sectarian, pagan, or atheistical dogmas. Leave the matter of religion to the family altar, the church, and the private school, supported entirely by private contributions. Keep the church and state forever separated." "The President's Speech at Des Moines," 22 Catholic World 433, 434-35 (1876).

So strong was this conviction, that rather than rest on the comprehensive prohibitions of the First and Fourteenth Amendments, President Grant urged that there be written into the United States Constitution particular elaborations, including a specific prohibition against the use of public funds for sectarian education,[6] such as had been written into many State constitutions.[7] By 1894, in urging the adoption of such a provision in the New York Constitution, Elihu Root was able to summarize a century of the nation's history: "It is not a question of religion, or of creed, or of party; it is a question of declaring and maintaining the great American principle of eternal separation between Church and State." Root, Addresses on Government and Citizenship, 137, 140.[8] The extent to which this principle was deemed a presupposition of our Constitutional system is strikingly illustrated by the fact that every State admitted into the Union since 1876 was compelled by Congress to write into its constitution a requirement that it maintain a school system "free from sectarian control."[9]

Prohibition of the commingling of religious and secular instruction in the public school is of course only half the story. A religious people was naturally concerned about the part of the child's education entrusted "to the family altar, the church, and the private school." The promotion of religious education took many forms. Laboring under financial difficulties and exercising only persuasive authority, various denominations felt handicapped in their task of religious education. Abortive attempts were therefore frequently made to obtain public funds for religious schools.[10] But the major efforts of religious inculcation were a recognition of the principle of Separation by the establishment of church schools privately supported. Parochial schools were maintained by various denominations. These, however, were often beset by serious handicaps, financial and otherwise, so that the religious aims which they represented found other directions. There were experiments with vacation schools, with Saturday as well as Sunday schools.[11] They all fell short of their purpose. It was urged that by appearing to make religion a one-day-a-week matter, the Sunday school, which acquired national acceptance, tended to relegate the child's religious education, and thereby his religion, to a minor role not unlike the enforced piano lesson.

Out of these inadequate efforts evolved the week-day church school, held on one or more afternoons a week after the close of the public school. But children continued to be children; they wanted to play when school was out, particularly when other children were free to do so. Church leaders decided that if the weekday church school was to succeed, a way had to be found to give the child his religious education during what the child conceived to be his "business hours."

The initiation of the movement[12] may fairly be attributed to Dr. George U. Wenner. The underlying assumption of his proposal, made at the Interfaith Conference on Federation held in New York City in 1905, was that the public school unduly monopolized the child's time and that the churches were entitled to their share of it.[13] This, the schools should "release." Accordingly, the Federation, citing the example of the Third Republic of France,[14] urged that upon the request of their parents children be excused from public school on Wednesday afternoon, so that the churches could provide "Sunday school on Wednesday." This was to be carried out on church premises under church authority. Those not desiring to attend church schools would continue their normal classes. Lest these public school classes unfairly compete with the church education, it was requested that the school authorities refrain from scheduling courses or activities of compelling interest or importance.

The proposal aroused considerable opposition and it took another decade for a "released-time" scheme to become part of a public school system. Gary, Indiana, inaugurated the movement. At a time when industrial expansion strained the communal facilities of the city, Superintendent of Schools Wirt suggested a fuller use of the school buildings. Building on theories which had become more or less current, he also urged that education was more than instruction in a classroom. The school was only one of several educational agencies. The library, the playground, the home, the church, all have their function in the child's proper unfolding. Accordingly, Wirt's plan sought to rotate the schedules of the children during the school-day so that some were in class, others were in the library, still others in the playground. And some, he suggested to the leading ministers of the City, might be released to attend religious classes if the churches of the City cooperated and provided them. They did, in 1914, and thus was "released time" begun. The religious teaching was held on church premises and the public schools had no hand in the conduct of these church schools. They did not supervise the choice of instructors or the subject matter taught. Nor did they assume responsibility for the attendance, conduct or achievement of the child in a church school; and he received no credit for it. The period of attendance in the religious schools would otherwise have been a play period for the child, with the result that the arrangement did not cut into public school instruction or truly affect the activities or feelings of the children who did not attend the church schools.[15]

From such a beginning "released time" has attained substantial proportions. In 1914-15, under the Gary program, 619 pupils left the public schools for the church schools during one period a week. According to responsible figures almost 2,000,000 in some 2,200 communities participated in "released time" programs during 1947.[16] A movement of such scope indicates the importance of the problem to which the "released time" programs are directed. But to the extent that aspects of these programs are open to Constitutional objection, the more extensively the movement operates, the more ominous the breaches in the wall of separation.

Of course, "released time" as a generalized conception, undefined by differentiating particularities, is not an issue for Constitutional adjudication. Local programs differ from each other in many and crucial respects. Some "released time" classes are under separate denominational auspices, others are conducted jointly by several denominations, often embracing all the religious affiliations of a community. Some classes in religion teach a limited sectarianism; others emphasize democracy, unity and spiritual values not anchored in a particular creed. Insofar as these are manifestations merely of the free exercise of religion, they are quite outside the scope of judicial concern, except insofar as the Court may be called upon to protect the right of religious freedom. It is only when challenge is made to the share that the public schools have in the execution of a particular "released time" program that close judicial scrutiny is demanded of the exact relation between the religious instruction and the public educational system in the specific situation before the Court.[17]

The substantial differences among arrangements lumped together as "released time" emphasize the importance of detailed analysis of the facts to which the Constitutional test of Separation is to be applied. How does "released time" operate in Champaign? Public school teachers distribute to their pupils cards supplied by church groups, so that the parents may indicate whether they desire religious instruction for their children. For those desiring it, religious classes are conducted in the regular classrooms of the public schools by teachers of religion paid by the churches and appointed by them, but, as the State court found, "subject to the approval and supervision of the Superintendent." The courses do not profess to give secular instruction in subjects concerning religion. Their candid purpose is sectarian teaching. While a child can go to any of the religious classes offered, a particular sect wishing a teacher for its devotees requires the permission of the school superintendent "who in turn will determine whether or not it is practical for said group to teach in said school system." If no provision is made for religious instruction in the particular faith of a child, or if for any reasons the child is not enrolled in any of the offered classes, he is required to attend a regular school class, or a study period during which he is often left to his own devices. Reports of attendance in the religious classes are submitted by the religious instructor to the school authorities, and the child who fails to attend is presumably deemed a truant.

Religious education so conducted on school time and property is patently woven into the working scheme of the school. The Champaign arrangement thus presents powerful elements of inherent pressure by the school system in the interest of religious sects. The fact that this power has not been used to discriminate is beside the point. Separation is a requirement to abstain from fusing functions of Government and of religious sects, not merely to treat them all equally. That a child is offered an alternative may reduce the constraint; it does not eliminate the operation of influence by the school in matters sacred to conscience and outside the school's domain. The law of imitation operates, and non-conformity is not an outstanding characteristic of children. The result is an obvious pressure upon children to attend.[18] Again, while the Champaign school population represents only a fraction of the more than two hundred and fifty sects of the nation, not even all the practicing sects in Champaign are willing or able to provide religious instruction. The children belonging to these non-participating sects will thus have inculcated in them a feeling of separatism when the school should be the training ground for habits of community, or they will have religious instruction in a faith which is not that of their parents. As a result, the public school system of Champaign actively furthers inculcation in the religious tenets of some faiths, and in the process sharpens the consciousness of religious differences at least among some of the children committed to its care. These are consequences not amenable to statistics. But they are precisely the consequences against which the Constitution was directed when it prohibited the Government common to all from becoming embroiled, however innocently, in the destructive religious conflicts of which the history of even this country records some dark pages.[19]

Mention should not be omitted that the integration of religious instruction within the school system as practiced in Champaign is supported by arguments drawn from educational theories as diverse as those derived from Catholic conceptions and from the writings of John Dewey.[20] Movements like "released time" are seldom single in origin or aim. Nor can the intrusion of religious instruction into the public school system of Champaign be minimized by saying that it absorbs less than an hour a week; in fact, that affords evidence of a design constitutionally objectionable. If it were merely a question of enabling a child to obtain religious instruction with a receptive mind the thirty or forty-five minutes could readily

be found on Saturday or Sunday. If that were all, Champaign
might have drawn upon the French system, known in its American
manifestation as "dismissed time," whereby one school day is short-
ened to allow all children to go where they please, leaving those
who so desire to go to a religious school.[21] The momentum of the
whole school atmosphere and school planning is presumably put
behind religious instruction, as given in Champaign, precisely in
order to secure for the religious instruction such momentum and
planning. To speak of "released time" as being only half or three
quarters of an hour is to draw a thread from a fabric.

We do not consider, as indeed we could not, school programs not
before us which, though colloquially characterized as "released
time," present situations differing in aspects that may well be
constitutionally crucial. Different forms which "released time" has
taken during more than thirty years of growth include programs
which, like that before us, could not withstand the test of the Constitution; others may be found unexceptionable. We do not now
attempt to weigh in the Constitutional scale every separate detail or
various combination of factors which may establish a valid "released time" program. We find that the basic Constitutional principle of absolute separation was violated when the State of Illinois,
speaking through its Supreme Court, sustained the school authorities of Champaign in sponsoring and effectively furthering religious
beliefs by its educational arrangement.

Separation means separation, not something less. Jefferson's
metaphor in describing the relation between Church and State
speaks of a "wall of separation," not of a fine line easily overstepped.
The public school is at once the symbol of our democracy and the
most pervasive means for promoting our common destiny. In no
activity of the State is it more vital to keep out divisive force than
in its schools, to avoid confusing, not to say fusing, what the Constitution sought to keep strictly apart. "The great American principle
of eternal separation," — Elihu Root's phrase bears repetition —
is one of the vital reliances of our Constitutional system for assuring
unities among our people stronger than our diversities. It is the
Court's duty to enforce this principle in its full integrity.

We renew our conviction that "we have staked the very existence
of our country on the faith that complete separation between the

state and religion is best for the state and best for religion." Everson, v. Board of Education, 330 U.S. at page 59, 67 S. Ct. at page 532. If nowhere else, in the relation between Church and State, "good fences make good neighbors."

NOTES

1. For an exposition of the religious origins of American education, see S. W. Brown, The Secularization of American Education (1912) cc. I, II; Knight, Education in the United States (2d rev. ed. 1941) cc. III, V; Cubberley, Public Education in the United States (1934), cc. II, III.

2. See Boese, Public Education in the City of New York (1869) c. XIV; Hall, Religious Education in the Public Schools of the State and City of New York (1914) cc. VI, VII; Palmer, The New York Public School (1905) cc. VI, VII, X, XII. And see New York Laws 1842, c. 150, §14, amended, New York Laws 1844, c. 320, §12.

3. S. M. Smith, The Relation of the State to Religious Education in Massachusetts (1926) c. VII; Culver, Horace Mann and Religion in Massachusetts Public Schools (1929).

4. It has been suggested that secular education in this country is the inevitable "product of 'the utter impossibility of harmonizing multiform creeds.'" T. W. M. Marshall, Secular Education in England and the United States, 1 American Catholic Quarterly Review 278, 308. It is precisely because of this "utter impossibility" that the fathers put into the Constitution the principle of complete "hands-off," for a people as religiously heterogeneous as ours.

5. See Cubberley, Public Education in the United States (1934) pp. 230 et seq.; Zollmann, The Relation of Church and State, in Lotz and Crawford, Studies in Religious Education (1931) 403, 418 et seq.; Payson Smith, The Public Schools and Religious Education, in Religion and Education (Sperry, Editor, 1945) pp. 32 et seq.; also Mahoney, The Relation of the State to Religious Education in Early New York 1633-1825 (1941) c. VI; McLaughlin, A History of State Legislation Affecting Private Elementary and Secondary Schools in the United States, 1870-1945 (1946) c. I; and see note 10, infra.

6. President Grant's Annual Message to Congress, December 7, 1875, 4 Cong. Rec. 175 et seq.; Ames, The Proposed Amendments to the Constitution of the United States during the First Century of its History, H. Doc. No. 353, Pt. 2, 54th Cong., 2d Sess., pp. 277, 278. In addition to the first proposal, "The Blaine Amendment," five others to similar effect are cited by Ames. The reason for the failure of these attempts seems to have been in part "That the provisions of the State constitutions are in almost all instances adequate on this subject, and no amendment is likely to be secured." Id.

In the form in which it passed the House of Representatives, the Blaine Amendment read as follows: "No State shall make any law

respecting an establishment of religion, or prohibiting the free exercise
thereof; and no religious test shall ever be required as a qualification
to any office or public trust under any State. No public property, and
no public revenue of, nor any loan of credit by or under the authority
of, the United States, or any State, Territory, District, or municipal
corporation, shall be appropriated to, or made or used for, the support
of any school, educational or other institution, under the control of
any religious or anti-religious sect, organization, or denomination, or
wherein the particular creed or tenets of any religious or anti-religious
sect, organization, or denomination shall be taught. And no such particular creed or tenets shall be read or taught in any school or institution supported in whole or in part by such revenue or loan of credit;
and no such appropriation or loan of credit shall be made to any religious or anti-religious sect, organization, or denomination, or to promote its interests or tenets. This article shall not be construed to
prohibit the reading of the Bible in any school or institution; and it
shall not have the effect to impair rights of property already vested
* * *." H. Res. 1, 44th Cong., 1st Sess. (1876).

7. See Constitution of the States and United States, 3 Report of the New
York State Constitutional Convention Committee (1938) Index, pp.
1766, 1767.

8. It is worthy of interest that another famous American lawyer, and indeed one of the most distinguished of American judges, Jeremiah S.
Black, expressed similar views nearly forty years before Mr. Root:
"The manifest object of the men who framed the institution of this
country, was to have a *State without religion* and a *Church without
politics* — that is to say, they meant that one should never be used
as an engine for any purpose of the other * * *. Our fathers seem to
have been perfectly sincere in their belief that the members of the
Church would be more patriotic, and the citizens of the State more
religious, by keeping their respective functions entirely separate. For
that reason they build up a wall of complete and perfect partition
between the two." From Religious Liberty (1856) in Black, Essays and
Speeches (1886) 51, 53; cf. Brigance, Jeremiah Sullivan Black (1934).
While Jeremiah S. Black and Elihu Root had many things in common,
there were also important differences between them, perhaps best illustrated by the fact that one became Secretary of State to President
Buchanan, the other to Theodore Roosevelt. That two men, with such
different political alignment, should have shared identic views on a
matter so basic to the well-being of our American democracy affords
striking proof of the respect to be accorded to that principle.

9. 25 Stat. 676, 677, applicable to North Dakota, South Dakota, Montana
and Washington, required that the constitutional conventions of those
States "provide, by ordinances irrevocable without the consent of the
United States and the people of said States * * * for the establishment
and maintenance of systems of public schools, which shall be open to
all the children of said States, and free from sectarian control. * * *"
The same provision was contained in the Enabling Act for Utah, 28
Stat. 107, 108; Oklahoma, 34 Stat. 267, 270; New Mexico and Arizona,

36 Stat. 557, 559, 570. Idaho and Wyoming were admitted after adoption of their constitutions; that of Wyoming contained an irrevocable ordinance in the same terms. Wyoming Constitution, 1889, Ordinances, §5. The Constitution of Idaho, while it contained no irrevocable ordinance, had a provision even more explicit in its establishment of separation. Idaho Constitution, 1889, art. IX, §5.

10. See, e.g., the New York experience, including, inter alia, the famous Hughes controversy of 1840-42, the conflict culminating in the Constitutional Convention of 1894, and the attempts to restore aid to parochial schools by revision of the New York City Charter, in 1901, and at the State Constitutional Convention of 1938. See McLaughlin, A History of State Legislation Affecting Private Elementary and Secondary Schools in the United States, 1870-1945 (1946) pp. 219-25; Mahoney, The Relation of the State to Religious Education in Early New York 1633-1825 (1941) c. VI; Hall, Religious Education in the Public Schools of the State and the City of New York (1914) pp. 46-47; Boese, Public Education in the City of New York (1869) c. XIV; Compare New York Laws 1901, vol. 3, §1152, p. 492, with amendment, id., p. 668; see Nicholas Murray Butler, Religion and Education (Editorial) in 22 Educational Review 101, June, 1901; New York Times, April 8, 1901, p. 1, col. 1; April 9, 1901, p. 2, col. 5; April 19, 1901, p. 2, col. 2; April 21, 1901, p. 1, col. 3; Editorial, April 22, 1901, p. 6, col. 1.

Compare S. 2499, 79th Cong., 2d Sess., providing for Federal aid to education, and the controversy engendered over the inclusion in the aid program of sectarian schools, fully discussed in, e.g., "The Nation's Schools," January through June, 1947.

11. For surveys of the development of private religious education, see, e.g., A. A. Brown, A History of Religious Education in Recent Times (1923); Athearn, Religious Education and American Democracy (1917); Burns and Kohlbrenner, A History of Catholic Education in the United States (1937); Lotz and Crawford, Studies in Religious Education (1931) Parts I and IV.

12. Reference should be made to Jacob Gould Schurman, who in 1903 proposed a plan bearing close resemblance to that of Champaign. See Symposium, 75 The Outlook 635, 636, November 14, 1903; Crooker, Religious Freedom in American Education (1903), pp. 39 et seq.

13. For the text of the resolution, a brief in its support, as well as an exposition of some of the opposition it inspired, see Wenner's book, Religious Education and the Public School (rev. ed. 1913).

14. The French example is cited not only by Wenner but also by Nicholas Murray Butler, who thought released time was "restoring the American system in the state of New York." The Place of Religious Instruction in Our Educational System, 7 Vital Speeches 167, 168 (Nov. 28, 1940); see also Report of the President of Columbia University, 1934, pp. 22-24. It is important to note, however, that the French practice must be viewed as the result of the struggle to emancipate the French schools from control by the Church. The leaders of this revolution, men like Paul Bert, Ferdinand Buisson, and Jules Ferry, agreed to this measure as one part of a great step towards, rather than a retreat from, the

principle of Separation. The history of these events is described in Muzzey, State, Church, and School in France, The School Review, March through June, 1911.

In effect, moreover, the French practice differs in crucial respects from both the Wenner proposal and the Champaign system. The law of 1882 provided that "Public elementary schools will be closed one day a week in addition to Sunday in order to permit parents, if they so desire, to have their children given religious instruction outside of school buildings." Law No. 11,696, March 28, 1882, Bulletin des Lois, No. 690. This then approximates that aspect of released time generally known as "dismissed time." No children went to school on that day, and the public school was therefore not an alternative used to impel the children towards the religious school. The religious education was given "outside of school buildings."

The Vichy Government attempted to introduce a program of religious instruction within the public school system remarkably similar to that in effect in Champaign. The proposal was defeated by intense opposition which included the protest of the French clergy, who apparently feared State control of the Church. See Schwartz, Religious Instruction under Pétain, 58 Christian Century 1170, Sept. 24, 1941.

15. Of the many expositions of the Gary plan, see, e.g., A. A. Brown, The Week-Day Church Schools of Gary, Indiana, 11 Religious Education 5 (1916); Wirt, The Gary Public Schools and the Churches, id. at 221 (1916).

16. See the 1947 Yearbook, International Council of Religious Education, p. 76; also New York Times, September 21, 1947, p. 22, col. 1.

17. Respects in which programs differ include, for example, the amount of supervision by the public school of attendance and performance in the religious class, of the course of study, of the selection of teachers; methods of enrolment and dismissal from the secular classes; the amount of school time devoted to operation of the program; the extent to which school property and administrative machinery are involved; the effect on the public school program of the introduction of "released time"; the proportion of students who seek to be excused; the effect of the program on non-participants; the amount and nature of the publicity for the program in the public schools.

The studies of detail in "released time" programs are voluminous. Most of these may be found in the issues of such periodicals as The International Journal of Religious Education, Religious Education, and Christian Century. For some of the more comprehensive studies found elsewhere, see Davis, Weekday Classes in Religious Education, U.S. Office of Education Bulletin 1941, No. 3; Gorham, A Study of the Status of Weekday Church Schools in the United States (1934); Lotz, The Weekday Church School, in Lotz and Crawford, Studies in Religious Education (1931) c. XII; Forsyth, Week-Day Church Schools (1930); Settle, The Weekday Church School, Educational Bulletin No. 601 of The International Council of Religious Education (1930); Shaver, Present-Day Trends in Religious Education (1928) cc. VII, VIII; Gove, Religious Education on Public School Time (1926).

18. It deserves notice that in discussing with the relator her son's inability to get along with his classmates, one of his teachers suggested that "allowing him to take the religious education course might help him to become a member of the group."

19. The divergent views expressed in the briefs submitted here on behalf of various religious organizations, as amici curiae, in themselves suggest that the movement has been a divisive and not an irenic influence in the community: The American Unitarian Association; The General Conference of Seventh Day Adventists; The Joint Conference Committee on Public Relations set up by the Southern Baptist Convention, The Northern Baptist Convention, The National Baptist Convention Inc., and the National Baptist Convention; The Protestant Council of the City of New York; and The Synagogue Council of America and National Community Relations Advisory Council.

20. There is a prolific literature on the educational, social and religious merits of the "released time" movement. In support of "released time" the following may be mentioned: The International Council of Religious Education, and particularly the writings of Dr. Erwin L. Shaver, for some years Director of its Department of Week-day Religious Education, in publications of the Council and in numerous issues of The International Journal of Religious Education (e.g., They Reach One-Third, Dec., 1943, p. 11; Weekday Religious Education Today, Jan., 1944, p. 6), and Religious Education (e.g., Survey of Week-Day Religious Education, Feb., 1922, p. 51; The Movement for Weekday Religious Education, Jan.-Feb., 1946, p. 6); see also Information Service, Federal Council of Churches of Christ, May 29, 1943. See also Cutton, Answering the Arguments, The International Journal of Religious Education, June, 1930, p. 9, and Released Time, id., Sept., 1942, p. 12; Hauser, "Hands Off the Public School?", Religious Education, Mar.-Apr., 1942, p. 99; Collins, Release Time for Religious Instruction, National Catholic Education Association Bulletin, May, 1945, pp. 21, 27-28; Weigle, Public Education and Religion, Religious Education, Apr.-June, 1940, p. 67; Nicholas Murray Butler, The Place of Religious Instruction in Our Educational System, 7 Vital Speeches 167 (Nov. 28, 1940); Howlett, Released Time for Religious Education in New York City, 64 Education 523, May, 1944; Blair, A Case for the Church School, 7 Frontiers of Democracy 75, Dec. 15, 1940; cf. Allred, Legal Aspects of Release Time (National Catholic Welfare Conference, 1947). Favorable views are also cited in the studies in note 17, supra. Many not opposed to "released time" have declared it "hardly enough" or "pitifully inadequate." E.g., Fleming, God in Our Public Schools (2d ed. 1944) pp. 80-86; Howlett, Released Time for Religious Education in New York City, Religious Education, Mar.-Apr., 1942, p. 104; Cavert, Points of Tension Between Church and State in America Today, in Church and State in the Modern World (1937) 161, 168; F. E. Johnson, The Church and Society (1935) 125; Hubner, Professional Attitudes toward Religion in the Public Schools of the United States Since 1900 (1944) 108-109, 113; cf. Ryan, A Protestant Experiment in Religious Education, The Catholic World, June, 1922; Elliott, Are Weekday Church Schools the Solution?, The International Journal

of Religious Education, Nov., 1940, p. 8: Elliott, Report of the Discussion, Religious Education, July-Sept., 1940, p. 158.

For opposing views, see V. T. Thayer, Religion in Public Education (1947) cc. VII, VIII; Moehlman, The Church as Educator (1947) c. X; Chave, A Functional Approach to Religious Education (1947) 104-107; A. W. Johnson, The Legal Status of Church-State Relationships in the United States (1934) 129-130; Newman, The Sectarian Invasion of Our Public Schools (1925). See also Payson Smith, The Public Schools and Religious Education, in Religion and Education (Sperry, Editor, 1945) 32, 42-47; Herrick, Religion in the Public Schools of America, 46 Elementary School Journal 119, Nov., 1945; Kallen, Churchmen's Claims on the Public School, The Nation's Schools, May, 1942, p. 49; June, 1942, p. 52. And cf. John Dewey, Religion in Our Schools (1908), reprinted in 2 Characters and Events (1929) 504, 508, 514. "Released time" was introduced in the public schools of the City of New York over the opposition of organizations like the Public Education Association and the United Parents Associations.

The arguments and sources pro and con are collected in Hubner, Professional Attitudes toward Religion in the Public Schools in the United States since 1900 (1944) 94 et seq. And see the symposia, Teaching Religion in a Democracy, The International Journal of Religious Education, Nov., 1940, pp. 6-16; The Aims of Week-Day Religious Education, Religious Education, Feb., 1922, p. 11; Released Time in New York City, id., Jan.-Feb., 1943, p. 15; Progress in Weekday Religious Education, id., Jan.-Feb., 1946, p. 6; Can Our Public Schools Do More about Religion?, 125 Journal of Education 245, Nov., 1942, id. at 273, Dec., 1942; Religious Instruction on School Time, 7 Frontiers of Democracy 72-77, Dec. 15, 1940; and the articles in 64 Education 519 et seq., May, 1944.

21. See note 14, supra. Indications are that "dismissed time" is used in an inconsiderable number of the communities employing released time. Davis, Weekday Classes in Religious Education, U.S. Office of Education Bulletin 1941, No. 3, p. 22; Shaver, The Movement for Weekday Religious Education, Religious Education, Jan.-Feb., 1946, pp. 6, 9.

List of Sources

Chapter 2

ROGER WILLIAMS: from *The Bloudy Tenent of Persecution for cause of conscience discussed in a conference betweene Truth and Peace.* As reprinted in *Publications of the Narragansett Club,* first series, Vol. III (Providence, Rhode Island, 1867), *passim.*

WILLIAM PENN: from *The Great Case of Liberty of Conscience once more briefly debated and defended by the Authority of Reason, Scripture, and Antiquity.* As reprinted in *The Select Works of William Penn* (London, 1782), Vol. III, *passim.*

Chapter 3

THOMAS JEFFERSON: "An Act for Establishing Religious Freedom." (Passed in the Assembly of Virginia in the beginning of the year 1786.) As reprinted in Henry W. Foote, *Thomas Jefferson, Champion of Religious Freedom: Advocate of Christian Morals* (Boston, 1947), pp. 22-24.

THOMAS JEFFERSON: from *Notes on Virginia.* As reprinted in H. A. Washington, ed., *The Writings of Thomas Jefferson* (New York, 1854), VIII, 398 ff.

JAMES MADISON: "A Memorial and Remonstrance on the Religious Rights of Man." As reprinted in *Letters and Other Writings of James Madison* (Philadelphia, 1867), I, 162 ff.

Chapter 4

JACOB HENRY: "Speech in the North Carolina House of Delegates." As reprinted in John H. Wheeler, *Historical Sketches of North Carolina from 1584 to 1851* (New York, 1925), II, 74-76.

H. M. BRACKENRIDGE: "Speech on the Maryland 'Jew Bill.'" As reprinted in *Speeches on the Jew Bill in the House of Delegates of Maryland* (Philadelphia, 1829), pp. 59 ff.

Chapter 5

RICHARD M. JOHNSON: "Report of the Committee of Post Offices and Post Roads of the United States House of Representatives." As printed in *Reports* of the 21st Congress, first session, No. 271.

Chapter 6

ZELOTES FULLER: *The Tree of Liberty: An Address in Celebration of the birth of Washington, delivered at the Second Universalist Church in Philadelphia, February 28, 1830* (Philadelphia, 1830).

Chapter 7

DAVID MOULTON and MORDECAI MYERS: "Report of the Select Committee of the New York State Assembly on the Several Memorials against Appointing Chaplains to the Legislature." As printed in *Documents of the Assembly of the State of New York,* Fifty-fifth session, 1832 (Albany, 1832), Vol. IV, No. 298.

Chapter 8

HORACE MANN: "Religious Education," from the *Twelfth Annual Report for 1848 of the Secretary of the Board of Education of Massachusetts.* As reprinted in *Life and Works of Horace Mann* (Boston, 1891), IV, 292 ff.

Chapter 9

FRANCIS ELLINGWOOD ABBOT: "Nine Demands of Liberalism." As printed in *The Index,* V (1874), 1.

BENJAMIN F. UNDERWOOD: from "The Practical Separation of Church and State." As printed in *Equal Rights in Religion: Report of the Centennial Congress of Liberals and Organization of the National Liberal League, at Philadelphia, on the Fourth of July, 1876* (Boston, 1876), pp. 92 ff.

Chapter 10

FELIX FRANKFURTER: "Concurring Opinion in the Vashti McCollum Case (People of the State of Illinois v. Board of Education)." As printed in 68 *Supreme Court Reporter* (1948), pp. 466 ff.

Index